I0896109

A NEW HANDBOOK OF RHETORIC

A New Handbook of Rhetoric

Inverting the Classical Vocabulary

EDITED BY MICHELE KENNERLY

The Pennsylvania State University Press
University Park, Pennsylvania

Library of Congress Cataloging-in-Publication Data

Names: Kennerly, Michele, editor.
Title: A new handbook of rhetoric : inverting the classical vocabulary / edited by Michele Kennerly.
Description: University Park, Pennsylvania : The Pennsylvania State University Press, [2021] | Includes bibliographical references and index.
Summary: "A collection of essays addressing the relevance, explanatory power, and exclusionary effects of the technical vocabulary of rhetorical theory"—Provided by publisher.
Identifiers: LCCN 2021011274 | ISBN 9780271091273 (hardback) | ISBN 9780271091839 (paperback)
Subjects: LCSH: Rhetoric—Handbooks, manuals, etc.
Classification: LCC P301 .N49 2021 | DDC 808—dc23
LC record available at https://lccn.loc.gov/2021011274

Printed in the United States of America
Published by The Pennsylvania State University Press,
University Park, PA 16802-1003

The Pennsylvania State University Press is a member of the Association of University Presses.

It is the policy of The Pennsylvania State University Press to use acid-free paper. Publications on uncoated stock satisfy the minimum requirements of American National Standard for Information Sciences—Permanence of Paper for Printed Library Material, ANSI Z39.48–1992.

To our students

CONTENTS

A NOTE FROM THE EDITOR

The so-called "handbook" tradition of rhetoric originates from the subsidiary meaning of both the ancient Greek word *technē* and the Latin *ars* as "instruction manual." *Technai* and *artes* rolled out conceptual systems abstracted from disparate instances of rhetorical practice judged to have gone well. Over time, certain rhetors, certain classifiers of their practices, and certain concepts came to be called not only "old" or "antecedent" but also "classical," from the Latin word *classicus,* meaning "first-class."

This original meaning of "classical" speaks to the outsized influence a subset of ancient material continues to exercise. For its part, this volume joins conversations underway in Rhetorical Studies about the pull of "classical" rhetoric in pedagogy, theory, criticism, and historiography. We invert the most well-known classical concepts to differentiate the classicizing attitude from ancient terms themselves.

An alpha privative, the ancient Greek grammatical feature upon which contributors to this volume rely to invert the terms of rhetorical theory, is like any other feature of grammar: once you know what it is, you see it everywhere. For those who don't know what it is, it is a particular use of alpha (α) that marks a condition of being without, and it comes into English as a certain "a" prefix. For instance, in the first six months of 2020, during which this volume was being revised, Sufjan Stevens and Lowell Brams released their album *Aporia* (from *a* [without] + *poros* [passageway]); ageusia, meaning lost or reduced sense of taste (from *a* [without] + *geūsis* [taste]), emerged as a common symptom of COVID-19 infection; asymptomatic carriers of that virus were thought to be the worst spreaders of it; it became necessary for millions to teach and learn asynchronously; and *Merriam-Webster Dictionary* tweeted about the difference between "immoral" and "amoral" during the protests against police violence and for Black liberation. Alpha privatives are all around, making meaning in underexplored ways. This volume makes a case for their usefulness to Rhetorical Studies at a time when the role of "the classical" is rightly being scrutinized.

MICHELE KENNERLY

JANUARY 2, 2021

ACKNOWLEDGMENTS

A few of us have benefited enormously from the high regard in which ancient rhetoric continues to be held within Rhetorical Studies, and we are aware of our privilege. We are also aware that ancient rhetorical concepts are used to block scholarship and scholars who do not want or need to use those concepts to pursue concerns far from the theorizing minds of élite ancient men or the generations of white scholars who have looked upon the writings of those men as sacrosanct. We hope this volume demonstrates *both* that ancient rhetoric is more than the "same-old" old concepts *and* that using ancient terms ought not to be a prerequisite for or the price of doing scholarship in Rhetorical Studies.

A lot happens between when writers get excited about an idea and when that idea takes book form. Major credit goes to the contributors, who wrote their pieces in the summer of 2019 and edited them during the very different summer of 2020. Many thanks to the lovely Ryan Peterson, our editor at the Press, for his enthusiasm and support, and for the generative reviews of the two anonymous readers of the initial manuscript. Thanks to Laura Reed-Morrisson for managing this volume's production, Dana Henricks for copyediting it, and to Natalie Shoch and Nicole de Lima for quick and immaculate help with back-matter materials. Cheers to Penn State's Center for Humanities and Information, which awarded me a teaching release and a grant (which I used to subsidize this book) during my time as a residential fellow in spring 2020. Thanks to John McCarthy and Carey Eckhardt, co-directors of the College of Liberal Arts Future Funded Faculty Program, from which I received various encouragements. My fellow rhetoricians in the department of Communication Arts and Sciences at Penn State—Mary Stuckey, Ekaterina Haskins, Brad Vivian, Jeremy Engels, Kirt Wilson, Rosa Eberly, Abe Khan, Michael Steudeman, Joshua Trey Barnett, and especially Debra Hawhee, Pamela VanHaitsma, and Steve Browne—help me channel my particular energies where they are most needed.

Though I had been thinking about *atopos*/*atopia* (strange/strangeness) for a while, Mari Lee Mifsud's work with the alpha privative in *Rhetoric and the Gift* was formative, getting me pondering the larger theoretical potential of alpha privatives. In the lead-up to the submission deadline for the 2018 Rhetoric Society of America convention, I invited Casey Boyle to collaborate on assembling a panel about the possibilities of the alpha privative for rhetorical theorizing. The original panelists were Casey on asomatic, Mari Lee on *atechnē*, John Muckelbauer on asignification, and myself on *atopos*. I express my abundant appreciation for everyone who attended that panel and for their encouragements, especially my Penn State colleagues Steve Browne (again) and Debra Hawhee (again), as well as Jen Buchan, Morgan Johnson, and Anthony Irizarry.

Harry C. Avery, an excellent Hellenist at the University of Pittsburgh, taught me about the variety of alpha prefixes in ancient Greek. I'm grateful. I'd be unforgivably remiss not to acknowledge, too, Mae Smethurst (1935–2019), a fierce advocate and much-missed friend who taught me to trust my own translations but also not to be fooled by them.

Introduction
Term Limits

MICHELE KENNERLY

Be they designated units of meaning, durative appointments, or conditions of an agreement, terms have endpoints. The matter of the ancient rhetorical terms that have organized Rhetorical Studies dramatizes the point. What are their limits? How much can they be stretched, conceptually and chronologically? When do they exceed their own edges? Are there areas into which they can never reach? For how long must we be beholden to ancient rhetorical terms? Because endpoints can be improperly negotiated when originating conditions are unclear, it makes sense to determine from the outset when and how ancient rhetorical terms entered Rhetorical Studies in the first place.

The rhetorical strain of what would become Communication Studies developed in the United States when, in the mid-1910s, a group of professors of speech invented a tradition originating in classical Athens—and inserted themselves into it.[1] The discipline's earliest scholars established themselves as such by intentionally annexing the authority of Protagoras, Gorgias, Isocrates, and Plato.[2] The rhetorical strain of English emerged when a group of English professors who taught composition turned to rhetoric—in particular, to ancient rhetoric—in the 1960s, thinking it might provide "practical guidance" to people who took teaching composition seriously and "intellectual substance" with which to ward off dismissive administrators or departmental colleagues in literature.[3] These professors readily connected with rhetoricians in Speech Communication, who, by that time, had been publishing about rhetoric in their own disciplinary journals for decades. According to one authoritative chronicle of those years, "classical rhetoric became an important element of this new cooperation."[4] Part of the reason was that, at that time, nobody else in academe was laying claim to ancient rhetoric; even among classicists the concerted study of rhetoric was (and remains) rare.

These many years later, Rhetorical Studies is one of very few intellectual formations that continues to understand and to authorize itself largely through its own originary assertions; that is, that the theory-based practice of "Public Address," or "Communication," or "Rhetorical Studies" started in ancient Athens, and that its rhetorical terms are therefore our terms.[5] A primary index of that understanding is a small subset of ancient Greek rhetorical terms—such as *technē* (system, art), *doxa* (opinion, reputation), *pathos* (emotion)—that features frequently in seminar discussions, conference papers, and published scholarship.[6] Generally, rhetoricians are expected not only to recognize those ancient terms but also to develop them through application to historical and contemporary forms and instances of symbolic action.

Certainly, then, such terms appear in conversations and publications that attend to ancient texts and contexts to retrieve from them fine-grained detail about those terms.[7] Far more commonly, though, the terms appear in scholarship not working with ancient texts much (or at all). There they receive theoretical development far beyond what ancient texts offer.[8] Although familiar ancient terms gain new folds and depths through both kinds of work, any given term has semantic recalcitrance, meaning it cannot be pushed too far. For rhetoricians who think these recurring ancient terms have outlived their usefulness or flat-out can never faithfully apply to the communicative realities of certain people or groups, even new takes on the same old terms do not go far enough. A related and toxic problem is that inquiries conducted *by rhetoricians trained in Rhetorical Studies* may be deemed insufficiently disciplinary (and disciplined) when lacking familiar ancient rhetorical terms.

Rhetoric's technical vocabulary has long been a site of struggle. From what seems to be the first time a teacher of speaking and writing mentions rhetoric handbooks (known as *technai*), already the vocabulary systems of public communication are said to result from a bad choice of technical terms. In the early fourth century BCE, Isocrates points to an earlier generation who wrote handbooks in which they "took it upon themselves to teach forensics, and picked hard to manage words," the kind that seemed more in line with those against education in speaking than those for it.[9] Isocrates himself prioritizes three principles, which take the form of terms: *to prepon* (the appropriate), *ho kairos* (the timely), and *ho kainos* (the new).[10] Apprais-ing as a whole the growing number of stipulated technical terms in the time of Isocrates, David Timmerman and Edward Schiappa credit the terms with bringing rhetoric into being.[11] In other words, the concept trails behind the terminology it organizes, with the terms leading the way. That seems to be the case now, too: ancient technical terms are sign evidence *par excellence* that "rhetorical study" is happening. It is, of course, a contestable claim—or, at least, it ought to be.

For us in the twenty-first century, that these technical terms are in ancient Greek or Latin makes them stick out in a way different from most other disciplinary terminologies. Yet, writing in Latin in the first century BCE about rhetoric's technical vocabulary, Cicero observes that "even the manuals of rhetoric, which belong entirely to the practical sphere and to the life of the world, nevertheless employ for purposes of instruction a sort of private and peculiar phraseology."[12] The Greekness and Latinity of rhet-oric's technical terms would have made them recede into the Greek and Latin spoken in the first century. Still, the terms had specialized meanings to which even knowledge of ancient Greek and Latin in themselves did not grant access. The meanings of these terms have always been adopted specially, as well as adapted to new cultures and circumstances.

The proliferation of words with particular meanings for rhetorical study and practice meant rhetorical handbooks in ancient Greek and in Latin had a lot to hold, teachers had a lot to command, and students had a lot to learn. In "The Old Rhetoric: an aide-mémoire," Roland Barthes observes that "all the treatises of Antiquity, especially the post-Aristotelian ones, show an obsession with classification (the very term of *partitio* in oratory is an example): rhetoric openly offers itself as a classification (of materials, of rules, of parts, of genres, of styles)."[13] In his thesaurus of technical terms at the back of his book *Rhetoric in Antiquity,* Laurent Pernot describes them as "a network taking the form of a multitude of lists."[14] He describes the lists as "juxtaposed, superimposed, and mesh[ed] with one another," as "endlessly modified, abridged, lengthened, debated," and as full of "numer-ous divergences on points of details among authors, not to mention actual contradictions between one list and another."[15] There are a lot of terms to know, not to mention their dynamic or agonistic interrelationships. Samuel Butler, in his 1663 poem *Hudibras,* carped that "for all a rhetorician's rules teach nothing but to name his tools."[16] The truth is, though, that despite there being dozens upon dozens of ancient rhetorical terms that crisscross a chronological and cultural range of ancient theorists, a few terms associated with Aristotle dominate US American rhetorical studies, especially the three genres he articulates (usually translated as "judicial," "deliberative," and "epideictic") and the three items generally called "proofs" or "means of persuasion" (these are usually kept in the ancient Greek as *ēthos, pathos,* and *logos*).[17] When all you have is Aristotle, the available means of explanation look nearly unvaryingly tripartite.[18]

What critical poses might rhetoricians two decades into the twenty-first century adopt toward the handful of overused ancient Greek terms and the expectation that all rhetoricians know and use them? I schematize four attitudes toward recurrent ancient rhetorical terms: affirmation, opposition, augmentation, and inversion. For each stance, I specify a few of its attractive and unattractive qualities. For the sake of cohesion, I pull examples pertaining to *pistis* (Aristotle's term for what's created between a speaker and the audience when the speaker uses *logos, pathos,* or *ēthos*) through the four-fold schema.

AFFIRMATION

One option is to affirm our commitment to the small set of ancient rhetorical terms already enumerated. That affirmation cannot be sentimental or defensive, however. It has to be radical; that is, undertaken with a suspicious regard for roots. Any given ancient Greek rhetorical term points far backward by virtue of its antiquity, but that mark should not be fixed as the only one that matters. In contrast to a fixation on origins, attendance to movement across time, space, and tongues puts emphasis on crossings. For that reason, translation presents itself as a foremost concern of this stance. First, I'll consider translation as *a taking across* of terms from one time and place to another and then in its conventional sense of *a taking across* from one language to another.

During the so-called "globalizing of rhetoric" debates of the 1990s, Carolyn Miller argued for the value of a capacious understanding of translation precisely because translation so often acts "as a metaphor for transhistorical appropriation and interpretation" in debates about the scope of rhetoric's applicability.[19] If the bounds of rhetoric are circumscribed by the terms—as in both scope and concepts—of its ancient Greek theorization, construed as faithfully as possible to their original conditions, then to call them narrow seems like lush overstatement.[20] One problem with drawing boundaries that way, of course, is that it ignores successive receptions of ancient rhetorical concepts and all the meanings and meaning that have accrued to them accordingly.

In her summary of prevalent approaches toward translation in the mid-1990s, Miller cites the translational distinction Richard Rorty makes between "contemporary appropriation" and "historical reconstruction," the first referring to efforts to pull the past into the present for dialogue and exchange, and the second describing efforts to understand past events on their own terms with as little anachronism as possible. Rorty's distinction—it is important to emphasize that he did not see it as *an opposition*—was zealously adopted by Edward Schiappa.[21] The debates in the early 1990s between Schiappa and John Poulakos largely amount to a disagreement over the historiographical limits of theorizing with or even about ancient Greek concepts, including *rhētorikē* (rhetoric) itself.[22] That Henry Johnstone felt he could adjudicate their debate in part by pointing out that neither of them accented "technē" in their transliterations is darkly funny: distinguishing an eta from an epsilon seems like the least of our worries when it comes to figuring out what to do with rhetoric's ancient terms and their eternal return.[23] Miller speaks to all the layers at play when she describes ancient rhetorical terms as "a conceptual vocabulary for interpretation which has itself been created by the process of interpretation. The rhetorical vocabulary has been appropriated and transformed from a tradition that is continually being appropriated and transformed."[24] The affirmative stance amounts to an acknowledgment of that accretion and of further acts of appropriation, transformation, and interpretation through translation that are to come.

Of course, translation also pertains to the matter of how to render ancient Greek and Latin technical terms into English. I mean by this kind of "translation" an interpretive process informed by the ingenuity-inspiring impossibility of achieving a one-to-one correspondence between one language and another. This impossibility does not put us at a loss, as in the Frost/Coppola commonplace "lost in translation"; moreover, with ancient languages in particular, the loss premise risks a dangerous fetishizing of pure, precious origins. One of the main objectives of translator Karen

Emmerich is to dispense with "the assumption that translation attempts a transfer of some semantic invariant" and to encourage a view of translation as "interpretive iteration."[25] Translating is not an exercise in copying (which would always be doomed to fail) but in copiousness: translators literally have to use words different from those they are translating, and thus cannot ever say the same thing as the text they are translating. And translations need to change with the times.

In her 1990 book *The Contemporary Reception of Classical Rhetoric*, Kathleen Welch highlights the use of outmoded translations as one source of dissatisfaction with what she calls classical keywords. "The keyword problem is made worse by the predominance of many English translations—particularly of Aristotle and Cicero—that are so old that they do not speak to many users of contemporary English," she writes.[26] In particular, "important Greek keywords such as pistis, ethos, and arete shrivel for many late-twentieth-century readers, when translators present them as, respectively, 'proof,' 'ethical proof,' and 'virtue.'"[27] New translations need to be undertaken periodically, and not because an English translation, for example, can help us get closer to what Aristotle meant *then* but because it can help us get closer to what we mean *now* than can an English translation undertaken decades ago.

Herein lies a constraint: translating ancient Greek or Latin texts afresh ourselves is an option viable only for rhetoricians who can set about doing intensive and extensive work in ancient Greek and Latin. Given increasing time-to-degree pressures, ancient rhetoric never having been a wildly in-demand specialty on the job market (even in those bygone years when there was a decent job market), and translations not counting toward tenure and promotion, that is work not many will have the privilege to dare to undertake.

The good news, however, is that we can locate and use updated translations, comparing translations diachronically to track shifts and sedimentations in how keywords are rendered, or even read a single ancient rhetoric text with priorities in mind that do not align with its translators and commentators (of whatever time period). Take *pistis*, for example, which Welch counted among the classical keywords whose common translation, in this case "proof," confines the word to a narrow sense of the evidentiary. Though James Kinneavy and C. Jan Swearingen wrote about *pistis* as "faith" and "belief" in the 1990s, their work was not adopted widely enough to shift the hegemony of "proof."[28] Furthermore, engaging with its role in Aristotle's *Rhetoric,* Danielle Allen renders *pistis* not as "proof" or "mode of persuasion" but as a means of "trust-production."[29] What could rhetorical pedagogy, criticism, and theory look like if "faith" or "trust" rather than "proof" were one of its central terms?[30]

The driving force behind affirmation as I articulate it here is a commitment to understanding common ancient rhetorical terms through fresh attitudes toward translation, variously conceived, which could generate new lines of research, unsettling the founding and foundational assumptions of Rhetorical Studies by means of the very material they are made of.

OPPOSITION

Outright opposition to predominant ancient Greek concepts is another solid stance, and it underlies several of the most consequential intercessions characterizing contemporary rhetorical theory. These interventions have converged on terms critics deem central to ancient rhetoric—such as "persuasion," "civility," and "citizenship"—and harmful to ethical interpersonal communication and to communal and coalitional efforts toward equity, diversity, access, and inclusion, both among our objects of study and within the ranks of Rhetorical Studies itself.[31]

For example, in "On White-Speak and Gatekeeping: Or, What Good Are the Greeks?," their contribution to a 2018 Race and Rhetoric forum in *Communication and Critical/Cultural Studies,* Martin Law and Lisa M. Corrigan identify a correlation between the grip ancient Greek concepts have on Rhetorical Studies and the whiteness of the discipline. The very few ancient rhetorical terms that have become focal points of contemporary rhetorical training and scholarship can—and sometimes *do*—block new ways of doing scholarship, new foci of scholarship, and new scholars from historically and currently underrepresented groups. Law and Corrigan vow that

> our concerns are shaped by the deployment of the Greeks in ways that we feel displace more contemporary theoretical literatures that describe phenomena that the Greeks were unconcerned with and silent about. To take one example, Aristotelian rhetorical theory focuses on locating the "appropriate" (*to prepon*) means of

> persuasion as determined by explicit rules and implicit conventions. It offers no recourse for rhetors (those that Blair calls "disturbers") whose ideas, voices, or bodies are considered inherently inappropriate (whether by rule or convention). This limitation makes the Greek canon ill-suited to account meaningfully for the disruptive tactics of contemporary antiracists and antifascists, for example. How can decorum-obsessed critical frameworks dominated by endless debates about the politics of [nonwhite] civility make sense of the radical rhetorics of, say, black liberal activists (or other radical leftists) who reject tactics like persuasion, identification, and political engagement?[32]

The solution they propose is to "think beyond *inclusion* and instead actively *exclude* those vocabularies that reinforce marginalization of nonwhite scholars. Failure to do so leaves us with a version of 'inclusion' that is limited to criticism *about* race rather than texts *for* the liberation of nonwhite writers and readers."[33] It is notable that Law and Corrigan stress, in particular, the harmful effects of a disciplinary focus on "'appropriate' means of persuasion," since that framing puts us back in the realm of *ēthos*, *pathos*, and *logos*. Surely one great irony of Rhetorical Studies is that, in 1970, Edward P. J. Corbett, the very scholar credited with pulling ancient rhetoric into Composition Studies in the 1960s, pointed to the need to theorize tactics of *ēthos* being deployed "in much of the rhetoric of confrontation," "including shocking or infuriating or alienating an audience with obscenities, threats, aspersions," which he also calls "'telling it like it is'" and "forthrightness."[34] He offers that, since it has met with a measure of success, "maybe the strategy of abrasiveness is a new 'available means of persuasion.'"[35] Despite Corbett's encouragements and hundreds of other inducements, *ēthos* has not been stretched significantly beyond its Aristotelian form. Further, though *pathos* is an Aristotelian means of persuasion, too many rhetoricians think, in contradiction to the evidence, that Aristotle has little time for it, the unstated premise being that his inattention sanctions ours. Corrigan opens the Acknowledgments portion of her most recent monograph, *Black Feelings: Race and Affect in the Long Sixties*, with anecdotes from her peer-review experiences at disciplinary journals, whose reviewers consistently and "lazily rejected any rhetorical analyses that took seriously the political theory of practical activism of radical black movement organizations.

I was tired of hearing that radical black leaders were 'too emotional' and weren't pragmatic enough."[36] Corrigan uses the word "pathos" only once in her book, and Aristotle is nowhere near.[37] She does not need him, and his exclusion ought not to be problematic.

A serious constraint, however, of the opposition stance as Law and Corrigan assume it, especially in the title of their piece, is that it dangerously distorts "the Greeks" when it cedes them to whiteness. Backdating the recent cultural construction of whiteness so dramatically that it applies to ancient cultures is the very move white supremacists make when they claim ancient Athens or ancient Rome as origin points of whiteness. That is why Nell Irvin Painter begins her history of white people with chapters on ancient Greeks and Romans. She writes, "Not a few Westerners have attempted to racialize antiquity, making ancient history into white race history and classics into a lily-white field complete with pictures of blond ancient Greeks. Transforming the ancients into Anglo-Saxon ancestors made classics unwelcoming to African American classicists."[38] Can we acknowledge that ancient Athens and ancient Rome have been mobilized symbolically by generations of overt or implicit racists *without* regarding ancient Athens and Rome as white cityscapes?[39] As classicist Rebecca Futo Kennedy insists, "The Classical texts and peoples themselves are not inherently 'Western' or 'white,' but there is a reason some people think so and we need to do better at teaching Classical antiquity in all its diversity and showing that we understand and own its racist uses—past and present."[40] The solution to the ugly side of ancient Greece and Rome and what people in subsequent periods—and that includes scholars—have carried out of them and amplified is not to exclude it but to teach it honestly and critically. At least, that's the solution for a classicist, who, after all, *must* teach about antiquity in some capacity. Rhetoricians need to ask themselves if they are under the same obligation. If we are, then we need to teach and use ancient rhetorical concepts radically differently. And this charge extends to peer review.

Ancient rhetorical concepts should not be used by gatekeepers to deem antiracist, anticapitalist, and antifascist rhetorical action insufficiently rhetorical. And, yet, so long as only a few ancient rhetorical terms—and unfavorably translated ones, at that—are held up again and again, regardless of suitability, as standards of rhetorical action, then such terms will be an impediment to fair peer review. The gatekeepers Law and Corrigan rightfully decry are making systems of ancient rhetoric small in addition to their other, more significant abuses. If mashing up a contemporary example with an overexposed ancient rhetorical term is a requirement of publication, then both the terms and disciplinary journals will be worse off. One result of a thoughtless insistence on the use of such terms is that the terms lose all dynamism. Welch points out that "appropriators of keywords who remain completely unaware of their escalating or de-escalating meanings over the seven hundred years of classical rhetoric and the similar fluctuations among postclassical readers, tend to base their single-level translations (their translations-as-substitutions) on the idea of classical rhetoric as a monolith."[41] The term *ēthos* is a good example. It looks very different in Aristotle than it does centuries later in Quintilian, the latter of whom categorizes it as a weak form of *pathos*.[42] What could rhetorical pedagogy, criticism, and theory look like if we understood *ēthos* to be a faint, loose, or sly emotional connection?

Reevaulations of ancient rhetorical terms, such as the kind offered in the previous stance and to be offered in the two subsequent stances, may go some way in making irrelevant or unnecessarily narrow applications of ancient rhetorical terms less likely, which may reduce the frequency of their being used to gatekeep. The next two stances presume there are ways to displace familiar ancient rhetorical terms without dispensing with them entirely; in particular, they ask whether the existence of other, less explored ancient terms makes an unquestioned, uncritical insistence on the same ancient terms by gatekeepers of the discipline much less acceptable.

AUGMENTATION

Another possibility is to inhabit what we have inherited from twentieth-century discipline building but to push the walls out, adding to the familiar terms by identifying within ancient sources their less well-known complements, counterparts, and even contraries. Augmentation cannot go on *ad infinitum*, since it is checked by the finite languages and cultures of the ancient world, but it can push far beyond the current conceptual contours. Some of the underexplored ancient Greek and Latin terms that have appeared in recent years include: *metanoia* (what occurs when a *kairos* is not grasped), *occultatio* (the opposite of clarity), *alloiostrophos* (which off-sets metaphor), *accumulatio* (a relation of *copia*), and *epicrisis* (amplification through allusion or citation).[43]

Admittedly, this growth model does not always include critical attention to the entailments of continuing to let ancient terms—and nearly always ancient Greek and Latin ones—occupy the foundation level of theory building in the discipline. The volume *Ancient Rhetorics and Digital Networks* takes on the matter, however, and largely out of the necessity of explaining why the titular combination seems incongruous if not ridiculous but is neither. We (Damien Smith Pfister and myself) justify our use of ancient rhetorics—Greek, Roman, Confucian, Buddhist, and Jainist—to study digitally networked communication a few ways, but here is one: "Historically, major media transitions and ancient rhetorical theory enjoy an iterative relation, linking and looping together at key junctures," such as the coincidence of print technology with the rediscovery of full works by ancient rhetoricians (e.g., Quintilian) in the early modern period and the frequent naming of digital programs after features or figures prominent in the rhetorical tradition.[44] Understood according to the schema I have been presenting here, *Ancient Rhetorics and Digital Networks* is an act of translation, but it also extends the inventory of rhetoric's ancient terms.

My pledge to use *pistis*-based examples, joined with the popularity of this chapter among readers of *Ancient Rhetorics and Digital Networks,* brings us to the chapter cowritten by Rosa Eberly and Jeremy David Johnson. In "Isocratean *Tropos* and Mediated Multiplicity," they explore Isocratean *tropos* (turn, "suggesting turning and mutability") as an alternative to Aristotelian *ēthos* (character, "suggesting dwelling and consistency").[45] As the authors put it, "The theoretical and practical chasms between Aristotelian *ēthos* and Isocratean *tropos* span a profound duplicity at the ancient heart of conceptions of self: Are we one? Are we many? Beyond theoretical conceptions of identity, how does actually existing identity-in-time—longitude—complicate even further how we make sense of ourselves and how others make sense of us? How can we trace the spaces between the turning places of multi-ply mediated identity?"[46] That digitality presses upon identity in distinctive ways gives exigency to philology.

A perhaps unintended attribute of the opposition stance as framed above is that it calls to mind the discipline's focus on the cultural productions associated with ancient Athens and Rome at the expense of an immense ancient world. Comparative ancient rhetorics, as represented by work done by Margaret Zulick on the ancient Hebrew vocabulary of persuasion, Xing Lu on ancient Chinese rhetoric in comparison to classical

Greek rhetoric, and Scott Church on ancient Buddhist concepts related to *imitatio* and *conformatio*, showcases instances of cultural congruity that enlarge upon the usual vocabulary.[47] There is also work that explicitly avoids comparison with ancient Greek rhetoric, such as that of Maulana Karenga on ancient African communicative practice, in which he uses "classical African sources, principally ancient Egyptian (Kemetic) texts, as a fundamental point of departure and framework for understanding and engaging African American rhetoric."[48] Arabella Lyon uses the thoroughly Confucian concepts *jiàn* (remonstration), *shù* (the recognition of oneself in others), and *zhōng* (acts of duty to others) to understand the 2014 Hong Kong protests known as the Umbrella Movement.[49] To position the terms of ancient Athenian and Roman rhetorical culture as the markers of rhetorical practice for which a scholar must find analogues is to limit our understanding of ancient rhetorical cultures and to constrict contemporary historiography, pedagogy, criticism, and theorizing.[50]

Even with all this building going on, or because of it, maybe, the small subset of ancient Greek rhetorical concepts still largely sets the terms of rhetorical history, pedagogy, theory, and criticism. The reluctance to part from them seems to come largely from contentment that their significance is not up for debate and we all know what they mean. As I have shown, that's certainly one feeling, but it is not the only feeling.

INVERSION

In several senses, this volume aims to change the terms of rhetorical theory. It uses a grammatical construction known as the alpha privative to alter the theoretical potential of some familiar ancient Greek rhetorical terms—namely, *technē*, *topos*, *kairos*, *doxa*, *gnōsis*, *pathos*, and *phantasia*—by turning them against themselves, but the contestation is not an outright opposition. To invert these terms is to engage in translation and augmentation informed by the opposition position, and the alpha privative performs those operations in a peculiar way.

The typical understanding of the alpha privative emphasizes how its construction (i.e., the alpha privative plus a noun or adjective stem) undercuts its stem, yielding words such as *a*pathy (without emotion) and *a*gnostic (without knowledge). Yet, an alpha privative overturns its stem in an unusual way. As Page duBois explains:

> More than other kinds of contraries, the alpha privative words preserve the presence of the contrary; it is as if instead of hate, we called the contrary of love unlove. The Greeks thus construct such concepts as a-letheia (unhiddeness) for truth, a-topia (placelessness) for eccentricity, a-ponia (nonexertion) for laziness, a-polis (a citiless person) for an outlaw. The kind of semantic formulations that occur in positive terms in English, or that have a variety of forms of negation, are in Greek endlessly and alliteratively rendered with this privation, this alpha that both preserves and takes away the sense of the word's meaning.[51]

A given alpha privative both underlines and undermines the concept at its base, making alpha privatives different from negation (signaled in Greek with the particle *ouk*) and antonymity. Ancient rhetoricians themselves do not say much about the effect of alpha privatives, but Aristotle (yes, him again) uses two alpha-privative examples in his *Rhetoric* when recognizing that "to speak from what is not had" packs amplificatory power.[52] Given the simplicity of its application, the alpha privative can be used to emphasize both "good and bad things that are not possessed, whichever of the two is useful."[53] Aristotle places this strategic use of alpha privatives into a stylistic category called *ongkos*, meaning capaciousness or expansiveness.[54] That an alpha privative takes up room in such a concentrated, suggestive form explains its appeal to Aristotle, who knows how influential condensed implications tend to be.[55] When truly noticed, an alpha privative prompts questions, such as: How can one account for the lack or the loss of what is missing? Was it ever there? What makes us assume it was, and are those assumptions just? An alpha privative pulls one into the culture of its use by backlighting normative assumptions and experiences, which are, by definition, not what everyone assumes and experiences.

A generative example of the theoretical power of understanding what the alpha privative does comes early in Debra Hawhee's book on animals and sensation in premodern rhetoric. Chapter 1 of *Rhetoric in Tooth and Claw* opens with a chapter on *alogos* (without *logos*), the adjective Aristotle notoriously uses to describe nonhuman animals in his *Politics*. The word is typically interpreted as a slight, but "the trick is to approach *alogos* as something other than the absence of *logos*, to identify in positive terms what takes the place of *logos*."[56] Accordingly, what Hawhee finds through her reading of Aristotle is that "an insistence on nonhuman animals being *aloga* is much an *attribution* as it is a denial or rejection, and this attribution of expansive, and oftentimes intense feeling to nonhuman animals helps account for their constitutive role in the teaching and shaping of rhetorical theory."[57] Hawhee centers *alogos* to see sensation better, not to make a case against reason.

The alpha privative has poignant implications for Rhetorical Studies, since its use allows one simultaneously to point to and away from persistent ancient terms. Such terms have been an undeniable part of the discipline, but that does not mean they need to continue to be in their usual forms. The alpha-privative guises of familiar concepts—*atechnē, atopos, akairos, adoxa, apatheia, aphantasia*—appear in ancient works, but not always in rhetorical handbooks, meaning their implications for rhetoric have been undertheorized or not theorized at all. We also avail of the alpha privative to make a case for the inclusion of some terms not often used in Rhetorical Studies in their nonprivative form (e.g., *a/nostos, a/poria, a/gnōstos*). There is also one instance of a Latinate alpha privative not used at all in ancient Roman texts: asignification.[58]

Inversions of well-known ancient rhetorical concepts yield perspectives on relational and communal life that are often ignored by the terms in their familiar forms. As Mari Lee Mifsud has argued, the alpha privative does not so much deprive as "free and invent something new."[59] Alpha privatives offer contrariness without outright opposition, which mirrors the critical intervention of this volume: we are unsettling familiar ancient Greek rhetorical terms but not unseating ancient Greek terms altogether. By presenting old terms in new forms, we hope to go some way in redressing critiques about their limits, mainly regarding their on-going relevance, explanatory power, or exclusionary effects.

ARRANGEMENT OF THIS VOLUME

Inverting Rhetoric bears similarities to the not uncommon keyword approach made famous by Raymond Williams in his 1976 book, *Keywords: A Vocabulary of Culture and Society*. For Williams, the concept of keywords has "two connected senses: they are significant, binding words in certain activities and their interpretation; they are significant, indicative words in certain forms of thought."[60] Most collections employing the keyword-based structure itemize one-word concepts that have undisputed if perhaps underappreciated importance in culture or a particular culture.[61] In Rhetorical Studies, the 2018 special issue of *Rhetoric Society Quarterly*, which marked the fiftieth anniversary of the founding of Rhetoric Society of America, offers a good example. Entitled "Keywords: A Glossary of the Pasts and Futures of the Rhetoric Society of America" and edited by Michelle Ballif, the issue forwards nine keywords—the body, the digital, energy, genre, *kairos*, memory, public, resistance, and sound—that emerged from a call that invited rhetoricians to submit one-hundred-word pitches.[62] The special issue provided a space for representatives of Rhetorical Studies to reflect on its past and project its potential futures, as seen through a given (well, chosen) disciplinary keyword. Keyword-based projects are usually preservative; that is, they are meant to articulate a relatively stable, orienting vocabulary. Ballif points out, however, that "although a collection of such words with ostensibly shared meanings serves to bind a community, those very keywords" can "render disciplinary homes unhomely."[63] There is nothing quite like feeling your discipline's keywords do not speak to you or are used to keep you out.

By inverting some of the most well-known, frequently taught theoretical concepts in Rhetorical Studies (including one from the *Rhetoric Society Quarterly* special issue), the contributors to this present volume offer what we hope is productive disorientation. Each chapter runs at approximately five thousand words, and that compactness makes for entries that are necessarily enthymematic and dynamic. Because, though, each contributor introduces a little-known term and explains how it differs from its more familiar form, even readers who are new to Rhetorical Studies will be able to keep up.

The first two chapters, grouped together under the heading of "Escape Velocity," demonstrate an evasion of the usual forces at work when theorizing is undertaken with ancient rhetorical terms. Mari Lee Mifsud takes on *atechnē*, meaning "without *technē*," specifically the *technē* of rhetoric, Aristotle's *Rhetoric* being the most famous place the distinction between *entechnē* and *atechnē* is drawn. By vexing the common translation of *technē* to "art" and arguing for "system" instead, Mifsud initiates a reframing of *atechnē* as that which is without, against, or in excess of systems, and pursues how we might use that reframing to understand equity and justice. In his chapter on asignification, John Muckelbauer seeks to divest the linguistic turn, with all its vibrating energy about signification, of any of its remaining inertia. What if rhetoric offers the possibility of attending to a dimension of language that is irreducible to the entire apparatus of signification? Because both Mifsud and Muckelbauer work on (and largely against) systems-thinking, their chapters break with the order of things considerably.

The second section, "(Out of) Place," takes on questions of belonging, fit, and fittingness. It unites chapters on *atopos* (without a place), *anostos* (without a homecoming), and *akairos* (without opportunity). *Atopos,* at the center of my chapter, literally means "without a place" or "out of place" but is more commonly translated as "strange," "odd," or even "unnatural." I organize and theorize "out of place" attributions into three types—the *atopos* of transgression, the *atopos* of exception, and the *atopos* of juxtaposition—to demonstrate variants of their rhetorical force. For im/migrants, *émigrés,* exiles, refugees, and asylees, "home" has a particular poignancy. Anthony J. Irizarry enters that space, writing about *anostos,* or a place of no return, which marks the limits of homecoming's rhetorical and democratic potential. This place of no return can manifest as the inability to realize home or work toward home, but it can also be the state of being-at-home, which would render the act of returning or homecoming unnecessary. Closing the section, Bess R. H. Myers uses eulogy to build a theory of the akairic, a fitting pairing since death is rarely perceived as falling at the right time and place in the lifespan of the deceased or the bereaved. Myers also considers whether *akairos* may be a better term to think with than *kairos,* since its paradoxical nature encourages experimentation with the inappropriate, the improper, and the unfitting.

The next section, "(Not) Knowing for Sure," attends to how and when what seem to be settled certainties are troubled. It holds chapters on *adoxa* (a state of being without the usual opinion), *aporia* (a state of being without a passageway), and *agnostic* (being without knowledge). Caddie Alford turns all the talk about the centrality of *doxa* to rhetorical life on its head and argues that it is actually *adoxa,* or "generally rejected" positions, that most motivate rhetorical theory, activism, and criticism. Also working with (un) conventions of disruption, Damien Smith Pfister plays with the meaning of *poros* as "pathway" to reclaim *aporia* from its dominant affective meaning of a frustrating impasse. In a time when all manner of companies are trying to track where we look, to refuse to offer up one's visual pathway for scrutiny is to refuse corporate commodification and control. "Aporia of the gaze," a concept of Pfister's coining, champions the wandering eye and its contributions to the sort of (relatively) unchanneled looking that is fundamental to serendipity, encounter, and democratic interaction. Keeping in the realm of the digital, Cory Geraths uses "Striking Vipers," a 2019 episode of the series *Black Mirror*, to theorize modes of being agnostic; in particular, he introduces the idea of *agnōstos erōs*, or desirous love that resists the usual maneuvers of a knower, such as classification, interpretation, and domination.

The final section, "(Not) Seeing It That Way," attunes to the spectrums and limits of perceptive-affective intensities, featuring chapters on *apathy* (without emotion) and *aphantasia* (without imagination). First, Nathaniel A. Rivers gives the usual line about apathy these days: it marks a lack of energy, engagement, and a shared sense of exigence. Then, using the 1983 film *WarGames*, he shows how apathy might be more generatively theorized as a redirection of destructively intense emotional engagement; not entirely, as with Stoic *apatheia*, but with certain *pathē*, in certain situations. In his chapter on *aphantasia*, Benjamin Firgens puts received rhetorical traditions and modern psychology into conversation to think through not only the practical and ethical implications of the unimagined but also the normative assumptions about visualizing capacities made in much of the literature about imagination.

The volume concludes with a short appendix of alpha-privative terms we did not explore here, replete with definitions, bibliographic pointers, and brief invitations for further use. Overall, contributors boast expertise in the following areas: ancient rhetoric, ancient and contemporary Christianity, gender and sexuality studies, im/migration studies, media studies, networked rhetorics, posthumanism, public address, public memory, science and technology studies, and visual rhetoric. As a result, each chapter both holds rhetoric at its hub and spokes toward other subject matters. The volume has, we think, an inviting miscellaneous quality as well as being unified by its insistence that alpha-privative concepts can make much-needed theoretical headway in Rhetorical Studies.[64] Fundamentally, this volume demonstrates that we rhetoricians do not need to limit ourselves to the "same old, same old" old terms; hopefully, it also communicates that use of their inverted forms is not a non-negotiable term of entry into Rhetorical Studies, either.

NOTES

1. See Herman Cohen, *The History of Speech Communication: The Emergence of a Discipline, 1914–1945* (Annandale, VA: Speech Communication Association, 1994), especially chapter 8.

2. Bromley Smith, "The Father of Debate: Protagoras of Abdera," *Quarterly Journal of Speech Education* 4, no. 2 (1918): 196–215; Bromley Smith, "Prodicus of Ceos: The Sire of Synonomy," *Quarterly Journal of Speech Education* 6, no. 2 (1920): 51–68; Everett Lee Hunt, "Plato on Rhetoric and Rhetoricians," *Quarterly Journal of Speech Education* 6, no. 3 (1920): 33–53; Bromley Smith, "Corax and Probability," *Quarterly Journal of Speech Education* 7, no. 1 (1921): 13–42; Bromley Smith, "Gorgias: A Study in Oratorical Style," *Quarterly Journal of Speech Education* 7, no. 4 (1921): 335–59; Russell H. Wagner, "The Rhetorical Theory of Isocrates," *Quarterly Journal of Speech Education* 8, no. 4 (1922): 323–37.

3. S. Michael Halloran, "The Growth of the Rhetoric Society of America: An Anecdotal History," *Rhetoric Society Quarterly* 48, no. 3 (2018): 234–41, at 235. For an example of the *topos* of utility, see Edward P. J. Corbett, "The Usefulness of Classical Rhetoric," *College Composition and Communication* 14, no. 3 (October 1963): 162–64. Robert J. Connors, Lisa S. Ede, and Andrea A. Lunsford judge that Edward P. J. Corbett's *Classical Rhetoric for the Modern Student*, first edition, 1965, "signaled the most vigorous use of classical rhetoric attempted in modern education." See their "The Revival of Rhetoric in America," in *Essays on Classical Rhetoric and Modern Discourse*, ed. Connors, Ede, and Lunsford (Carbondale: Southern Illinois University Press, 1984), 1–15, at 11. See also Kathleen E. Welch, *The Contemporary Reception of Classical Rhetoric: Appropriations of Ancient Discourse* (New York: Routledge, 1990), 6–7; Elizabeth Kalbfleish, "Anxieties of Legitimacy: The Origins and Influence of the 'Classicist Stance' in American Rhetoric Studies," *Advances in the History of Rhetoric* 16, no. 1 (2013): 82–106, at 84–87; Bryan J. McCann, Ashley Noel Mack, and Rico Self, "Communication's Quest for Whiteness: The Racial Politics of Disciplinary Legitimacy," *Communication and Critical/Cultural Studies* 17, no. 2 (June 2020): 243–52.

4. Connors, Ede, Lunsford, "Revival of Rhetoric in America," 11. Another outcome of the connection between the rhetoric-curious in Speech Communication and English was the founding of the Rhetoric Society of America in 1968. See Halloran, "Growth of the Rhetoric Society of America," 235. Out of ongoing conversations with rhetoricians in Europe came the International Society for the History of Rhetoric in 1977. The Society's own materials indicate debate over its title, with International Society for the *Study* of Rhetoric receiving less support (see https://ishr-web.org/aws/ISHR/asset_manager/get_file/81016).

5. Three of several volumes that rethink the rhetorical tradition as established in the twentieth century are Takis Poulakos, ed., *Rethinking the History of Rhetoric: Multidisciplinary Essays on the Rhetorical Tradition* (Boulder: Westview Press, 1993); Richard Graff, Arthur E. Walzer, and Janet M. Atwill, eds., *The Viability of the Rhetorical Tradition* (Albany: State University of New York Press, 2005); Michelle Ballif, ed., *Theorizing Histories of Rhetoric* (Carbondale: Southern Illinois University Press, 2013).

6. Carly S. Woods and I curated evidence of this early orientation toward Greek antiquity in the names and accompanying images of disciplinary societies and journals; see "Moving Rhetorica," *Rhetoric Society Quarterly* 48, no. 1 (January 2018): 3–27. Ira Allen has argued that "a fantastical continuity between the 'classical' and the 'modern' is key to, in some sense constitutive of, the spirit of rhetorical theory," and he explores the nature of that fantasy. See Ira J. Allen, *The Ethical Fantasy of Rhetorical Theory* (Pittsburgh: University of Pittsburgh Press, 2018), 37.

7. E.g., Takis Poulakos, "Isocrates' Use of 'Doxa,'" *Philosophy and Rhetoric* 34, no. 1 (2001): 61–78.

8. E.g., *megethos* (magnitude): Christa J. Olson, "American Magnitude: Frederic Church, Hiram Bingham and Hemispheric Vision," *Quarterly Journal of Speech* 48, no. 4 (2018): 380–404; Jenny Rice, "The Rhetorical

Aesthetics of More: On Archival Magnitude," *Philosophy and Rhetoric* 50, no. 1 (November 2017): 26–49; Stephanie R. Larson, "'Just Let This Sink In': Feminist *Megethos* and the Role of Lists in #MeToo," *Rhetoric Review* 38, no. 4 (2019): 432–44. *Kairos* (the timely): Joe Edward Hatfield, "The Queer Kairotic: Digital Transgender Suicide Memories and Ecological Rhetorical Agency," *Rhetoric Society Quarterly* 49, no. 1 (2019): 25–48.

9. Isocrates, *Against the Sophists* 19. My translation from *Isocrates II*. Edited by George Norlin (Cambridge: Harvard University Press, 1980).

10. Isocrates, *Against the Sophists* 13.

11. David M. Timmerman and Edward Schiappa, *Classical Greek Rhetorical Theory and the Disciplining of Discourse* (New York: Cambridge University Press, 2010).

12. Cicero, *On Ends* [*De finibus*] 3.1.4, trans. H. Rackham (Cambridge: Harvard University Press, 1914).

13. Roland Barthes, *The Semiotic Challenge*, trans. Richard Howard (New York: Hill and Wang, 1988), 47. Of the nearly innumerable tropes and figures, he gushes: "Why this rage for segmentation, for denomination, this sort of delirious activity of language upon language?" (85). The ancient treatise on "height" attributed to Longinus contains this line: "it would be a long and indeed interminable task to treat them all [the figures] in detail" (Longinus, *On the Sublime* [*Peri hupsous*] 16.1, trans. W. Hamilton Fyfe [Cambridge: Harvard University Press, 1932]).

14. Laurent Pernot, "Thesaurus: The System of Ancient Rhetoric," in his *Rhetoric in Antiquity*, trans. W. E. Higgins (Washington, DC: Catholic University of America Press, 2005), 215–32.

15. Ibid., 215.

16. Samuel Butler, "Hudibras," in *The Logic and Rhetoric of Hudibras*, lines 25–26, https://www.bartleby.com/380/poem/361.html. Riffing on this dig is Carolyn R. Miller, "Should We Name the Tools? Concealing and Revealing the Art of Rhetoric," in *The Public Work of Rhetoric*, ed. David Coogan and John Ackerman (Columbia: University of South Carolina Press, 2010), 19–38.

17. Ekaterina Haskins accounts for why in "Choosing Between Isocrates and Aristotle: Disciplinary Assumptions and Pedagogical Implications," *Rhetoric Society Quarterly* 36, no. 2 (Spring 2006): 191–201. See also Kalbfleish, "Anxieties of Legitimacy," 86–93.

18. Carolyn Miller speculates on what the past and present of genre theory in rhetoric might have looked like had Aristotle treated speech as variably as he treats biological life. See Carolyn R. Miller, "Genre in Ancient and Networked Media," in *Ancient Rhetorics and Digital Networks*, ed. Michele Kennerly and Damien Smith Pfister (Tuscaloosa: University of Alabama Press, 2018), 176–204.

19. Carolyn R. Miller, "Classical Rhetoric Without Nostalgia: A Response to Gaonkar," in *Rhetorical Hermeneutics: Invention and Interpretation in the Age of Science*, ed. Alan G. Gross and William Keith (Albany: State University of New York Press, 1997), 156–71, at 157 (quote), and 162–67.

20. For a reflection on the gendered nature of "faithfulness" as a criterion of a good translation, see Bess R. H. Myers, "Women Who Translate," *Eidolon*, August 5, 2019, https://eidolon.pub/women-who-translate-7966e56b3df2.

21. Miller, "Classical Rhetoric Without Nostalgia," 165. The adoption of Rorty is clear in, e.g., Edward Schiappa and Omar Swartz, "Introduction," in *Landmark Essays on Classical Greek Rhetoric*, ed. Edward Schiappa (Davis, CA: Hermagoras Press, 1994), xi–xiv, at xi.

22. These debates are easy to find.

23. Henry W. Johnstone Jr., "On Schiappa Versus Poulakos," *Rhetoric Review* 14, no. 2 (Spring 1996): 438–40, at 440, n. 3.

24. Miller, "Classical Rhetoric Without Nostalgia," 166.

25. Karen Emmerich, *Literary Translation and the Making of Originals* (New York: Bloomsbury, 2017), 1, n. 2. Thanks to Bess Myers for the gift of this wholly absorbing book.

26. Welch, *Contemporary Reception of Classical Rhetoric*, 12.

27. Ibid., 17. Since I will touch upon *pistis* and *ēthos* throughout, here I cite a piece on *aretē* that complicates its translation as "virtue": Debra Hawhee, "Agonism and Aretē,"

Philosophy and Rhetoric 35, no. 3 (2002): 185–207.

28. James L. Kinneavy, *Greek Rhetorical Origins of Christian Faith: An Inquiry* (New York: Oxford University Press, 1987); C. Jan Swearingen, "*Pistis*, Expression, and Belief: Prolegomenon for a Feminist Rhetoric of Motives," in *A Rhetoric of Doing: Essays on Written Discourse in Honor of James L. Kinneavy*, ed. Stephen P. Witte, Neil Nakadate, and Roger D. Cherry (Carbondale: Southern Illinois University Press, 1992), 123–43. See also Teresa Morgan, *Roman Faith and Christian Faith:* Pistis *and* Fides *in the Early Roman Empire and Early Churches* (New York: Oxford University Press, 2015), and for a short piece urging more work in the history of rhetoric and religion, see Martin Camper, "The Future of the History of Rhetoric is Religious," *Journal for the History of Rhetoric* 23, no. 1 (2020): 104–5.

29. Danielle Allen, *Talking to Strangers: Anxieties of Citizenship Since Brown v. Board of Education* (Chicago: University of Chicago Press, 2004), 141.

30. Jarron Slater is working on a project about renderings of *pistis* across twentieth- and twenty-first-century English translations of Aristotle's *Rhetoric*, and Scott Koslow is doing comparative work on English translations of Aristotle's definition of rhetoric. Both papers are, at this moment, unpublished.

31. Persuasion: Sally Miller Gearhart, "The Womanization of Rhetoric," *Women's Studies International Quarterly* 2 (1979): 195–201; Sonja K. Foss and Cindy L. Griffin, "Beyond Persuasion: A Proposal for an Invitational Rhetoric," *Communication Monographs* 62 (March 1995): 2–18. Civility: Nina M. Lozano-Reich (now Nina Lozano) and Dana L. Cloud, "The Uncivil Tongue: Invitational Rhetoric and the Problem of Inequality," *Western Journal of Communication* 73, no. 2 (2009): 220–26. Citizenship: Karma R. Chávez, "Beyond Inclusion: Rethinking Rhetoric's Historical Narrative," *Quarterly Journal of Speech* 101, no. 1 (2015): 162–72.

32. Martin Law and Lisa M. Corrigan, "On White-Speak and Gatekeeping: or, What Good Are the Greeks?," *Communication and Critical/Cultural Studies* 15, no. 4 (2018): 326–30, at 327, parentheses and brackets *sic*.

33. Law and Corrigan, "On White-Speak and Gatekeeping," 328. Law and Corrigan's piece appears in a forum on "Race and Rhetoric" edited by Matthew Houdek (*Communication and Critical/Cultural Studies* 15, no. 4 [2018]). In 2019, Darrel Wanzer-Serrano edited a forum on #RhetoricSoWhite (*Quarterly Journal of Speech* 105, no. 4 [2019]), and, in 2020, *Communication and Critical/Cultural Studies* published a special issue on whiteness and Communication Studies (17, no. 2), edited by Thomas K. Nakayama. Nikki Orth encouraged me to think through why this kind of critical race work is done outside the usual peer-review system.

34. Edward P. J. Corbett, "Rhetoric in Search of a Past, Present, and Future," in *The Prospect of Rhetoric*, ed. Lloyd F. Bitzer and Edwin Black (Englewood Cliffs, NJ: Prentice-Hall, 1971), 166–78. Law and Corrigan cite from Edwin Black (p. 327), who also appears in the *Prospect* volume.

35. Corbett, "Rhetoric in Search of a Past, Present, and Future," 174.

36. Lisa M. Corrigan, *Black Feelings: Race and Affect in the Long Sixties* (Jackson: University of Mississippi Press, 2020), ix.

37. Ibid., 116.

38. Nell Irvin Painter, *The History of White People* (New York: W. W. Norton, 2010), x.

39. On the dangers of white marble fantasies, see Sarah E. Bond, "Why We Need to Start Seeing the Classical World in Color," *Hyperallergic*, June 7, 2017, https://hyperallergic.com/383776/why-we-need-to-start-seeing-the-classical-world-in-color; Aimee Hinds, "Hercules in White: Classical Reception, Art and Myth," The Jugaad Project, June 23, 2020, https://www.thejugaadproject.pub/home/hercules-in-white-classical-reception-art-and-myth.

40. Rebecca Futo Kennedy, "Why I Teach About Race and Ethnicity in the Classical World," EIDOLON, September 11, 2017, https://eidolon.pub/why-i-teach-about-race-and-ethnicity-in-the-classical-world-ade379722170. On borders and/in Classics, see Dan-el Padilla Peralta, "Classics Beyond the Pale," EIDOLON, February 20, 2017, https://eidolon.pub/classics-beyond-the-pale-534bdbb3601b.

41. Welch, *Contemporary Reception of Classical Rhetoric*, 74.

42. Quintilian, *The Orator's Education* [*Institutio oratoria*] 6.1–2, vol. 3, trans. Donald A. Russell (Cambridge: Harvard University Press, 2001). For a strong summary, see Richard A. Katula, "Quintilian on the Art of the Emotional Appeal," *Rhetoric Review* 22, no. 1 (2003): 5–15.

43. *Metanoia*: Kelly A. Myers, "*Metanoia* and the Transformation of Opportunity," *Rhetoric Society Quarterly* 41, no. 1 (2011): 1–18; Adam Ellwanger, *Metanoia: Rhetoric, Authenticity, and the Transformation of the Self* (University Park: Penn State University Press, 2020). *Occultatio*: Donovan Conley and William O. Saas, "*Occultatio*: The Bush Administration's Rhetorical War," *Western Journal of Communication* 74, no. 4 (July–September 2010): 329–50. *Alloiostophos*: Jane S. Sutton and Mari Lee Mifsud, "Toward an Alloiostrophic Rhetoric," *Advances in the History of Rhetoric* 15, no. 2 (2012): 222–33. *Accumulatio*: Debra Hawhee, *Rhetoric in Tooth and Claw: Animals, Language, Sensation* (Chicago: University of Chicago Press, 2016), chapter 6; Jonathan L. Bradshaw, "Rhetorical Exhaustion and the Ethics of Amplification," *Computers and Composition* 56 (June 2020). *Epicrisis*: James J. Brown Jr., "Epicrisis for an Epic Crisis," *Amodern 9: Techniques and Technologies*, April 9, 2020, https://amodern.net/article/epicrisis.

44. Kennerly and Pfister, introduction to *Ancient Rhetorics and Digital Networks*, ed. Michele Kennerly and Damien Smith Pfister (Tuscaloosa: Alabama University Press, 2018), 1–27, at 1 and 9. An example Pfister found more recently is NESTOR, a computer program that monitors students for signs of inattention (Rose Eveleth, "The Biggest Lie Tech People Tell Themselves—and the Rest of Us," *Vox*, October 8, 2019, https://www.vox.com/platform/amp/the-highlight/2019/10/1/20887003/tech-technology-evolution-natural-inevitable-ethics?__twitter_impression=true). Nestor is most famous in the rhetorical tradition for his "words sweeter than honey" (Homer, *Iliad* 1.249, trans. A. T. Murray, 2 vols. [Cambridge: Harvard University Press, 1924]) and for teaching Achilles to be a "doer of deeds and a speaker of words" (*Iliad* 9.443).

45. Rosa A. Eberly and Jeremy David Johnson, "Isocratean *Tropos* and Mediated Multiplicities," in *Ancient Rhetorics and Digital Networks*, ed. Michele Kennerly and Damien Smith Pfister, 132–53, at 132.

46. Ibid., 133.

47. Margaret D. Zulick, "The Active Force of Hearing: The Ancient Hebrew Language of Persuasion," *Rhetorica* 10, no. 4 (Autumn 1992): 367–80; Xing Lu, *Rhetoric in Ancient China, Fifth to Third Century B.C.E.: A Comparison with Classical Greek Rhetoric* (Columbia: University of South Carolina Press, 1998); Scott Haden Church, "Remix, *Śunyatā*, and *Prosōpopoeia*: Projecting Voice in the Digital Age," in *Ancient Rhetorics and Digital Networks*, ed. Michele Kennerly and Damien Smith Pfister, 229–51. Also, Keith Lloyd, ed., *The Routledge Handbook of Comparative World Rhetorics: Studies in the History, Application, and Teaching of Rhetoric Beyond Traditional Greco-Roman Contexts* (New York: Routledge, 2020).

48. Maulana Karenga, "Nommo, Kawaida, and Communicative Practice: Bringing Good into the World," in *Understanding African American Rhetoric: Classical Origins to Contemporary Innovations*, ed. Ronald L. Jackson II and Elaine B. Richardson (New York: Routledge, 2003), 3–22, at 3.

49. Arabella Lyon, "Imagining Confucian Audiences: Tactical Media and the Umbrella Movement," in *Ancient Rhetorics and Digital Networks*, ed. Michele Kennerly and Damien Smith Pfister, 48–66.

50. For a guide to teaching the history of African rhetoric, see this resource credited by Omedi Ochieng, "African Philosophy and Rhetoric," ASHR.org, https://ashr.org/teaching-resources/diversifying-teaching/african-philosophy-rhetoric, and for a guide to teaching the history of Chinese rhetoric, see this resource created by Xing Lu, "Chinese Rhetoric in Classical and Contemporary Times," ASHR.org, https://ashr.org/teaching-resources/diversifying-teaching/chinese-rhetoric-in-classical-and-contemporary-times.

51. Page duBois, "A Passion for the Dead: Ancient Objects and Everyday Life," in *Representing the Passions: Histories, Bodies, Visions*, ed. Richard Evan Meyer (Los Angeles: Getty Publications, 1999), 270–88, at 270–71. Throughout the humanities, there is a surprising lack of sustained attention to the alpha

privative and its communicative power. For an analysis of the alpha privatives in Aeschylus's trilogy, see Naomi Finkelstein, "Unmentionables: The Erinyes as the Culmination of Alpha Privative and Negated Language in Aeschylus's *Oresteia*," unpublished dissertation (Columbia University, 2010).

52. The alpha privatives he uses are τὸ ἄχορδον and τὸ ἄλυρον, which an unnamed poet used to describe a musical strain "without chords" and "without a lyre" (1408a6–7). From these details, we are meant to conclude a flute was used, and a flute connotes wildness (!). From Aristotlelis, *Ars Rhetorica*, ed. W. D. Ross (Oxford: Oxford University Press, 1959), 1408a1. Hereafter, I cite this source as Aristotle, *Rhetoric*.

53. Aristotle, *Rhetoric* 1408a4–6. Translation mine.

54. Aristotle, *Rhetoric* 1407b26.

55. See, e.g., his treatment of *gnōmai* and enthymemes in his *Rhetoric*.

56. Hawhee, *Rhetoric in Tooth and Claw*, 13.

57. Ibid., 14 (italics original).

58. Though *significatio* is a Latin word, which first appears as a rhetorical term in the *Rhetorica ad Herennium*, in fact, *asignificatio* is not ([Cicero,] *Rhetorica ad Herennium* 4.67, trans. Harry Caplan [Cambridge: Harvard University Press, 1954]).

59. Mari Lee Mifsud, *Rhetoric and the Gift: Ancient Rhetorical Theory and Contemporary Communication* (Pittsburgh: Duquesne University Press, 2015), 146–47.

60. Raymond Williams, introduction to his *Keywords: A Vocabulary of Culture and Society*, rev. ed. (New York: Oxford University Press, 1985), 11–26, at 15.

61. See, e.g., Benjamin Peters, ed., *Digital Keywords: A Vocabulary of Information Society and Culture* (Princeton: Princeton University Press, 2016).

62. Michelle Ballif, "Introduction: Keywords; A Prelude and an Appendix," *Rhetoric Society Quarterly* 48, no. 3 (2018): 232–33, at 232. Ballif, Susan Jarratt (*Rhetoric Society Quarterly* editor at the time), and two members of the editorial board evaluated the approximately sixty proposals they received (232).

63. Ballif, "Keywords," 232.

64. Thanks to Damien Smith Pfister for his encouragements and suggestions during the initial composition of this introduction.

Escape Velocity

Atechnē

MARI LEE MIFSUD

TECHNĒ

Much intellectual attention has been given to *technē*. From philosophy to media theory to writing studies, to cybernetics, considerations of *technē* attend to the systems that produce, and reproduce, social life.[1] Perhaps this is especially so in the study of rhetoric, where the arrival of *technē rhētorikē* in fourth-century BCE Attica marks the arrival of a system for producing and performing civic discourse in the service of what Paul Woodruff terms First Democracy.[2] For ancient Athenians, creating a new polity to resist tyranny, essential practices of political deliberation, judicial decision-making, and cultural orchestration of norms to live by could not be left to the whims of tyrants or the (so-called) wisdom of kings. Instead, a new polity needed to be produced by a *technē* of persuasive public argument using practical reasoning in proofs about probabilities of political, judicial, and cultural matters.

I launch this essay considering *technē* as a "system" and not so much an "art," as traditional translations and scholarly works would have it. From the media arts, to the creative arts, to the practical arts, "art" carries a sense of something good, elevated and elevating, something that heightens our senses and sensibilities and marks a positive achievement of being human. No doubt the *technai* of media, philosophy, cybernetics, and rhetoric all share in this sense of "art." Yet something about *technē* slips past "art," and something about "art" captures too little of *technē*. A *technē* more broadly can be a system to produce, and reproduce, social, cultural, civic life, rather than an ethical or elevated accomplishment of a cultural practice. Something about "art" as the translation of *technē* misses the banality of systems.

A wide range of contemporary scholarship offers reasons why the banality of systems poses threats to living justly together sans brutalizing and deadly psychic and physical violence. Hannah Arendt's critique of fascism shows evil as produced in the banality of bureaucratized systems.[3] Beyond Arendt, from intersectional and decolonial feminisms to critical race theories, we know well that patriarchy, misogyny, white supremacy, racism, ethnocentrism, ableism, homophobia, transphobia, and the like are systemic, operating in and as systems producing and reproducing policies, laws, cultural norms and practices.[4] When seen as systems producing society and cultural life, *technai* can be acknowledged as just as likely to produce art as hate. Defining *technē* only through "art" is inadequate, even dangerous. *Technē* as art needs upending. I explore in this chapter the possibilities of *technē* inverted: *atechnē*.

ATECHNĒ

In classical rhetorical theory, *atechnē* refers to the so-called "inartistic" proofs (*pisteis atechnoi*), external to the "art" of rhetoric, as in already existing proofs needing only to be used by the rhetor, not generated by the rhetor, as in not the primary concern of rhetoric but of something other, something artless.[5] Translations of the ancient Greek to English tend to emphasize the "a" of the alpha privative as an absence of artistic proofs; that is, not *ēthos, pathos, logos,* but oaths, witnesses, torture, contracts, and law.[6] The resulting binary of art and its absence signals the way classical rhetorical theory uses *technē* as a privileged principle. Exploring atechnic inversions upends this privilege.

I explore *technē* inverted as *atechnē*, and I explore inversions of *atechnē*. Alpha privatives cannot be reduced to alpha negatives. The root *privare* can suggest liberation, not necessarily negation.[7] Through inversion, with the alpha privative signaling liberation and *technē* signaling a system, *atechnē* poses ways to be before and beyond systems, ways to intervene in them, not to serve them in their noninverted ends. The system in rhetorical history I focus on is the classical one of persuasive argument in the civic sphere. Mostly when contemporary critical theory addresses rhetoric, it does so negatively, in the name of rhetoric's classical system. This classical system in critical theory is exposed as the Master's *technē* to bring the Othered into control.[8] *Technē* inverted as *atechnē* could offer a means of freedom.

This freedom, of course, is not totalizing. The trace of *technē* remains in this inversion. Yet, the alpha privative's liberatory inversion of *technē* can be studied for theoretical and practical resources for living more justly civic life, sans the foundation in domination and death of those who are othered by the system.[9]

What happens outside of the *technē* of rhetoric—that is, *atechnē* in this inverted sense—packs power and is still, and even more so, rhetorical in its orchestration of attitudes, affects, feelings, beliefs, sensations, understandings, meanings, actions, values, norms, and the like. Prior to and in excess of technical rhetoric, a more general rhetoric is active. This more general rhetoric I am theorizing here as atechnical, in an inverted sense of the term, from a technical term in Aristotle's *Rhetoric* as proofs existing beyond the rhetor's immediate situation, to a general term meaning a rhetoric operating prior to and in excess of the presentation of proof and persuasion. In a Burkean way, this general rhetoric is akin to human motives in the drama of life.[10] In Ernesto Laclau's work, this general rhetoric, along with the *technē* of rhetoric, form the foundations of society.[11] For Thomas Rickert, this general rhetoric is ambient.[12] To some, this general rhetoric is "Big Rhetoric," characterized by Victor Vitanza as a rhetoric without a plan, just "rhetoricking," just "energized, moving, possessing."[13] For George Kennedy, this general rhetoric is the very energy of life.[14] In more recent work, Megan Eatman's *Ecologies of Harm* shows the entanglement of rhetoric and violence is less about conscious persuasion and more about a general rhetorical ecology gradually shaping public identity.[15]

Thinking rhetoric as *atechnē* is thinking rhetoric in these general ways. Whereas each of these examples just mentioned theorizes this general rhetoric beyond the *technē* of rhetoric, their scope is society, and as Eatman's work in particular shows the general rhetoric gradually shaping public identity has its systems that form, too, even though in a way not necessarily conscious. I focus, inspired as always by my studies with Henry W. Johnstone Jr., on an atechnic rhetoric that can act in a way to liberate from systems, even those forming in the general rhetorical ambience. I focus on theorizing atechnic rhetoric as a means of offering the conditions of possibility for the emergence of a rhetorical self.[16] Johnstone's work was primarily focused on dismantling the idea of formal logic in philosophical argumentation by showing its rhetorical foundations and character, namely, the emergence of a self as a perspective on dilemma made visible by a rhetoric acting as a wedge—not an art. I have used Johnstone's work to try to dismantle notions of the self as they operate in the history of rhetoric and classical rhetorical theory—namely, as an entity of enacting will upon the world through various strategic/clever/artful (*technē*-based) choices among available means of persuasion.[17] In this chapter, I focus on dismantling notions of "the self" to explore the rhetorical dimensions of the self that can be seen anew as *atechnē*.

The classical binary of self/other that shapes civic norms and what is possible for our relations with each other is a dualism of death, as Hélène Cixous writes, for both the self and the "other/ed."[18] She writes herself out of this dualism by exposing its violence and redefining all of us as a bunch of others, no self. But the self as a concept is not going to go away, meaning it must not just be dismantled and discarded, but dismantled and imagined radically anew. Johnstone's theory of rhetoric as a wedge, not an art, makes possible dismantling the notion of the self as a stable entity enacting control through persuasion instead to theorize (see/imagine) a self as a contingent rhetorical phenomenon, born in situations of contradiction and dilemma to bear witness, attacking unawareness, evoking consciousness, then going away as a perspective upon rendering a decision, leaving a person with the embodied experience and memory of this self-perspective, but now in a state of being a person. A self as an atechnical rhetorical phenomenon is situational in that it arises and resolves in particular relational situations, whether personal or public. The self from this view is not stable and is master of nothing, just a way of holding space to see contradiction, dilemma. Drawing from Johnstone, I write a self (not *the* self) as an emergence from the rhetorical wedge, occupying as perspective the space split open by the rhetorical wedge for reflexive action in the face of contradiction. Rhetoric acting as a wedge is not a technical system of orchestrating proofs and persuasion in civic life, but an atechnical rupture, a splitting open of space for reflexive action.

What does the splitting? What is the cause of this rupture? In the context of philosophical argumentation, Johnstone focuses on one's experience with dilemma. In the context in which I explore Johnstone's rhetorical wedge, the history of rhetoric prior to and at the dawning of the arrival of its *technē*, I focus on the archaic terms of Homeric epic, namely, one's experience of being "torn asunder," divided in mind and heart. One cannot exist long in such a state, the suffering of being torn asunder too great. A perspective on the whole comes to save the torn-asunder person. The self is this perspective emerging in the space held open by the rhetorical wedge. This rhetorical self, that is prior to and in excess of a technical system of rhetoric, in its bearing witness makes possible the experience of dilemma that then must be resolved. The rhetorical self is a reflexive self.

A rather big problem with this theory of the rhetorical wedge was posed to me one time many years ago by Maurice Charland at a Canadian Society for the Study of Argumentation conference, a question to which I could not respond then or barely even now: What guarantees a dilemma will be experienced? Sometimes, as Carroll Arnold points out, the driver of the wedge is an initializing technical rhetoric of appeal that forces one to undergo an experience of contradiction, of dilemma.[19] But while technical rhetoric is good at effecting persuasion, it has no guarantee. Technical rhetoric of appeal can have the opposite effect of forcing opposition to shore up their position rather than go through the experience of being torn asunder.

What activates experiencing dilemma? Although Arnold gives the answer of an initiating rhetoric of appeal that pushes one into a reflexive frame of consciousness, this answer misses the sharpest point of the rhetorical wedge. A general rhetoric as a wedge is not a rhetoric of technical appeal, a rhetoric dedicated to persuasion of others even if that other is internal—that is, a prior "self" addressed by a present "self"—rather it is an atechnical attention to objects of consciousness, the attention is held by a "self" perspective that emerges to bear witness to the gap between oneself as a person and the objects of consciousness before them. The self as perspective emerges from the wedge attacking unawareness and evoking consciousness, not necessarily through overt appeal but through awareness of contradiction, however that can be brought about. Johnstone points out that sometimes even the most mundane of questions could trigger the rupture for self-emergence. So still the question remains, what makes one aware of contradiction, especially in an age in which irony has been pronounced dead?

EQUITY

This one word: equity. Equity may very well hold unending (*atelic*) possibilities for driving that rhetorical wedge. Equity is the example I will work with in this essay for two reasons: (1) it is an understudied, yet deeply inscribed, part of *atechnē* in Aristotle's *Rhetoric*, and (2) it is currently prominent in urgent discourse dealing with racism and intersectional oppression. This atechnic rhetoric of equity is specifically about treating people and matters "outside of the system," and its rhetorical energy orchestrates the general conditions for treatment of those whose human dignity and rights are not affirmed and kept secure by "the system," for those who experience more of the burdens of public life than the benefits.

As I revise this chapter, situated in the United States, we are experiencing a global pandemic, the most severe economic downturn in the United States since the Great Depression, and the most widespread civil rights activism in the United States since 1968. Racism is being called a public health crisis along with the COVID-19 virus, and the effects of both racism and the virus are piling the unfair additional burdens on Black people and those made to be "Other" in the traditional sense of that self/other dualism of death. When the "Black & Prideful" LGBTQ+ protest march was announced for Friday, June 12, 2020, in Richmond, Virginia, the organizers, Black Pride RVA, sent this message out on social media: "We live at an identity intersection prime for multiple layers of discrimination, exclusion, and omission not to mention exposure to levels of hate, violence, and death. We march in protest and awareness to the forces that would seek to silence and extinguish us."[20] In response to these crises in public health and public life, calls for equity escalate, as the Black & Prideful LGBTQ+ March called for people to "Take an oath of accountability with action demanding institutional EQUITY & RESPECT for BLACK LGBT."[21]

In this pivotal situation, in which systems are being ruptured, rhetorics of equity abound, though they were already at an all-time high usage before this collision of crises. Institutions of higher education especially have been appealing to equity as "the new term" to advance diversity and inclusion efforts.[22] When equity is only a technical rhetoric, designed to appeal to audiences and persuade, its exquisite opportunity for justice is wasted. But hope is not lost—atechnic rhetoric offers an escape from a brutalizing *technē*. In what follows, working from Aristotle's *Rhetoric* and the idea of atechnic rhetoric as Johnstone's rhetorical wedge, I show equity can be an initiation of a rhetorical self. This rhetorical self would be capable of the reflexive action required for bearing witness to the dilemma of unfair distribution of the burdens and benefits of public life. In acting as such, this atechnic rhetoric of equity can hold space so that poles of dilemmas can be objects of consciousness and offer the conditions of possibility for resolution in ways that bend our moral arc toward justice.

The term *equity* (translated from ancient Greek *epieikes*) is used in both a general and a particular way in Aristotle's *Rhetoric*. In general usage, *epieikes* is translated to virtue. In particular usage, *epieikes* is translated to equity in a legal setting as a form of justice exceeding and superior to the justice of written law.

First let's consider *epieikes* as virtue in general. Why do translations substitute "virtue" for "equity" and that which is "equitable"? How does "virtue" make sense, knowing *epieikes* is the ancient Greek word in play? The virtue that is equity is nearly rendered invisible in English translations, leaving an abstract notion of virtue, as if virtue were a universal idealized natural good possessed by some men (i.e., not women, enslaved people, or foreigners). But *epieikes* by the time of Aristotle had a long-standing role in displaying virtue in very specific ways, namely, as fair exchange.

When we find *epieikes* used in Homeric epics, we see an active virtue that is relational and situational and about exchange.[23] The specific cultural norms of Homeric exchange are certainly not to be carried forward as virtues, but the relational and situational dynamics of equity as a virtue is sense-making for what "virtue" means in English translations of *epieikes* in Aristotle. The dynamics are that of gift-exchange and what is considered meet, fit, and fair on the occasions of such exchange. Achilles's fury with Agamemnon that opens the *Iliad* and drives the story throughout arises from a violation of *epieikes*—Agamemnon's taking back Briseis, the enslaved girl he traded to Achilles in exchange for Achilles's heroism on the battlefield. That exchanging women for winning at war is a norm, one that could give rise to an epic tale of inequity when that exchange goes wrong, shows the cultural contingency of the norms (let's not still trade women in these ways or any ways). What transcends the specific Homeric norms is the gift culture and economy of exchange at play in the use of *epieikes*, and that a person or situation can be judged virtuous or good depending on how they act or operate when exchanging benefits and burdens of life together.

Fairness in exchange orchestrating social and intimate relations circulates in cultural norms, opinions, attitudes, and beliefs in the Homeric epics, continuing to Aristotle's *Rhetoric*. Giving well, as in being fair, is a high virtue for first democracy. *Epieikes*, then, as a general virtue circulating in the *endoxa* as fairness in the exchange of benefits and burdens, is not a passive, abstract virtue but an act of checking fair exchange. These archaic norms of fair giving are atechnic, prior to and in excess of the *technē* of rhetoric. They circulate as a general rhetoric, an ambience, an energy, an ecology gradually shaping identity, beyond *technē*, but they are amendable to *technē*, able to be appropriated by *technē*. *Epieikes* as equity in giving is a pervasive virtue circulating in the cultural attitudes, opinions, beliefs, *endoxa*, from which technical proofs are invented. As Demosthenes is said to have spoken in *On the Crown*, equity is recognized among all the Greeks for their oaths taken to the principle.[24] *Epieikes* as acting to ensure equity in exchange is the given knowledge when Aristotle uses the term in this general sense translated flatly to "virtue." *Epieikes* is not a passive, abstract, universal virtue, but an action, both relational and situational, intervening in exchange to ensure the benefits and burdens of life together are given fairly.

Speaking of Demosthenes, he has more to say on equity, namely, "that nothing becomes a democratic people more than zeal for equity and justice."[25] Demosthenes's use of equity here moves to a more particular use of the term *epieikes*; namely, the use it has in forensic rhetoric, the rhetoric of law and the courtroom.

Considering this particular use of *epieikes*, and returning to Aristotle's *Rhetoric*, equity can be found to be doubly so atechnic. First, equity is part of the category of atechnic proof of law as the classical rhetorical tradition holds. Second, equity is atechnic for operating in excess of the technical system of written law.[26] "Equity is justice that goes beyond the written law," Aristotle writes.[27] Equity contains what is omitted in the written law, and these omissions are sometimes involuntary, sometimes voluntary, on the part of lawmakers, involuntary when it may have escaped notice, voluntary when, being unable to define for all cases, lawmakers are obliged to make a universal statement, which is not applicable to all, but only to most cases, and whenever it is difficult to give a definition owing to the infinite number of cases. When no exact definition is possible, but law is necessary, we must have recourse to general terms. This is a case for equity.[28] In the *Nicomachean Ethics*, Aristotle puts forward this point even more clearly about equity being an act of correction. This act is "the essential nature of the equitable: it is a rectification of law where law is defective because of its generality."[29] Sumali Hurri describes this statement as "a remarkable event in the history of jurisprudence, in that it depicts the fact that the legal system can look upon itself critically. In other words, the practice of law is self-reflective [*sic*] in its business of administration of justice and injustice."[30]

Equity as an atechnic rhetoric is at once a corrective of the written system of law and a part of the system of law, hence the importance of the alpha privative: the *technē* resides as a trace element in the term. In this case, the trace of *technē* is the inclusion of equity as part of the legal system to query justice in the written laws, querying whether the process of law has been fair and appropriate by way of intervening in the law, including the normalization of "facts" that underwrite the law.

We can keep in mind these two definitions of equity: (1) Equity and being equitable are synonymous with, translated to, virtue and being virtuous for fairness in exchange; (2) Equity is a praxis of forging a superior justice beyond the written law. Keeping these definitions in mind, we can start to see how equity works as an atechnic rhetoric driving the rhetorical wedge. Equity as an atechnic rhetoric in the vision of Johnstone's rhetorical wedge can be characterized by (at least) three key features:

- Atechnic rhetoric of equity is active—not an abstract, passive, inert virtue but a radically energized intervention, a wedge being driven.
- Atechnic rhetoric of equity is reflexive—intervening in the binary of self/other, attacking unawareness, evoking consciousness of an imbalance and the need for corrective action in relational and civic, especially legal, matters.
- Atechnic rhetoric of equity holds space to observe and query fairness in exchanging the benefits and burdens of personal and public life.

As the rhetorical wedge of equity holds space, a deliberative calculus can proceed as a praxis of technical rhetoric, a deliberation about various rhetorical appeals for judging one way or another, and these deliberations can be internalized or directed outward to an audience other than oneself; nonetheless, they remain technical. The *telos* of this deliberation is a decision, one that creates new systems, whether law or policy or the like, one available for rupturing by the general atechnic rhetoric of equity.

MOVING FORWARD

By translating and theorizing *atechnē* otherwise, as a means of liberation from systems, I am not denying the classical texts; rather, I am seeing them through an inverted lens that allows different dimensions of possibility in the rhetorical orchestration of self and society to be seen. Theorizing inversions of *atechnē* makes visible "sorties," as Cixous writes, exits, pathways, escapes, to create a new world, a new people, a new humanism.[31] This inverted humanism (ahumanism) would be characterized by liberation from systems of domination by performing equity as an unending (*atelic*) act of intervening in systems, not just the writing of new systems that take on the name of being equitable systems. Theorizing *atechnē* through various inversions creates escape routes from systems and signals the making of a new self, a new human rhetorical doing, enacting equity's justice.

This utopian vision of atechnic rhetoric may be naïve, but, too, an act of determination to imagine and create something other than brutalization in the orchestration of self and society. Theorizing atechnic rhetoric as I have in this essay is driven by a desire for something other, as Cixous writes,[32] than the same old story of death, something like love, friendship, happiness, not in a liberal way, and certainly not neo-liberal way, but a radical way: joy that can emerge only after the killjoy's call for equity ruptures the system, turns us reflexively, and holds space for the praxis of equity's justice.[33] This makes love that comes from revolution, as Houria Bouteldja inspires.[34]

But this cannot end yet, or ever. Equity calls for the very exchange of this essay to be interrupted and queried for its justice. Interpersonal equity theory makes predictions about what people in relationships will do when they sense an imbalance in their relationship.[35] This imbalance (inequity) is based on the perception of imbalance by a participant in a given relationship, which may appear as under-benefit or over-benefit. Under-benefit occurs when someone is putting in more work or getting fewer rewards than their partner; over-benefit occurs when someone is putting in less work or getting more rewards than their partner. When people sense an imbalance, they act to restore equity. Applied studies in equity theory show grim results: under-benefited people restore equity by forgiving their partners, and over-benefited people restore equity by derogating their partners. Derogating victims of inequity alleviates the discomfort of the over-benefited. The over-benefited justify inequity as equity by way of considering the victim's lowliness deserves no rewards.

We can see this pattern maintaining in the transition from interpersonal to public life. An ancient Greek history exists for this equity theory for public life. Aristotle's *Politics* offers a quite transparent account: justice is not for everybody but only for those who are equals, and it is thought that inequality is just, for so indeed it is, though not for everybody, but for those who are unequal.[36] Inscribed into justice is this hierarchy of people, and whose personhood matters for being just. In ancient Athens, those people were land-owning, Athenian-born men, not lower-class men, foreigners, enslaved people, or women. This normalization of equals being treated equally and unequals unequally has not changed so much since then.

So, even if equity as an atechnic rhetoric were to make more likely a rhetorical wedge in which dilemma can be experienced, no guarantee can be had that the resulting deliberation will produce an equitable result. And every decision based on equity creates new law, new policy, new systems, new *technai* for orchestrating civic life. As an action of intervention, reflexivity, correction, equity as an atechnic rhetoric must drive a rhetorical wedge continually. Equity as a praxis of questioning fairness is always moving, never stable; even though new decisions and laws get made post equity's intervention, equity must next upend them. When being equity-minded, one must be prepared for an endless process of intervention. The search for idealized origins and ends of atechnic rhetoric in justice is a mistake, for rhetoric that is *atechnē* is *atelic* in its praxis, unending in its action, and therein lies hope.

NOTES

1. See, for example, Timothy Campbell, *The Techne of Giving: Cinema and the Generous Form of Life* (New York: Fordham University Press, 2017); Kelly Pender, *Techne, from Neoclassicism to Postmodernism: Understanding Writing as a Useful, Teachable Art* (Anderson, SC: Parlor Press, 2011); Jeff Pruchnic, *Rhetoric and Ethics in the Cybernetic Age: The Transhuman Condition* (Abingdon: Routledge, 2013); David Roochnik, *Of Art and Wisdom: Plato's Understanding of Techne* (University Park: Penn State University Press, 1996); Henry Staten, *Techne Theory: A New Language for Art* (New York: Bloomsbury, 2019); Bernard Stiegler, *The Age of Disruption: Technology and Madness in Computational Capitalism*, trans. Daniel Ross (Cambridge: Polity, 2019); Jonathan Sterne, "Communication as Techné," in *Communication as . . . : Perspectives on Theory*, ed. Gregory J. Shepherd, Jeffrey St. John, and Ted Striphas (Thousand Oaks, CA: Sage, 2006), 1–98.

2. Paul Woodruff, *First Democracy* (New York: Oxford University Press, 2005). A sample of scholars in rhetoric focusing on *technē*, including those praising as well as subverting: Janet M. Atwill, *Rhetoric Reclaimed: Aristotle and the Liberal Arts Tradition* (Ithaca: Cornell University Press, 1998); Sharon Crowley and Debra Hawhee, *Ancient Rhetorics for Contemporary Students*, 3rd ed. (New York: Pearson, 2004); Byron Hawk, *A Counter-History of Composition: Toward Methodologies of Complexity* (Pittsburgh: University of Pittsburgh Press, 2007), and "Toward a Post-Techne—Or, Inventing Pedagogies for Professional Writing," *Technical Communication Quarterly* 13, no. 4 (2004): 371–92; James A. Herrick, *The History and Theory of Rhetoric*, 3rd ed. (New York:

Pearson, 2005); Andrew Maura and Byron Hawk, "Posthuman Rhetorics and Technical Communication," *Technical Communication Quarterly* 19, no. 1 (2019): 1–10; Edward Schiappa, *The Beginnings of Rhetorical Theory in Classical Greece* (New Haven: Yale University Press, 1999).

3. Hannah Arendt, *Eichmann in Jerusalem: A Report on the Banality of Evil* (New York: Viking Press, 1963).

4. For a sample of critical scholarship informing this essay, see Sara Ahmed, *Living a Feminist Life* (Durham: Duke University Press, 2018); Mary Beard, *Women in Power: A Manifesto* (New York: Liveright Publishing Corporation, 2017); Hélène Cixous, "Sorties: Out and Out: Attacks / Ways Out / Forays," in *The Newly Born Woman*, ed. Hélène Cixous and Catherine Clément, trans. Betsy Wing (Minneapolis: University of Minnesota Press, 1986), 63–131; Kimberlé Crenshaw, "Demarginalizing the Intersection of Race and Sex: A Black Feminist Critique of Antidiscrimination Doctrine, Feminist Theory and Antiracist Politics," *University of Chicago Legal Forum* 8 (1989): 139–67; Kate Manne, *Down Girl: The Logic of Misogyny* (Oxford: Oxford University Press, 2018); Raka Shome, "Post-Colonial Interventions in the Rhetorical Canon: An 'Other' View," in *Contemporary Rhetorical Theory: A Reader*, ed. John Louis Lucaites, Celeste Michelle Condit, and Sally Caudhill (New York: Guilford Press, 1999), 591–608; Gayatri Spivak, *An Aesthetic Education in an Era of Globalization* (Cambridge: Harvard University Press, 2012).

5. Christopher Carey, "'Artless' Proofs in Aristotle and the Orators," in *Oxford Readings in the Attic Orators*, ed. Edwin Carawan (Oxford: Oxford University Press, 2007), 229–46; Crowley and Hawhee, *Ancient Rhetorics*; Michael de Brauw, "The Parts of Speech," in *A Companion to Greek Rhetoric*, ed. Ian Worthington (Malden, MA: Blackwell, 2007), 187–202; David Mirhady, "Non-Technical Pisteis in Aristotle and Anaximenes," *American Journal of Philology* 112, no. 1 (1991): 5–28.

6. For the key passage introducing "inartistic" proofs, see Aristotelis, *Ars Rhetorica*, ed. W. D. Ross (Oxford: Oxford University Press, 1959), 1375a22–1377b12. Hereafter, I cite this source as Aristotle, *Rhetoric*.

7. See for additional comment, Mari Lee Mifsud, *Rhetoric and the Gift: Ancient Rhetorical Theory and Contemporary Communication* (Pittsburgh: Duquesne University Press, 2015), 146–47.

8. See for example Cixous, "Sorties"; Foucault, *Fearless Speech* (Cambridge: MIT Press, 2001).

9. Victor Villanueva, afterword to *Rhetorics Elsewhere and Otherwise: Contested Modernities, Decolonial Visions*, ed. Romeo García and Damián Baca (Urbana, IL: Conference on College Composition and Communication of the National Council of Teachers of English, 2019), 223–25.

10. Kenneth Burke, *Attitudes Toward History* (Los Altos: Hermes, 1959); and *Rhetoric of Motives* (Berkeley: University of California Press, 1969).

11. Ernesto Laclau, *The Rhetorical Foundations of Society* (London: Verso Books, 2014).

12. Thomas Rickert, *Ambient Rhetoric: The Attunements of Rhetorical Being* (Pittsburgh: University of Pittsburgh Press, 2013).

13. Victor J. Vitanza, "Big Rhetoric," interviewed by Jimmy Butts, *Itineration* (2013), https://vimeo.com/62108351.

14. George A. Kennedy, "A Hoot in the Dark: The Evolution of a General Rhetoric," *Philosophy and Rhetoric* 25, no. 1 (1992): 1–21.

15. Megan Eatman, *Ecologies of Harm: Rhetorics of Violence in the United States* (Columbus: Ohio State University Press, 2020).

16. This essay draws from the following writings of Henry W. Johnstone Jr.: "Bilaterality in Argument and Communication," in *Advances in Argumentation Theory and Research*, ed. Robert J. Cox and Charles Willard (Carbondale: Southern Illinois University Press, 1983), 95–102; "Communication: Technology and Ethics," in *Communication, Philosophy, and the Technological Age*, ed. Michael J. Hyde (Tuscaloosa: University of Alabama Press, 1982), 38–53; "Philosophical Argument and the Rhetorical Wedge," *Communication and Cognition* 24, no. 1 (1991): 77–91; "Rhetoric as a Wedge: A Reformulation," *Rhetoric Society Quarterly* 20, no. 4 (1990): 333–38; *The Problem of the Self* (University Park: Penn State University Press, 1970); *Validity and Rhetoric in Philosophical Argument: An Outlook in Transition* (University Park: The Dialogue Press of *Man and World*,

1978); "Response to Carroll Arnold and George Yoos," *Philosophy and Rhetoric* 20, no. 2 (1987): 129–134; Henry W. Johnstone Jr. and Mari Lee Mifsud, "Wedge and Bridge: A Note on the Rhetoric of Distinction and Identification," *Rhetoric Society Quarterly* 29, no. 2 (1999): 75–78.

17. See, for example, Mari Lee Mifsud, "Revision and Immortality in Philosophical Argumentation: Reconsidering the Rhetorical Wedge," *Informal Logic* 21, no. 1 (2001): 51–60; *Rhetoric and the Gift*; "On Being a Simple Judge: Exploring Rhetorical Citizenship in Aristotelian and Homeric Rhetorics," in *Contemporary Rhetorical Citizenship*, ed. Christian Kock and Lisa S. Villadsen (Leiden: Leiden University Press, 2014), 223–38; "Oh Popoi! Henry Johnstone, Homer, and the History of Rhetoric," *Communication Annual: Journal of the Pennsylvania Communication Association* 60 (2004): 73–90; "On Rhetoric as Gift/Giving," *Philosophy and Rhetoric* 40 (2007): 89–107; "On the Idea of Reflexive Rhetoric in Homer," *Philosophy and Rhetoric* 35, no. 1 (1998): 41–54.

18. Cixous, "Sorties."

19. Carroll Arnold, "Johnstone's 'Wedge' and Theory of Rhetoric," *Philosophy and Rhetoric* 20, no. 2 (1987): 118–28.

20. Black Pride RVA, "Black & Prideful LGBTQ+ March," photo 2, Richmond, VA, accessed June 12, 2020, https://twitter.com/BlackPrideRVA/status/1271249646845931523/photo/2.

21. Black Pride RVA, "Black & Prideful LGBTQ+ March," photo 1, Richmond, VA, accessed June 12, 2020, https://twitter.com/BlackPrideRVA/status/1271249646845931523/photo/1.

22. A sample of works advancing the call for equity in higher education: Estela Mara Bensimon and Lindsey Malcom, *Confronting Equity Issues on Campus: Implementing the Equity Scorecard in Theory and Practice* (Sterling, VA: Stylus, 2012); Joseph Ralina, "What's the Difference with 'Difference'?: Equity, Communication, and the Politics of Difference." *International Journal of Communication* 11 (2017): 3306–26; Frank Tuitt, Chayla Haynes, and Saran Stewart, eds., *Race, Equity, and the Learning Environment: The Global Relevance of Critical and Inclusive Pedagogies in Higher Education* (Sterling, VA: Stylus, 2016); Keith Witham, Lindsey Malcom-Piqueux, Alicia Dowd, Estela Mara Bensimon, *America's Unmet Promise: The Imperative for Equity in Higher Education* (Washington, DC: Association of American Colleges and Universities, 2015).

23. See, for example, Homer, *Iliad*, trans. A. T. Murray, 2 vols. (Cambridge: Harvard University Press, 1985), 19.21, 19.147, 23.50, 23, 537; Homer, *Odyssey*, trans. A. T. Murray, 2 vols. (Cambridge: Harvard University Press, 1984), 2.207, 8.389, 12.382.

24. Demosthenes, *On the Crown*, ed. Harvey Yunis (New York: Cambridge University Press, 2001), section 181.

25. Demosthenes, "On the Accession of Alexander," in *Orations*, vol. 1, trans. J. H. Vince and C. A. Vince (Cambridge: Harvard University Press, 1926), section 1.

26. Aristotle, *Rhetoric* 1374a22–44; Aristotle, *Nicomachean Ethics*, trans. H. Rackham (Cambridge: Harvard University Press, 1975), 1137a31–1138a3.

27. Aristotle, *Rhetoric* 1374a.28.

28. Ibid., 1374a22–44. See also Aristotle, *Nicomachean Ethics* 1137a31–1138a3.

29. Aristotle, *Nicomachean Ethics* 1137b.

30. Samuli Hurri, "Justice *Kata Nomos* and Justice as *Epieikeia* (Legality and Equity)," in *Aristotle and the Philosophy of Law: Theory, Practice and Justice*, ed. Liesbeth Huppes-Cluysenaer and Nuno M. M. S. Coelho (New York: Springer, 2013), 153.

31. Cixous, "Sorties."

32. Ibid.

33. See Ahmed, *Living a Feminist Life*, for more on the feminist killjoy, including a toolkit.

34. Houria Bouteldja, *Whites, Jews, and Us: Toward a Politics of Revolutionary Love*, trans. Rachel Valinsky (South Pasadena, CA: Semiotext(e), 2016).

35. Catherine Y. Kingsley Westerman, "How People Restore Equity at Work and Play: Forgiveness, Derogation and Communication," *Communication Studies* 6, no. 3 (July–August 2013): 296–314.

36. Aristotle, *Politics*, trans. H. Rackham (Cambridge: Harvard University Press, 1994), 1280a.

Asignification

JOHN MUCKELBAUER

LINGUISTIC V. RHETORICAL TURNS

In the mid-1990s, when I was just beginning to study rhetoric, I found it vaguely curious that many scholars aligned its study with the so-called "linguistic turn" in the human and social sciences. Even today, I still occasionally encounter rhetoric scholars who refer to a supposed "rhetorical turn" in humanistic scholarship that they treat as more or less synonymous with the "linguistic turn" of the last thirty or so years. As many of us likely recall, this "linguistic turn" refers to an intellectual trajectory wherein, in Jacques Derrida's words, "language invaded the universal problematic."[1] That is, this turn refers to a historico-theoretical moment in which the signifying movement of language (and the relational or differential quality of meaning) became the paradigm for analyzing a whole host of diverse social phenomena. With Ferdinand de Saussure's *Course on General Linguistics* as a key origin text, prominent thinkers from Derrida to Jacques Lacan to Julia Kristeva to Henry Louis Gates pursued the literary, psychological, and broadly social consequences of this "semiotic" analysis. Conversely, throughout the 1990s, a whole host of scholars of rhetoric, particularly those involved in rhetorical theory, pointed to an important kinship between these intellectual directions and their own work.[2]

Of course, what all this work has in common is that it prioritizes and emphasizes language, pointing to its importance across the social field (and at times even claiming that language constitutes that field by constructing the "terministic screens" of human perception—but more on this later). The first point I'd like to make, then, is simply that there are many different ways of prioritizing language and that not all of them are entirely compatible with each other. That is, the simple fact that a work "emphasizes the role of language" does not necessarily indicate very much; not only are there (obviously) quite different senses of what "language" is, but less obviously, there are multiple, often conflicting senses of what counts as "emphasizing" or "prioritizing."[3]

For the discourses usually associated with the linguistic turn, the emphasis is on language *as a signifying operation*. That is, the linguistic turn's commitment to language is a commitment to language as a signifying system that is directed toward meaning, to either the production of meaning or to the attempt to understand or interpret meaning/s. This is language thought "symbolically," by which I mean only that it works primarily in the realm of symbol systems that are conceived as forms of mediation between human consciousness and the world "out there" (as I will argue below, "signifying" language requires this dualist ontological diagram as well as the mediation that links them). Now, even this "symbolic and mediating" version is not simply univocal: there are a series of different possible variations on the question of *how* language mediates; for instance, one crucial hinge *within* signifying conceptions of language is whether or not the formation of "signifieds" (meanings or "thought images") requires the presence of "signifiers" (words or "sound images"). Saussure thought it did; Noam Chomsky thinks it doesn't. But in the most straightforward examples of signifying language, subjects use signifiers to transmit signifieds to another consciousness, endeavoring to reproduce, as accurately as possible, the signified meaning in the mind of its audience.

Now, it is also the case that most of the more provocative versions of the "linguistic turn's" approach to signification (such as can be found in Roland Barthes or Paul de Man) demonstrate language's inability to *finally* mean, its structural incapacity for a signified meaning to ever become self-present. Hence, one of the more intriguing conclusions that sometimes issues from this approach (particularly in literary studies) is that any interpretation will always be incomplete, will always have to be deferred to the next (also indeterminate) articulation. The most important aspect of this point is that such incompleteness is not a product of any actual interpreter's inadequacy or failure (or an author's greatness), but of the structure and function of language itself. However, the point that I want to call attention to here is simply that whether one is concerned with producing a meaning, understanding a meaning, or demonstrating the indeterminacy of meaning, it's not self-evident that any of this concern with meaning is simply synonymous with rhetoric.

In other words, to my mind, rhetoric has always encouraged something different than this signifying approach to language. More precisely, I think rhetoric offers the possibility of attending to a dimension of language that is irreducible to the entire apparatus of signification. Indeed, what originally attracted me to the study of rhetoric back then was that, even in its classical Greek incarnation, rhetoric seems largely indifferent to signification and to the processes of either producing or interpreting a signified meaning. While signifying versions of language might ask questions about how language means, how we can come to understand it, or whether or not we can finally ever approach meaning (or a signified), even the most instrumental, classical versions of rhetoric pose different questions. They ask, for instance, what force does language have? How can it impact actions? What effects does it produce (one of which may be "meaning")? In its classical incarnation, in the work of Gorgias and other "sophists," if I want to persuade the polis of something, I'm not necessarily trying to get them to simply comprehend my message or even trying to get them to understand anything at all; I'm primarily just trying to get them to *do* something. (Of course in this classical version, I would likely want them to at least understand what I want them to do, but such understanding would not be the *goal* of my discourse, only a hinge toward that goal.)

So while signification seems inclined toward issues of meaning, understanding, and perhaps indeterminacy, rhetoric seems inclined toward a focus on forces, effects, and actual actions (an inclination that, following Deleuze and Guattari, I simply call "asignifying").[4] In other words, and staying with the classical version of rhetoric as persuasion, persuasion's relationship to the proposition it supplements is not primarily to the proposition's meaning or content, but to its capacity to exert a compelling force, its ability to evoke particular responses in specific audiences (often in the interest of producing political or juridical actions).

Another way of saying this is that the traditional act of persuasion is not primarily interested in *what the proposition is,* nor with the entire apparatus that follows from this: signification, the goal of identical reproduction, an emphasis on understanding and consciousness. Instead, it emphasizes *what the proposition does,* the actual responses it provokes and the effects it engenders. This distinction between prioritizing "being" (what the proposition *is*) and prioritizing "doing" (what the proposition *does*) is, to my mind, a crucial distinction for rhetoric. For classical thinkers, the distinction indicates that in order to reproduce the proposition rhetorically, one need not reproduce a particular content or a particular meaning so much as provoke a certain array of responses and effects. To take one of the most frequently discussed consequences of this distinction throughout antiquity, through asignifying rhetoric, one need not transmit the truth as a content in order to incite a response or persuade someone to act.

And it is precisely because the ancients were well aware of this difference between signifying and asignifying dimensions of language—and the consequences of each—that some, following Plato, believed rhetoric to be morally dangerous. If rhetoric was not tethered to some kind of (dialectical) method for discerning the truth, it could easily encourage people to act without knowing that truth. But even more profoundly, people could *appear* to be acting in accordance with justice and virtue without truly knowing what justice or virtue *was*. For Plato, of course, acting without knowing the truth (of virtue, of justice, of anything) meant that one was *not really* acting in accordance with virtue or justice. And this was the basis for much of the Platonic dialogues: Socrates's task was to show his interlocutor that they did not really know, for instance, what virtue really *was*, such that their actions were only *apparently* virtuous (see, for example, the *Protagoras*).[5] In other words, the danger of rhetoric for this lineage of thinkers is that it simply isn't primarily concerned with knowing the truth or understanding the meaning—it just wants to move people to some kind of action. And any movement to action (any doing) that was not guided by a prior understanding of the truth (a being) was, at best, intellectually and morally suspect.

Unlike those ancient thinkers, I do not want judge this difference as a shortcoming, but I do want to point to it *not only as a difference, but as a crucial, even definitive difference for rhetoric*: asignification focuses primarily on forces, effects, and actions (doing) while signification focuses on content, meaning, and understanding (being). And we could even construct a provisional twentieth-century intellectual lineage focused on asignification, beginning, perhaps, with J. L. Austin's *How to Do Things with Words*, and proceeding through Derrida's "Signature Event Context," Judith Butler's *Gender Trouble*, Deleuze and Guattari's *A Thousand Plateaus*, and Karen

Barad's "Posthuman Performativity."[6] Of course, none of those theorists explicitly connect their work to "rhetoric," although it's important to note that, with the exception of de Man, neither did the "signifying" tradition. While this asignifying approach to language may not be the prevalent orientation of many scholars of rhetoric today, it was not only one of the distinguishing features of rhetorical theory in antiquity, but it is also one that offers a vibrant intellectual tradition today.[7]

Now, all that said, it is also important to emphasize that, despite how I have largely presented them to this point, these two dimensions of language are certainly not mutually exclusive: in the traditional, managerial diagram of antiquity, I most likely want my audience to understand what it is that I want them to do (though not necessarily; persuasion might even be most effective when my audience thinks that they alone have reached the decision to act). It may even be the case that these two dimensions of language actually require each other; certainly, much traditional rhetoric assumes that at least rhetors themselves should understand what they are trying to accomplish.[8] But the possible interplay between these two dimensions does not make them identical. For this reason, it is crucial not to imply an either/or logic between these different dimensions of language; for my part, I have elsewhere tried to render the distinction between signification and asignification merely as different inclinations or different emphases in any particular encounter.[9] Asignifying rhetoric engages with symbolic practices of meaning and understanding; these simply aren't its primary orientation. And meaningful language also has actual effects beyond the realm of the symbolic; these just aren't its principal concern. The fact that these two dimensions of language—that is, signifying meaning and asignifying force—exist in close proximity does not indicate that they are the same. And maintaining and emphasizing the distinction, *as well as rendering their complex and messy interplay*, is, I believe, crucial for rhetoric as an intellectual tradition.

LANGUAGE AS (NON)SYMBOLIC ACTION

To develop this line of thinking a bit further, I would like to schematically take up a couple moments in the work of Kenneth Burke, the mid-twentieth-century thinker who portrayed rhetoric as a crucial aspect of human interaction. To my knowledge, Burke never draws explicitly on Saussure or the language of semiotics, and he rarely seems interested in what we would call a "signified meaning." In fact, unlike many of his contemporaries, he opts instead to focus on what he calls the "hortatory" or "suasory" force of language, on what language *does*. Obviously, this emphasis on action would seem to make Burke an interesting figure to consider in the lineage of "asignifying" thinkers. However, to my reading, his approach to thinking about rhetorical action shares two key aspects in common with the signifying approach to language: (1) a dualist ontology and (2) the privileging of "being" prior to "doing." For me at least, it is precisely the ambiguous status of his treatment of language (not exactly signifying; not exactly asignifying) that makes his work an interesting site through which to pursue the messy delineation of asignification.

While Burke clearly wants to think of language as an action, for him, that action is consistently modified as "symbolic": "Such considerations are involved in what I mean by the 'dramatistic,' stressing language as an aspect of 'action,' that is, as 'symbolic action.'"[10] I am not aware if he ever attempted to directly define what he meant by this domain of "the symbolic" in much detail, but attending to some of the ways he uses the term can allow me to develop (and then hopefully blur) the distinction between signification and asignification.

For instance, in his famous "Definition of Man" essay, Burke begins by taking up the classical characterization of humans as "the symbol-using animal." However, unlike many before him who have used this phrase, Burke is quick to distinguish himself from the simple verbal realist perspective that thinks of language as simply something we "use." For Burke, humans are not symbol users in the same way that we are, for example, tool users, because language is not simply something outside of us that we employ in order to accomplish some nonlinguistic task in the so-called "real world." As he writes, "The 'symbol-using animal,' yes, obviously. But can we bring ourselves to realize just what that formula implies, just how overwhelmingly much of what we mean by 'reality' has been built up for us through nothing but our symbol systems."[11] Indeed, I think it is due to the fact that Burke pushes against a simple conception of symbolicity in this way, and even points toward a kind of asignifying orientation, that makes him so appealing to scholars of rhetoric: "Though man [*sic*] is typically the symbol-using animal, he clings to a kind of naïve verbal realism that refuses the full extent of the role played by symbolicity in his notions of reality."[12] This verbal realism that we humans cling to is the oversimplified understanding of "the symbolic" that most humans implicitly possess (the belief that we see things and then simply attach words to them), but this understanding requires that we "forget the kind of relation that really prevails between the verbal and the nonverbal."[13] Here, Burke offers a kind of provisional understanding of how "symbols" actually function: "In being a link between us and the nonverbal, words are by the same token a screen separating us from the nonverbal."[14] That is, the "symbolic" is not just a series of names for things; it functions much more deeply as a mediating screen between us and the world, both connecting us to that world and keeping us forever separated from it. In effect, then, "the symbolic" is a kind of epistemic force that forms not only how humans perceive the world, but even what we see. Think here of his famous definition of symbolic action: "Even if any given terminology is a *reflection* of reality, by its very nature as a terminology it must be a *selection* of reality, and to this extent it must function as a *deflection* of reality."[15]

But Burke doesn't stop at the realization that language may be constitutive of how we, as humans, perceive reality. He continues, ". . . though the statement [that symbols both connect us to and separate us from reality] gets tangled in its own traces, since so much of the 'we' that is separated from the nonverbal by the verbal would not even exist were it not for the verbal (or for our symbolicity in general, since the same applies to the symbol systems of dance, music, painting and the like)."[16] Burke's moves in this brief and famous passage are worth unpacking a bit.

He begins by debunking the realist assertion that words are simply names that humans attach to things so that we can refer to them more easily. His first move, then, is to set up a dualist diagram with humans on one side and "reality" on the other, with "symbol systems" acting as a mediating screen between the two. But in Burke's version of this diagram, words are very much constitutive of our capacity to see things at all. That is, symbol systems are "terminisitic screens" that direct our attention to some aspects of the world and encourage us to ignore others (elsewhere, he likens symbols to colored photographic filters of the same object, enabling one to perceive different aspects of the "same" picture). But second, he goes even further and claims that not only are symbols essential to human perceptions of reality, but "so much of the 'we'" of our perceptions wouldn't even be imaginable without these symbol systems. In other words, these mediating screens are not simply something located between humans and objects, but are even constitutive of "so much of" one side of that diagram—the human.[17]

This is a pretty heady diagram of language—a thinking of symbolicity that portrays it as a mediating force between human perception and the world "out there"—but also a thinking of symbolicity that hints that one side of that diagram (human perception) is deeply dependent upon the existence of these mediating symbolic screens to even exist. And yet, there is one classic question that he never raises here: whether the basic dualist diagram he sets up (human perception / (mediating language) / reality) is not itself already a terministic screen. In fact, I would argue that he actually can't attend to that possibility because he is fundamentally committed to a dualist diagram that involves, first, symbolic action that is distinctly human, and, second, nonsymbolic action (or what he will elsewhere call "motion") that is the case for all the nonhuman things out there. This also explains why he hedges his phrasing even as he troubles the epistemological diagram ("so much of the 'we' that is separated from the nonverbal by the verbal"): it is only "so much of" the human that is at stake—not *all* of the human—because there are parts of the human (its materiality, for example) that, for Burke, are *not* of the same order as symbol systems.

What I want to point to through all of this is that thinking of language as "symbolic"—*even if it is constitutive of perception or constitutive of subjectivity*—irreducibly separates (and almost certainly elevates) human consciousness from the world itself. If "language referring to the realm of the nonverbal is necessarily talk about things in terms of what they are not," this is only the case if you think that language is a *symbolic* action and not an actual action.[18]

And for Burke, as for many others, this dualist diagram becomes a way of a establishing a kind of prior "being" (the nonsymbolic real world) that preexists the "doing" of the symbolic, rhetorical world of human perception. Now this sentence may seem surprising to scholars of Burke who are very much drawn to an image of him as an anti-foundationalist or linguistic constructionist who is invested in the contingency of language and human existence. But it seems to me that throughout his prolific career, Burke's dualistic orientation nearly always encouraged him to note (and often to pursue) a sense of "being" that is "logically prior" to all "doing" (his commitment to the "logical priority" of being is pervasive). For instance, as he writes in the introduction to *A Grammar of Motives,* after "formulating the basic stratagems which people employ" as Symbolic and Rhetorical, he found that the "project needed a *grounding in formal considerations logically prior* to both the rhetorical and psychological."[19] This is also why, in searching for the commonalities among the language games of differing philosophical schools through his dramatistic method, he explicitly states that he is not looking for *just another language,* but "an Edenic prelanguage."[20] And also why, in a symposium, when an interlocutor pointed out to him that "dramatism is a perspective on reality, but it is not the only perspective," Burke responded that dramatism "functions on another level [than perspectives and 'isms']."[21] And lest one think that his commitment to discovering the dramatistic features that are "logically prior" and that "underly" the world of human symbolic action has no connection to an emphasis on the priority of "being" over "doing," consider this passage: "'Principles' are 'firsts' but they are absolute firsts, not the kind of firsts that require a temporal succession as we go from a first to a second. They just *are.* They have logical, rather than temporal, priority."[22]

So, it would certainly be inadequate to claim that for Burke, there is nothing but mediated symbolic perspectives and terministic screens. The *Grammar*'s investment in dramatism and dialectic is an investment in rendering visible the underlying logical foundations (the being) of rhetoric. When he turns to the realm of symbolic action, he is turning to a terrain on which these more fundamental relations are simply playing themselves out and being enacted by people—but not where they are *really* constituted. Whatever Burke's deep and abiding interest in the social and in the contingency of "doing"—and it seems to me that it is clearly abiding, though not terribly deep—the dialectical logic of "being" (which he at times calls "unity and division," at times "grammar," at times "the negative") remains the structuring, transcendent principle of the social.[23]

Now to be clear, I find no necessary fault with the establishment of transcendent grounds, and it is my sense that all claims to "anti-foundationalism" are finally foundational in their commitment to, for example, an originary principal of negation (this, to me, is a basic lesson of Hegel's *Phenomenology of Spirit*).[24] Here, I simply want to indicate that a commitment to "language as action" can take many different forms, not all of which are compatible. And in this case, the commitment to action/doing can be undercut through the employment of a dualist ontological diagram and a (logical) prioritizing of being.

BURKE CONTRA BURKE

Of course, essays and books are complex artifacts made of up many different directions and movements; their apparent unity will always be a bit of a joke. My goal, then, is not to try to "recharacterize" Burke as a signifying thinker who merely appears as an asignifying one (whatever those terms might mean), but merely to think through some of the complexities implicit in thinking asignification. And there are also moments in Burke in which his thinking and writing push up against these complications quite explicitly.

For instance, Burke explains that the original project for *A Grammar of Motives* was to develop a logic of constitutions, documents whose writing (a doing) establishes the basis for a nation (a being). What interested him about constitutions is that they are practical examples of a so-called language game in which the rules of the game are perpetually at stake. Indeed, one of the particularly interesting characteristics of constitutions is that they are commonplace, human documents that function like "God" terms: they are both the condition of possibility for all laws, but simultaneously neither part of those laws nor answerable to them (one could never say that a provision of the constitution was "illegal"). According to Burke, the pentad itself grew out of his work on constitutions as a supplement, though it was later placed in front of the section on constitutions (in fact, for reasons that will become apparent, the belief that this supplement should be located prior to the section on constitutions is itself a symptom of the belief in the logical—and in this case, textual—priority of "being").

One of the most intriguing moments in his analysis of constitutions demonstrates the ways in which the dialectic of constitution confuses the demand for "logical priority" through which what something "is" precedes what it "does." As he writes, "Logically, of course, we should go from substance to command; but in proposing a constitution we reverse this process, going from command to substance, and thereby trying to so frame the statement of substance that it implies or contains the command."[25] In these constitutional moments, Burke points toward a dimension of language that appears in some sense prior to its signified: its "doing" *comes before* its "being." And this reversal presses Burke to try to "so frame the statement of substance that it implies or contains a command." In other words, the reversal of logic exhibited by constitutions encourages him to try to think a sense of "being" that must already include a force of "doing."

Here, Burke gestures toward a dimension of language that not only acts rather than signifies, but also one that doesn't merely act "symbolically" but acts on the world itself (it makes an actual nation). In order to uncover this dimension, however, he has had to suspend the "logical" priority of "being" over "doing," which, in his terms, he describes as requiring him to frame "being" or substance with a sense of "doing"—to my mind, a very intriguing conjunction of asignification and signification.

This framing explains why the "paradox of substance" that interests Burke so much in the *Grammar* is not merely a logical paradox, nor does it simply demonstrate some indeterminacy about our ways of knowing. To put it succinctly, this paradox is not just an epistemic phenomenon, limiting the ways in which we come to know things; for Burke, it is part of the world itself. "Men's linguistic behavior reflects real paradoxes in the world," he writes, though even here the notion of "reflection" reinscribes the dualism; otherwise "men's linguistic behavior" wouldn't "reflect" anything at all, but would simply act as one of many "real paradoxes in the world."[26]

But by inverting the supposedly "logical" relation of "being' and "doing" in the context of constitutions, Burke is able to temporarily problematize his dualist diagram, indicating the force of an asignifying, active dimension of language. While I do not believe that Burke follows out the consequences of this revision to nearly the extent that some of the other thinkers I mentioned above do, one of them would be that language could no longer be reduced (or elevated) to a symbol system; instead, it must be thought as an action (a doing) that is merely one force among many others in a larger "ontology" of rhetorical becoming.

NOTES

1. Jacques Derrida, *Writing and Difference*, trans. Alan Bass (Chicago: Chicago University Press, 1978), 280.

2. See, e.g., Stanley Fish, *Doing What Comes Naturally* (Durham: Duke University Press, 1989); Alan G. Gross and William M. Keith, eds., *Rhetorical Hermeneutics: Invention and Interpretation in the Age of Science* (Albany: State University of New York Press, 1997). For a survey of the "rhetoric of inquiry," see John S. Nelson and Allan Megill, "Rhetoric of Inquiry, Projects and Prospects," *Quarterly Journal of Speech* 72, no. 1 (1986): 20–37.

3. Much of the point of this essay is simply to say that this logic also holds true for the word "rhetoric."

4. Gilles Deleuze and Felix Guattari, *A Thousand Plateaus: Capitalism and Schizophrenia*, trans. Brian Massumi (Minneapolis: University of Minnesota Press, 1987).

5. Plato, *Protagoras*, trans. W. K. C. Guthrie, in *Plato: Collected Dialogues*, ed. Edith Hamilton and Huntington Cairns, 308–52 (Princeton: Princeton University Press, 1989).

6. J. L. Austin, *How to Do Things with Words* (Cambridge: Harvard University Press, 1962);

Jacques Derrida, "Signature Event Context," in *Limited INC*, ed. Gerald Graff, trans. Samuel Weber, 1–24 (Evanston: Northwestern University Press, 1988); Judith Butler, *Gender Trouble*, 10th anniversary ed. (New York: Routledge, 1999); Deleuze and Guattari, *A Thousand Plateaus*; Karen Barad, "Posthumanist Performativity: How Matter Comes to Matter," *Signs: Journal of Women in Culture and Society* 28, no. 3 (2003): 801–31.

7. To be clear, my purpose in this essay is not at all to make a historical argument about the "linguistic turn" or "signification." While scholars rarely explicitly consider this linguistic turn anymore, the two key features of signification that I discuss below—a dualist ontology and prioritizing of being over doing—are alive and well in the constructionist and identitarian thinking that are prevalent in rhetorical scholarship today.

8. Indeed, the way that I have distinguished signifying language from asignifying rhetoric here is entirely "traditional" in that it is premised on what a speaker is trying to accomplish (to produce understanding versus to produce action). This approach, however, is not at all necessary to the distinction.

9. John Muckelbauer, *The Future of Invention: Rhetoric, Postmodernism, and the Problem of Change* (Albany: State University of New York Press, 2008), 17–8 and 34–6.

10. Kenneth Burke, *Language as Symbolic Action* (Berkeley: University of California Press, 1966): 44. Also, though Burke made a distinction between the domains of the Rhetorical (addressed to others) and the Symbolic (more psychological), he seems to always think of rhetorical action as symbolic action, so for the purpose of developing the distinctions I am pursuing here, I will provisionally treat them more or less synonymously.

11. Ibid., 5.

12. Ibid.

13. Ibid.

14. Ibid.

15. Ibid., 45.

16. Ibid., 5.

17. I do not believe that Burke ever pursues this implication for the other side of his diagram, the object side. Nor do I think he could have, as doing so would have forced him to complicate (to the point of erasure) the whole dualist diagram with which he begins.

18. Burke, *Language*, 5. Given the emergence of a posthumanist tone in rhetorical studies, I should also say that "separating human consciousness from the world itself" isn't *necessarily* an objectionable move; at least, there are all kinds of understandable motives for doing so. In this case, one of Burke's lifelong targets was a reductive social scientific behaviorism that he (and many others) linked to the commodification of human life—so it makes sense that he would want to resist the reduction of the human to "object" status. These days, however, there are also good reasons to think differently than he did about the relationship between human exceptionalism and the "objectification" of others.

19. Burke, *A Grammar of Motives* (Berkeley: University California Press, 1945), xviii, emphasis mine.

20. Ibid., 127, emphasis mine.

21. Kenneth Burke, with Bernard Brock and Parke G. Burgess, "Dramatism as Ontology or Epistemology: A Symposium," *Communication Quarterly* 33 (Winter 1985): 17–33, 27.

22. Burke, *Grammar*, 73.

23. In this, Burke is much like Aristotle, who, despite our modern handwringing over the term "antistrophos" seems to me to clearly articulate dialectic as the fundamental logical ground (the Being) of rhetorical contingency.

24. I do not make this point to show a logical contradiction (I certainly don't believe that so-called logical contradictions are *necessarily* a fault or deficiency). Instead, it is my suspicion that work under the vague rubric of "anti-foundationalism" dramatically underestimates the role that something like "critique" (the "anti-") plays in the generation of "foundations"; perhaps negation itself is the very movement of "foundations"?

25. Burke, *Grammar*, 358.

26. Ibid., 56.

(Out of) Place

Atopos

MICHELE KENNERLY

Henri Lefebvre opened his celebrated 1974 book *The Production of Space* with this claim: "Not so many years ago, the word 'space' had a strictly geometrical meaning: the idea it evoked was simply that of an empty area. In scholarly use it was generally accompanied by some such epithet as 'Euclidean,' 'isotropic,' or 'infinite,' and the general feeling was that the concept of space was ultimately a mathematical one. To speak of 'social space,' therefore, would have sounded strange."[1] Maybe. But the practice of applying spatial terms to social relations so as to assign certain people to certain social and actual spaces plainly goes back centuries. Consider "stations" and "spheres," whose social meanings the *Oxford English Dictionary* (OED) traces to the sixteenth and seventeenth centuries, respectively.[2] By the next century, Oliver Goldsmith's 1773 stage comedy *She Stoops to Conquer* could suggest the artful manipulation of social space only if a spatial understanding of social relations was commonplace.[3] In the subsequent century, spatial metaphors made up a prominent proportion of metaphors used in recorded oratory. Parsing those metaphors, Michael Osborn observed that those used by men conveyed "a relatively simple, linear, two-dimensional conception of space," whereas those used by women conveyed "a far more complex, three dimensional, often exquisitely painful sense of space."[4] In particular, women orators "had a spherical point of reference for their lives," and, "thus, 'women's sphere' and 'women's place' for the feminist orators were most often metaphors of opprobrium."[5] For other women, though, they were metaphors of corrective approbation.[6] As Nan Johnson narrates, all manner of nineteenth-century discourses attempted "the rhetorical repatriation of women" to "their former place in the home."[7] By the end of that century, French sociologists were writing of "géographie sociale," and German ones of "Soziologie des Raumes."[8] Lefebvre's estimation of when space became social seems, therefore, a bit off.

Because place and space, both actual and social, are central to public life, contemporary rhetoricians theorize them amply.[9] There are even multiple versions of "rhetorical space."[10] And the conceptual grounds keep growing; for instance, in her work on *mestiza* rhetorics of Mexican women journalists and activists, Cristina Devereaux Ramírez uses the Spanish word *puesto* (post, position, place, situation, stall, market stand) to enlarge upon the usual social-conceptual circumference of "space."[11] In addition, two ancient Greek spatial terms—*topos* (space, place) and more recently *khōra* (place, spot, ground, countryside, land)—appeal on occasion.[12] There has been, however, no obvious ancient term through which to theorize social space, making it yet another feature of public life for which traditional rhetorical terms cannot account.[13] Strictly speaking, *topos* does not apply to the hierarchical relations of social space, applying instead to repeating features of what Stephen Gersh calls "dialectical and rhetorical space."[14] In her work on Ecuadorian national identity, Christa Olson, though, created a hybrid *topos* when she used the word to describe a repeatable (and thus able to be imitated and appropriated) set of rhetorical features that indicate actual or fanciful social/subject position, thereby showing that *topos* can be used to evaluate how social hierarchies are sustained by communicative patterns.[15] Here is where *atopos* enters the picture: adding an alpha privative to *topos* fundamentally changes its zone of applicability, because *atopos* is adjectival—that it is always attributed, and so not an inherent feature, underscores its constructed status—and thoroughly spatial-social.

Literally, *atopos* means "without a place" or "out of place." In use, though, *atopos* means "strange," "odd," or "eccentric," and sometimes with the force of "unnatural," or even "disgusting."[16] The underlying semantic unity is that whoever or whatever are deemed to warrant the adjective *atopos* have dared disturb someone's sense of the order of things, such that sorting things out has become necessary once again, in either an aggressively preservative mode or an imaginatively generative one, but more typically the former. *Atopos* is thus a compelling concept through which to organize discourse about and from people for whom space (and the way they take it up) and place (and whether they keep in and to it) are always dangerously policed and politicized. As Nirmal Puwar explains, "Some bodies are deemed as having the right to belong, while others are marked out as trespassers, who are, in accordance with how both spaces and bodies are imagined (politically, historically and conceptually), circumscribed as being 'out of place.'"[17]

That Puwar puts the phrase "out of place" in quotes indicates its ascribed, discursive quality and the caution it is necessary to exercise when the phrase is used so what one hears where it is coming from.

In this chapter, I suggest how and why we might develop the concept of *atopos* as a term of and for rhetorical theory and criticism. I begin with its emergence in ancient Greek texts, from its potential geometrical origins, to Plato's use of *atopos* to describe Socrates. Through its association with Socrates, several consequential Continental thinkers picked up the term in the twentieth century, and it has appeared, sparsely, in the work of rhetoricians. My contribution here amounts to using *atopos* to organize a topology (an atopology, really) of social space around attributions—including self-attributions—of being "out of place." By social space, I refer to "a relational setting of positions," and, since how we are habituated to think about where we fit in the scheme of things results from where we are allowed to be, as well as impinges on where we go, and what we say and do when we get there, when we talk about social space, we are usually talking about actual spaces, too.[18] One could organize and theorize "out of place" attributions any number of ways, but here are the three I propose: the *a/topos* of transgression, the *a/topos* of exception, and the *a/topos* of juxtaposition.

Naturally, given the organizing premise of this volume, I am interested in the privative component of *atopos*: Of what is someone denied, deprived, or divested when they are seen or felt to be "out of place"? In what place are they thereby presumed to belong? I am also interested, though, in when this deprivation can be additive: when can a denial of belonging or a refusal to be stuck in a social slot not of one's choosing be constructive and creative? *Atopos* tends to be constructive and creative when it is a self-attribution that anticipates and thereby manages the reactions of those most likely to police social space for violations. Some self-attributions of being out-of-place, though, can be mistaken, which I show in the penultimate section. I conclude with a gesture toward *atopia*.

ATOPOS, IN THEORY

The most obvious place to start an account of *atopos* is with *topos*, since the latter is both semantically prior and more familiar. At least, we tend *to think* we know it. As Michael Leff observed, "Classical rhetoricians are not very scrupulous in defining the key term."[19] For instance, Aristotle enumerates over three hundred *topoi* in *Topics* and nearly thirty in the *Rhetoric*, but, in the words of Sara Rubinelli, "he never defined exactly what a *topos* is."[20] Richard McKeon adds that place terms were "as ambiguous in ordinary Greek as they are in ordinary English, and the nature of 'place' and 'space' was a subject of dispute in the beginnings of Greek physical science."[21] Tormond Eide argues that Aristotle borrowed the word from geometry ("Voilà!" shouts Lefebvre), where a *topos* was what is now called a "geometrical locus," or "the set of all points that satisfy a given requirement."[22] Eide builds this supposition from *Rhetoric* 1403a17–18, which Eide says is "the closest we ever come to a definition of topos in Aristotle," and which reads, "I regard *stoicheīon* and *topos* as the same, since a *stoicheīon* or a *topos* is that under which many enthymemes fall [*empiptei*]."[23] Eide shows that the verb *empiptō* means "'fall on to' (a line) or 'fall into' (a figure) in ancient Greek geometry, which suggests that Aristotle thinks "many enthymemes 'fall into' a certain type or pattern determined by the topos."[24] Eide also points out that "locus-theorems seem to have intrigued the Greeks, geometers and philosophers alike, in that they exemplify an infinity of particulars showing one and the same property."[25] Here, then, we have an intriguing account of *topos* as an organizer of shared properties that locates *topos* first on a geometrical plane and follows it into the spaces of rhetoric.

Eide claims that, by extension from the geometrical leaning of *topos*, *atopos* first meant "'impossible,' 'contradictory,' 'illogical.'"[26] It describes some element that does not fit. Though one can find grammatical variants of *atopos* 8 times in Aristotle's *Rhetoric*, and 15 in Isocrates, they appear close to 250 times in the Platonic corpus.[27] The word, therefore, is typically tied to Plato; more precisely, it is typically tied to Socrates, whom his interlocutors deem odd. For example, Callicles calls Socrates *atopos* in the *Gorgias*, Phaedrus calls Socrates atopos in the *Phaedrus*, and Alcibiades calls Socrates *atopos* in the *Symposium*.[28] In the *Symposium* we learn Socrates has only ever left Athens—where he was born and reared—to fight as a foot soldier for its interests. It is in Athens that he is and feels at home, yet it is there that he is constantly told he is out of place and weird. *Atopos* holds a certain lexical space, and it is different from the space held by *xenos*, meaning "strange" in the sense of "foreign."[29] Atopos allows us, therefore, to be more precise in how we talk about "outsiders within" and the discourses applied to and availed of by them.

By dint of its application to Socrates, *atopos* was taken up in the twentieth century by the consequential Continental thinkers Jacques Lacan, Hans-Georg Gadamer, and Roland Barthes, who refer to Socratic *atopia* within accounts of transference, understanding, and love, respectively. In 1960–61, Lacan structured a seminar around Plato's *Symposium*, paying particular attention to the exchange between Alcibiades and Socrates, during which the former calls the latter *atopos*, because, only by talking to people, Socrates directs their desire, including away from himself.[30] Lacan maps their relationship onto that which forms between an analyst and an analysand. In the subsequent decade, Gadamer drew upon *atopon* to describe interpretive encounters that challenge understanding.[31] *Atopon*, he explains, "actually means 'the placeless,' that which cannot be fitted into the categories of expectation in our understanding and which therefore causes us to be suspicious of it. The famous Platonic doctrine that philosophizing begins with wonder, has this suspicion in mind, this experience of not being able to go any further with the pre-schematized expectations of our orientation to the world, which therefore beckons to thinking."[32] New encounters challenge our categories. In *A Lover's Discourse*, his alphabetical lexicon from later that decade, Roland Barthes includes *atopos* (one of two Greek words total) among the eighty words he calls "figures," recognizable and memorable shapes or scenes encountered or uttered by a lover *qua* lover.[33] "It is as if there were an amorous Topic, whose figure was a site (*topos*)," he writes.[34] What Barthes offers is not a progression of feeling but an "encyclopedia of affective culture" that no two lovers will draw upon in the same way or in the same sequence.[35] The header to *atopos* reads, "The loved being is recognized by the amorous subject as 'atopos' (a qualification given to Socrates by his interlocutors), i.e., unclassifiable, of a ceaselessly unforeseen originality."[36] To convey the befuddlement one feels in the presence of the loved one, Barthes draws on descriptions of the feeling Socrates produces in his interlocutors and admirers. To love is to scramble for a meaningful vocabulary. "Being Atopic," Barthes writes, "the other makes language indecisive: one cannot speak *of* the other, *about* the other; every attribute is false, painful, erroneous, awkward: the other is *unqualifiable* (this would be the true meaning of *atopos*)."[37] Be it coupled with exasperation or exhilaration, this estimation of another's atopia renders one without "*topo*," Barthes puns, *topo* being colloquial French for "talk."[38]

Neither *atopos* nor its reception has made deep inroads into Rhetorical Studies, but the bit of groundwork that has been laid merits mention. In *Negation, Subjectivity, and the History of Rhetoric*, Victor Vitanza tries to articulate the challenge of, "in rewriting histories of rhetoric, how to include what, heretofore, has been excluded or purged."[39] He articulates histories of rhetoric through "three notions of the possible, namely, *topos*, *e/utopos*, and *atopos*," the first two of which are oppositional pairs.[40] "Whereas the first two engage in territorializing and reterritorializing (both editorializing), the third dis/engages in perpetual deterritorializings (decodings, denegations)."[41] Whereas topical and utopian discourses occupy space, atopical discourse does not settle in anywhere; in fact, it unsettles. *Atopos* powers his effort to rewrite histories of rhetoric because of its "exuberance."[42] In his article on commemoration, Joshua Reeves builds on Gadamer's use of *atopon* to argue that unconventional works of public memory jolt observers out of place, and observers come out the other side of the strange encounter "feel[ing] newly in place vis-à-vis one's rearranged and recharged surroundings."[43] Further, José Cortez uses his own concept of "atopic peripheries" to question the centrality of *mestizaje* in Latinamericanist thought about identity and decolonial resistance.[44] I applied *atopos* in a study of archaeological efforts to locate Socrates in his historical context and critical efforts to understand references to Socrates out of context, specifically in the speeches and writings of Rev. Dr. Martin Luther King Jr., and James Baldwin.[45]

Largely, this section has pointed to the work done on *atopos*, and much of that work celebrates the excesses and strangeness of that and those to whom the word is applied. The atopology I propose in the next section employs the structural capacities of *topos* to categorize recurrent attributions of being "out of place," attending in the first two instances to the harm that often follows those attributions and in the third instance to the empowerment that can come from embracing an "outsider" position.

ATOPOLOGY

The First A/topos *Is That of Transgression*

The *atopos* of transgression organizes place-based injunctions—that someone should "know or stay in their place"—that emphasize a perceived transgressor's being out of place, with the potential additional attributes of being odd or even disgusting. Those who use this type of *atopos* attribution have no intention of ceding ground within the social or actual spaces they inhabit.

Kate Manne's book *Down Girl,* a treatment of the logic of misogyny from the perspectives of analytic philosophy, abounds with attention to perceived transgression. Consider, first, its title. "Down" could be adjectival, modifying girls and women, who have good reason to be downcast and forlorn. "Down" could be prepositional, part of an imperative "Get down, girl!" as issued by someone who likens empowered women to energetic and unmannerly female dogs (and this interpretation of the title means the command is not punctuated correctly, like much digital "commentary" from angry men).[46] Prepositions, of course, locate in space; in this case, the idea is to subjugate women and bring them low. The image on the cover of the cloth copy of *Down Girl* is a loose leash, and, for a time, Manne used the poodle emoji when responding to trolls on Twitter. Of course, the cover image also resembles a ligature, and Manne begins the book with a chapter on strangulation.

Down Girl contains at least 25 instances of the "know your place" injunction, a performance of the frequency with which women are told—directly or indirectly—that they have wandered into territory that does not belong to them and to which they do not belong.[47] Their arrival is viewed as an incursion, a violation of social and literal borders that is often met with violence. In Manne's account of misogyny, "misogyny primarily targets women because they are women in a *man's world* (i.e., a historically patriarchal one, among other things), rather than because they are women in a *man's mind,* where that man is a misogynist."[48] For Manne, misogyny is a set of "*maneuverings*" that "put women in their place when they seem to have 'ideas beyond their station.'"[49] Citing Moya Bailey's coining of and work on misogynoir—what Bailey describes as a referent to "the particular brand of hatred directed at black women in American visual & popular culture"—Manne underlines that Black women face distinctive forms of misogyny.[50]

If misogyny is to blame for Hillary Clinton not having been elected president in 2016, then misogynoir likely played a role in Donald Trump having been elected. Koritha Mitchell frames the election of Donald Trump in 2016 in terms of high-achieving Black and POC women, such as Michelle Obama, and white anxiety about them: "By voting for Donald Trump, sixty-three million Americans communicated their belief that successful people of color, especially women, had forgotten their 'proper' place. Trump's election and the hate crimes that attended it reiterated what was already painfully clear: the United States remains committed to its tradition of *know-your-place aggression*."[51] Mitchell defines the concept as "the flexible, dynamic array of forces that answer the achievements of marginalized groups such that their success brings aggression as often as praise. Any progress by those who are not straight, White, and male is answered by a backlash of violence—both literal and symbolic, physical and discursive—that essentially says, *know your place*!"[52] Mitchell classifies know-your-place aggression as a longstanding US American tradition.[53] In his book on desegregation debates during Reconstruction, Kirt Wilson supplies the deep background of this "rhetoric of place," as does Ersula Ore in her book about lynching, particularly in her consideration of "how one's sense of 'place' within the polity is rhetorically constituted through lynching and customary acts of display and spectatorship associated with the practice."[54] Attributions of transgressive *atopia* are aggressions that often escalate to outright violence, including murder.

The Second A/topos *Is That of Exception*

It organizes attributions of being "out of place" that work to set apart an "exceptional" member of a group commonly deemed by the attributor to be troublesome or inferior. Think of the discourses of "the extraordinary Negro," "the model minority," or "the cool girl."[55] This discourse either attempts to persuade members of an "out" group to comport or present themselves in ways an "in" group perceives itself to do, though that latter self-perception is usually abundantly aggrandizing, or it praises a particular person or subgroup for being *surprisingly* excellent.

Writing about the particular strains heard by Black people in the United States, Ibram Kendi calls such discourse "uplift suasion" and marks it as a type of persuasion dear to assimilationists.[56] Assimilationist positions are still racist (or classist or sexist), because assimilation norms to extant systems rather than abolishes them. For Kendi, "the widespread belief in the extraordinary Negro" from the eighteenth through the twenty-first century, a belief shared even among extraordinarily racist people, demonstrates the inefficacy of the "uplift" approach: "When Black people rose, racists either violently knocked them down or ignored them as extraordinary. When Black people were down, racists called it their natural or nurtured place, and denied any role in knocking them down in the first place."[57] Kendri's vertical-spatial ("uplift," "rose," "down," "place") vocabulary highlights the metaphors in which this discourse has been and continues to be pitched.

The *a/topos* of exception works by making an exception for the exceptional. That which is exceptional is literally "seized out of," and this seizure speaks to what the *a/topos* of exception does for the attributor and the attributed. For the attributor, the *a/topos* of exception seizes on particular qualities they do not typically impute to members of the out-group. For the attributed, the attribution of exceptional makes them still an outlier within the in-group, and also esteemed at the expense of others in their out-group. In terms of social space, there is a relaxation of some rules of inclusion but they come with the stricter reinforcement of others.

The life-writings of W. E. B. Du Bois are the US American *locus classicus* for examples of the *a/topos* of exception. In "The White World," a chapter from his 1940 book *Dusk of Dawn*, Du Bois shows the contours of that world "by personifying the white and colored environment" by way of an invented but not fictive conversation between himself and two white "friends."[58] The first says to Du Bois that it must be "'horrible' to be an Exception. By this he means me. He is more than certain that I prove the rule" about Black inferiority.[59] The second "friend" concludes a rant about the social place of Black people in this way: "Of course, there may be a few exceptions, but the mass of the colored world can't think, they can't rule, they can't direct, and we mustn't let them try. And to keep them from trying we've got to pound them back into their places every time they show their heads above the ramparts." When the "friend" comes out of his rant, he recalls Du Bois's presence: "'Of course,' he stammered, 'I don't exactly mean you—you are an Exception, at least in some respects—.'"[60] The *a/topos* of exception and the *a/topos* of transgression reinforce one another, and the person deemed an "outlier" serves as the exception that proves the rule.

The Third A/topos *Is That of Juxtaposition*

And it describes a self-attribution of outsiderness that comes as a result of anticipating or knowing full well that one will face the *a/topoi* of transgression or exception. The juxtaposition *a/topos* acknowledges not only that one or one's kind is not included, but also that exclusions force or allow to develop certain ways of seeing and being that are not available to people who occupy dominant social and actual spaces by cultural default. So, Rev.

Dr. Martin Luther King Jr., an outright admirer of *atopos* Socrates, extols being "creatively maladjusted."[61] Audre Lorde articulates the position of "sister outsider."[62] Patricia Hill Collins theorizes the status of "the outsider within."[63] *The Home Place*, a memoir by J. Drew Lanham, whom, among other things, is a Black ecologist, birder, and poet, tropes with incongruities extensively. For instance, Lanham begins the work with this self-reflection:

> I am as much a scientist as a black man; my skin defines me no more than my heart does. But somehow my color often casts my love affair with nature in shadow. Being who and what I am doesn't fit the common calculus. I am the rare bird, the oddity: appreciated by some for my different perspective and discounted by others as an unnecessary nuisance, an unusually colored fish out of water.
>
> But in all my time wandering I've yet to have a wild creature question my identity. . . . Responses in forests and fields are not born of any preconceived notions of what "should be." They lie only in the fact that I *am*. Each of us is so much more than the pigment that orders us into convenient compartments of occupation, avocation, or behavior. It's easy to default to expectation. But nature shows me a better, wilder way. I resist the easy path and claim the implausible, indecipherable, and unconventional.[64]

The *a/topos* of juxtaposition places inside and outside, the expected and the eccentric, close together purposefully to dramatize the constructedness of the distinction between the pairs: their history, their functions, their outcomes. This *a/topos* also affords core standing to the experience of the "odd" person, making their perspective central rather than marginal.

Poignant examples of this *a/topos* undergird Saidiya Hartman's book *Wayward Lives, Beautiful Experiments: Intimate Histories of Social Upheaval.* Hartman celebrates the liberatory energies and practices of certain young Black women living in Philadelphia and New York from 1890–1935 who are part of the historical record because authorities from various bureaucratic orders deemed them to be problems; that is, categorized them under the a/*topos* of transgression. Sorting through that evidence, Hartman "craft[s] a counter-narrative liberated from the judgment and classification that subjected young black women to surveillance, arrest, punishment, and confinement, and offer[s] an account that attends to beautiful experiments—to make living an art—undertaken by those often described as promiscuous, reckless, wild, and wayward."[65] Hartman credits to these young Black women "a revolution in a minor key," an "upheaval or transformation of black intimate life [that] was the consequence of economic exclusion, material deprivation, racial enclosure, and social dispossession; yet it, too, was fueled by the vision of a future world and what might be."[66] Hartman's study locates these "wayward" women at the juxtaposition of restriction and liberation. In general, the *a/topos* of juxtaposition speaks to the energy to be found when the ground breaks.

OUT-OF-PLACE *ATOPIA*

The trifold atopology of social space I propose is but one way to build on *atopos* for Rhetorical Studies. Another way is to attend to out-of-place "out-of-place" attributions; that is, when a person or group enjoying certain or many advantageous characteristics adopts the language of the outsider or marginalized. For example, there are successions of intensifying expressions of feeling among people in parts of North America and Europe who (believe they) are white that displacement or replacement by "others" is imminent.[67]

Consider Arlie Russell Hochschild's 2016 book, *Strangers in Their Own Land: Anger and Mourning on the American Right*. The result of five years of interviews, *Strangers in Their Own Land* details Hochschild's efforts to learn "a deep story"—that is, is "a *feels-as-if* story"—from conservative white voters in the parishes of Louisiana's bayous.[68] Hochschild attempts to locate what is behind "the disorientation, fear, and resentment" she hears during her interviews.[69] The white people with whom she speaks feel snapped out of place by what they see as a cultural and, depending on the administration, governmental focus on "oppressed blacks, dominated women, weary immigrants, closeted gays, [and] desperate refugees."[70] As she puts it, using a second-person perspective: "You have the impulse to call out, 'I'm part of a minority *too*!' But you have criticized just such appeals for sympathy when others have made them on similar grounds."[71] This struggle—between wanting to claim a minoritized status and yet despising such claims when they come from people more egregiously oppressed by systems and structures that often intersect—is yet another dimension of felt estrangement from a "proper" place. That place, of course, is the ostensibly unassailable heights of whiteness.

The year Hochschild's book came out, an anxiety about where they stood in the scheme of things led the majority of white people who voted to cast their vote for Donald Trump. In his work on what he calls Donald Trump's demagogic art of masculine victimhood, Paul Johnson describes how "demagogues encourage audiences to self-identify as victims on the basis of felt precarity, encouraging the well-off and privileged to adopt the mantle of victimhood at the expense of those who occupy more objectively fraught positions."[72] He continues, "Far from seeming forthrightly illogical, claims of White, masculine victimhood encourage objectively well-off members of society to interpret the presence of difference and uncertainty as threatening the subject with unjust marginalization, coding a 'diverse and diffuse range of experiences'—or in the case of Trump, political topoi ranging from immigration to terrorism to trade—as part of a single trauma: the subject's exile from politics."[73] Johnson's use of "exile" here emphasizes the angst about social space and being ousted from one's ostensibly "rightful place" within it.

The discourse of being out-of-place, just like the discourse of diversity and of intersectionality, is first mocked and then occupied and turned against those of and for whom it has meaning and heft historically and currently. Out-of-place "out-of-place" grievances take up serious room in collective rhetorical space, and they ought to be confronted.[74]

TOWARD *ATOPIA*

Undeniably, the ancient Greek rhetorical term *topos* is familiar to rhetoricians. It is mentioned even in theoretical work on space and place that moves far beyond the structures of invention catalogued in the ancient world. One deft adapter of *topos* to contemporary theorizing, Christa Olson, spoke accurately of the positions of many rhetoricians when she urged, "Since the majority of rhetorical historians locate our work in places where the rhetorical theories that originated in classical Greece and Rome overlap with, appropriate, or are washed away by other practices of persuasion, careful attention to terrain, to common and uncommon places, and to shifting constitutional scenes is essential for all of us."[75] Years prior, Jacqueline Jones Royster used a landscaping analogy to frame what she called "contemporary challenges in the history of rhetoric."[76] The essential challenge she identifies is that "habitual systems," including terminological ones, "easily filter out aberrations, making it abundantly clear that such deviations from normed understanding are not computable, that they are alien, distracting, unproductive, and likely the result of insanity, that is, non-rationality."[77] When traditional rhetorical terms, such as *topos*, are used on their own terms, they often do not sufficiently accommodate what is difficult to accommodate: the out of place, the exceptional, the eccentric, and that which seems convinced it is so. It is precisely there, however, that *atopos* is most at home. The atopology I proposed unites *topos* and *atopos* to classify discourses about purported classification breakers, thereby making the point that being "out of place" is a designation whose patterns of use are of significance to historians, theorists, and critics of rhetoric. Further, perhaps the very notion of *atopia* can move theorists of utopia to imagine a new space: a society where being deemed "out of place" would not be a harbinger of violence.

NOTES

1. Henri Lefebvre, *The Production of Space*, trans. Donald Nicholson-Smith (Oxford: Basil Blackwell, 1991 [1974]), 1.

2. *Oxford English Dictionary* (OED), s.v. *station* ^ 10 ("A person's position in life as determined by external circumstances or conditions"), ^ 11 ("A position in a sequence, series, or (esp.) hierarchy"), ^ 12 ("Position in the social scale; a person's social status"); s.v. *sphere* ^ 6. "A province or domain in which one's activities or faculties find scope or exercise, or within which they are naturally confined." Pertinent to my argument, it was around the same time that "eccentric" took on meaning as a social descriptor.

3. Oliver Goldsmith, *She Stoops to Conquer; Or, the Mistakes of a Night: A Comedy*. Open access through Project Gutenberg: http://www.gutenberg.org/ebooks/383.

4. Michael Osborn, "Patterns of Metaphor Among Early Feminist Orators," in *Rhetoric and Community: Studies in Unity and Fragmentation*, ed. J. Michael Hogan (Columbia: University of South Carolina Press, 1998), 3–26, 10.

5. Ibid., 11.

6. Take, for example, Catharine Beecher's 1837 "Essay on Slavery and Abolitionism with Reference to the Duty of American Females," an open letter to Angelina Grimké written in response to Grimké's "Appeal to the Christian Women of the South," penned the year prior. In the last third of her letter, Beecher writes plentifully about spheres and circles, rightful subordination, and the "true place" of woman, all furnished and reinforced by Christianity. These letters can be found at http://utc.iath.virginia.edu/abolitn/grimkehp.html.

7. Nan Johnson, *Gender and Rhetorical Space in American Life, 1866–1910* (Carbondale: Southern Illinois University Press, 2002), 49. See also Jessica Enoch, "A Woman's Place Is in the School: Rhetorics of Gendered Space in Nineteenth-Century America," *College English* 70, no. 3 (2008): 275–95, and, for a study of how Victorian-age, white Englishmen adjusted spatially to social gains for white women, see John Tosh, *A Man's Place: Masculinity and the Middle-Class Home in Victorian England* (New Haven: Yale University Press, 1999). For an overview of how Anna Julia Cooper complicated the dominant domestic sphere discourse, see Hannah Giorgis, "How Black Suffragettes Subverted the Domestic Sphere," *Atlantic*, August 18, 2019, https://www.theatlantic.com/entertainment/archive/2019/08/how-black

-suffragettes-subverted-domestic-sphere /596284.

8. G. S. Dunbar, "Some Early Occurrences of the Term 'Social Geography,'" *Scottish Geographical Magazine* 93, no. 1 (1977): 15–20. In 1908, the German scholar Georg Simmel wrote "Der Fremde [The Stranger]," an outgrowth of his work on "the sociology of space." The essay appears in Georg Simmel, *Soziologie: Untersuchungen über die Formen der Vergesellschaftung*, 685–91 (Leipzig: Duncker & Humbolt, 1908). For a history of "social distancing" that includes Simmel's contribution, see Lily Scherlis, "Distantiated Communities: A Social History of Social Distancing," *Cabinet Magazine*, April 30, 2020, http://cabinetmagazine.org/kiosk/scherlis_lily_30_april_2020.php.

9. For a thorough overview and extensive bibliography, see Joan Faber McAllister, "Space in Rhetorical Theory," in the *Oxford Research Encyclopedia of Communication*, 2019, https://oxfordre.com/communication.

10. For "rhetorical space," see Roxanne Mountford, "On Gender and Rhetorical Space," *Rhetoric Society Quarterly* 31, no. 1 (2001): 41–71; Johnson, *Gender and Rhetorical Space in American Life, 1866–1910*; Carly S. Woods, *Debating Women: Gender, Education, and Spaces for Argument* (East Lansing: Michigan State University Press, 2018), 14–18. For a germane review essay that appeared during the brief window in which this volume was in copyedit stage, see Jean Bessette, "Making Space," *Journal for the History of Rhetoric* 23, no. 3 (2020): 366–69.

11. Cristina Devereaux Ramírez, *Occupying Our Space: The Mestiza Rhetorics of Mexican Women Journalists and Activists, 1875–1942* (Tucson: University of Arizona Press, 2015, 3–4). For a critique of Ramírez on account of her book's reinforcement of "the very topoi of essentialism (racial difference, nativism) ascribed to non-Western cultures that she attempts to displace," see José M. Cortez, "Of Exterior and Exception: Latin American Rhetoric, Subalterity, and the Politics of Cultural Difference," *Philosophy and Rhetoric* 51, no. 2 (2018): 124–50, at 134.

12. For *topos*, see, e.g., Scott Consigny, "Rhetoric and Its Situations," *Philosophy and Rhetoric* 7, no. 3 (Summer 1974): 175–86, at 181–84; for *khōra*, e.g., see Thomas Rickert, *Ambient Rhetoric: The Attunements of Rhetorical Being* (Pittsburgh: University of Pittsburgh Press, 2013), 41–73.

13. *Khōra* actually can be used to refer to the "station, place, position" of a person (s.v. *khōra* in Henry George Liddell, Robert Scott, and Henry Stuart Jones, *A Greek-English Lexicon*, 9th ed. (Oxford: Clarendon Press, 1996), 1 ^ 3, 4, 5), but that meaning has not been taken up in contemporary theory. For a study of ancient Greek spatial concepts, see Keimpe Algra, *Concepts of Space in Greek Thought* (New York: Brill, 1995), especially chapter 2.

14. This seems to be a sort of abstract discursive space without a location. Stephen Gersh, "Dialectical and Rhetorical Space: The Boethian Theory of Topics and Its Influence During the Middle Ages," in *Raum und Raumvorstellungen im Mittelalter*, ed. Jan A. Aersten and Andreas Speer (New York: W. de Gruyter, 1998), 391–401. For a critique of what he calls "the topo-centric accounts of rhetoric" due to everything and everyone it displaces, see Kundai Chirindo, "Rhetorical Places: From Classical Topologies to Prospects for Post-Westphalian Spatialities," *Women's Studies in Communication* 39, no. 2 (April 2016): 127–31, 128.

15. Christa J. Olson, "Performing Embodiable Topoi: Strategic Indigeneity and the Incorporation of Ecuadorian National Identity," *Quarterly Journal of Speech* 96, no. 3 (August 2010): 300–323.

16. Liddell, Scott, and Jones, *Greek-English Lexicon*, s.v. *atopos*. "Without a place" and "out of place" seem importantly different, but there is no distinction in the Greek *atopos*. In modern Greek, *atopos* means "absurd, inept, incongruous."

17. Nirmal Puwar, *Space Invaders: Race, Gender, and Bodies Out of Place* (New York: Bloomsbury, 2004), 8. Tim Cresswell writes that "a sustained investigation of the 'out of place' metaphor points to the fact that social power and social resistance are always already social," in his *In Place / Out of Place: Geography, Ideology, and Transgression* (Minneapolis: University of Minnesota Press, 1996), 11. Understanding being in and out of place is also

the subject of Edward S. Casey, *Getting Back into Place: Toward a Renewed Understanding of the Place-World* (Bloomington: Indiana University Press, 1993). *Atopos* appears on ix–xi.

18. The definition of "social space" is from Katharina Manderscheid, "Social Space," *Encyclopedia of Urban Studies*, vol. 2, ed. Ray Hutchison (Thousand Oak, CA: SAGE Reference, 2010), 747–51, at 747. For examples of the relationships between actual and social space, see: Elijah Anderson, "The White Space," *Sociology of Race and Ethnicity* 1, no. 1 (2015): 10–21; Brandi Thompson Summers, *Black in Place: The Spatial Aesthetics of Race in a Post-Chocolate City* (Chapel Hill: University of North Carolina Press, 2019); Kevin M. Kruse, "A Traffic Jam in Atlanta Would Seem to Have Nothing to Do with Slavery. But Look Closer . . ." The 1619 Project. *New York Times Magazine*, August 18, 2019: 48–49.

19. Michael C. Leff, "The Topics of Argumentation in Latin Rhetorical Theory from Cicero to Boethius," *Rhetorica* 1, no. 1 (Spring 1983): 23–44, 24. Leff continues, "Even when limited to its technical use in rhetoric, 'topic' incorporates a bewildering diversity of meanings. Hence, among modern authors we find conceptions of the topics ranging from recurrent themes in literature, to heuristic devices that encourage the innovation of ideas, to regions of experience from which one draws the substance of an argument" (23–24). For an analysis of the argumentative power of the common topics precisely because of their wide scope of applicability, see Lucia Calboli Montefusco, "Die Topik in der Argumentation," in *Rhetorik zwischen den Wissenschaften*, ed. Gert Ueding (Tübingen: Max Niemeyer Verlag, 1991), 21–34.

20. Sara Rubinelli, *Ars Topica: The Classical Technique of Constructing Arguments from Aristotle to Cicero* (New York: Springer, 2009), viii.

21. Richard McKeon, "Creativity and the Commonplace," *Philosophy and Rhetoric* 6, no. 4 (Fall 1973): 199–210, at 199.

22. Tormond Eide, "Aristotelian *Topos* and Greek Geometry," *Symbolae Osloenses* 70, no. 1 (1995): 5–21, at 9.

23. Ibid., 11. A *stoicheīon* is "an element of a series" or "part of a structured whole," meaning "it is used of any element that fills a place in a system and thus is capable of wide generalizations" (Eide, 14). My translation uses the Greek in Aristotelis, *Ars Rhetorica*, ed. W. D. Ross (Oxford: Oxford University Press, 1959).

24. Eide, "Aristotelian *Topos* and Greek Geometry," 12.

25. Ibid., 13.

26. Ibid., 19.

27. *Atopos*: Aristotle, *Rhetoric* in 1.1, 1.15, 2.23, 2.24, 3.15, 3.18; Isocrates, *To Demonicus* 42; *Helen* 1; *Busiris* 8 and 37; *Panathenaicus* 92 and 149; *Antidosis* 1, 74, 150, and 243; *Against Callimachus* 14; *Nicocles* 2; *Panegyricus* 127; *To Philip* 18, 41. All these texts are available on Perseus (http://www.perseus.tufts.edu/hopper/collection?collection=Perseus:collection:Greco-Roman).

28. Plato, *Gorgias* 494d1, Plato, *Phaedrus* 229c6, Plato, *Symposium* 175a10, 215a2, 221d2. Also available via Perseus.

29. Though I am using *atopos* to understand outsider-insiders, *atopos* could be used to analyze discourses about and from asylum seekers, immigrants, migrants, and exiles. For example, the title of Edward W. Said's memoir is *Out of Place* (New York: Vintage, 2000), one potential rendering of *atopos*. Pierre Bourdieu uses *atopos* poignantly in his preface to Abdelmalek Sayad, *The Suffering of the Immigrant*, trans. David Macey (Malden, MA: Polity, 2004), xi–xiv, at xiv. See also Annika McPherson, "From Utopia to Atopia to Diaspora? Narratives of Social (Re-)Organization in a German Refugee Home," in *Transcultural Modernities: Narrating Africa in Europe*, ed. Elisabeth Bekers, Sissy Helff, and Daniela Merolla (New York: Editions Rodopi, 2009), 363–75.

30. Jacques Lacan, *Le séminaire livre VIII: Le transfert*, ed. Jacques-Alain Miller (Paris: Editions du Seuil, 1991). For a study of the sorts of love at play in this seminar, see Bruce Fink, "Love and/in Psychoanalysis: A Commentary on Lacan's Reading of Plato's *Symposium* in Seminar VIII: Transference," *Psychoanalytic Review* 102, no. 1 (February 2015): 59–91. For Lacan's attempt to wrest *atopia* from Socrates for himself, see Guy Le Gaufey, "Le plus atopique des deux . . . ," in *Lacan avec les Philosophes*, ed. Natalia S. Avtonomova (Paris: Albin Michel, 1991), 166–70.

31. Hans-Georg Gadamer, "Language and Understanding (1970)," trans. Richard E. Palmer, *Theory, Culture and Society* 23, no. 1 (2006): 13–27, at 14,; Hans-Georg Gadamer, "Rhetoric, Hermeneutics, and Ideology-Critique," in *Rhetoric and Hermeneutics in Our Time: A Reader*, ed. Walter Jost and Michael J. Hyde, trans. G. B. Hess and R. E. Palmer (New Haven: Yale University Press, 1997), 313–34, at 318. See also Donatella Di Cesare, "Atopos: Die Hermeneutik und der Ausser-Ort des Verstehens," in *Das Erbe Gadamers*, ed. Andrzej Przylebski (Frankfurt: Peter Lang, 2006), 85–94.

32. Gadamer, "Language and Understanding (1970)," 14.

33. Roland Barthes, *A Lover's Discourse. Fragments*, trans. Richard Howard (New York: Hill and Wang, 2010 [1977]), 4. For development of the claim that "classification—and associated activities of *de*classifying or unclassifying—is a key theme, if not the key theme, in the work of Roland Barthes," see Andy Stafford, "*Classé, Surclasser, Déclassé*, or, Roland Barthes, Classification without Class," *L'Esprit Créateur* 55, no. 4 (Winter 2015): 148–64, at 148.

34. Barthes, *A Lover's Discourse*, 5.

35. Ibid., 7.

36. Ibid., 34.

37. Ibid., 35.

38. Ibid., 36.

39. Victor J. Vitanza, *Negation, Subjectivity, and the History of Rhetoric* (Albany: State University of New York Press, 1997), 67.

40. Ibid., 62.

41. Ibid., 63.

42. Ibid., 68.

43. Joshua Reeves, "Suspended Identification: *Atopos* and the Work of Public Memory," *Philosophy and Rhetoric* 46, no. 3 (2013): 306–27, at 308.

44. José M. Cortez, "Atopic Peripheries: Rhetoric, Hybridity, and the Latin American Resistance," unpublished dissertation, University of Arizona, 2017. Cortez makes generative use of quick references to atopic and atopia in Derrida (15) and Foucault (191).

45. Michele Kennerly, "Socrates *Ex Situ*," *Advances in the History of Rhetoric* 20, no. 2 (2017): 196–208.

46. Kate Manne, *Down Girl: The Logic of Misogyny* (New York: Oxford University Press, 2018). Manne details: "Misogynist hostility encompasses myriad 'down girl' moves—so many as to make the list seem likely to be indefinitely extensible. But, to generalize: adults are insultingly likened to children, people to animals or even objects" (68). Thanks to Jen Buchan for the gift of this book some time back.

47. E.g., Manne, *Down Girl*, xi, xvii–xviii, xix, 19, 21, 24; 49; 64; 68–69; 75; 77; 83; 149; 152; 155; 157; 160; 169; 171; 217; 234; 289.

48. Manne, *Down Girl*, 64, italics original.

49. Ibid., 69, italics original.

50. Ibid., 64. For the coining, see Moya Bailey, "They aren't talking about me . . ." Crunk Feminist Collective, March 14, 2010, http://www.crunkfeministcollective.com/2010/03/14/they-arent-talking-about-me.

51. Koritha Mitchell, "Identifying White Mediocrity and Know-Your-Place Aggression: A Form of Self-Care," *African American Review* 51, no. 4 (Winter 2018): 253–62, 253. Throughout his presidency, Trump harassed and demeaned Black women reporters, including April Ryan, Joy-Ann Reid, Abby Phillip, and Yamiche Alcindor, with particular vehemence.

52. Mitchell, "Identifying White Mediocrity and Know-Your-Place Aggression," 253.

53. Ibid.

54. Kirt H. Wilson, *The Reconstruction Desegregation Debate: The Politics of Equality and the Rhetoric of Place, 1870–1875* (East Lansing: Michigan State University Press, 2002), 12, 190–96; Ersula J. Ore, *Lynching: Violence, Rhetoric, and American Identity* (Jackson: University of Mississippi Press, 2019), 33 (see also 19 and 21).

55. Ibram X. Kendi, *Stamped from the Beginning: The Definitive History of Racist Ideas in America* (New York: Nation Books, 2016), 96, 125, 483; Ellen D. Wu, *The Color of Success: Asian Americans and the Origins of the Model Minority* (Princeton: Princeton University Press, 2013); Anne Helen Peterson, "Jennifer Lawrence and the History of Cool Girls," BuzzFeed, February 28, 2014, https://www.buzzfeed.com/annehelenpetersen/jennifer-lawrence-and-the-history-of-cool-girls.

56. Kendi, *Stamped from the Beginning*, 124–5.

57. Ibid., 125.

58. W. E. B. Du Bois, "The White World," in *Dusk of Dawn*, in *W. E. B. Du Bois Writings*, ed. Nathan Huggins (New York: Library of America, 1986), 652–80, at 656.

59. Ibid., 656.

60. Ibid., 677. In 1903, much earlier than *Dusk of Dawn*, Du Bois offered his idea of "the talented tenth," starting and concluding his essay of that title with this line: "The Negro race, like all races, is going to be saved by its exceptional men" (in "The Talented Tenth," in "Essays and Articles," in *W. E. B. Du Bois Writings*, ed. Nathan Huggins (New York: Library of America, 1986), 842–61, at 842 and 861). In "The Colored World Within," another chapter of 1940s *Dusk of Dawn*, Du Bois revisits the notion of "the talented tenth" (692), in Huggins, ed., 681–715. On the development of Du Bois's thinking from centered on Black men to focused, too, on the particular kinds of oppression faced by Black women, see Nneka D. Dennie, "Black Male Feminism and the Evolution of Du Boisian Thought, 1903–1920," *Palimpsest* 9, no. 1 (2020): 1–27.

61. Martin Luther King Jr., "Letter from Birmingham Jail," in *Why We Can't Wait* (New York: Signet Classic, 2000 [1963]).

62. Audre Lorde, *Sister Outsider: Essays and Speeches by Audre Lorde* (Berkeley: Crossing Press, 2007 [1984]).

63. Patricia Hill Collins, "Learning from the Outsider Within: The Sociological Significance of Black Feminist Thought," *Social Problems* 33, no. 6 (October–December 1986): s14–s32.

64. J. Drew Lanham, *The Home Place: Memoirs of a Colored Man's Love Affair with Nature* (Minneapolis: Milkweed Editions, 2016), 4. This chapter was drafted in May of 2018; in May of 2020, Lanham's scholarly and public writing was widely tweeted after a white woman called the cops on the Black birder Christopher Cooper because he asked her to leash her dog in Central Park, in accordance with the Park's policy.

65. Saidiya Hartman, *Wayward Lives, Beautiful Experiments: Intimate Histories of Social Upheaval* (New York: W. W. Norton, 2019), xiv. Hartman uses the language of "utopia" (e.g., xiii, xv).

66. Ibid., xv.

67. For a history, see Sarah E. Bond, "The Origins of White Supremacists' Fear of Replacement," *Hyperallergic*, August 22, 2019, https://hyperallergic.com/514034/the-origins-of-white-supremacists-fear-of-replacement.

68. Arlie Russell Hochschild, *Strangers in Their Own Land: Anger and Mourning on the American Right* (New York: The New Press, 2016), 135.

69. Ibid., 147; 135–51. What Hochschild finds is in keeping with what rhetoricians doing critical race analyses in the 1990s noticed about whiteness. See, e.g., Thomas K. Nakayama and Robert L. Krizek, "Whiteness: A Strategic Rhetoric," *Quarterly Journal of Speech* 81, no. 3 (1995): 291–319; Ronald L. Jackson II, "White Space, White Privilege: Mapping Discursive Inquiry into the Self," *Quarterly Journal of Speech* 85, no. 1 (1999): 38–54.

70. Hochschild, *Strangers in Their Own Land*, 139.

71. Ibid., 144–45.

72. Paul Elliott Johnson, "The Art of Masculine Victimhood: Donald Trump's Demagoguery," *Women's Studies in Communication* 40, no. 3 (2017): 229–50, at 230. For a regional approach to discourses of white victimhood, see Brandon Inabinet and Christina Moss, "Complicit in Victimage: Imagined Marginality in Southern Communication Criticism," *Rhetoric Review* 38, no. 2 (2019): 160–72.

73. Johnson, "Art of Masculine Victimhood," 231. It is important to emphasize that many of Trump's most steadfast supporters and enablers are white, college-educated, and comparatively well-off economically.

74. And obviously not only in the United States. In her aforementioned work with *topos*, Christa Olson shows how and why white-mestizo Ecuadorians "desire[d] simultaneously to invoke a legitimate and popular national sovereignty through the incorporation of a stylized indigenous subjectivity and to remain separate from the negative social and economic realities of actually being indigenous" (Olson, "Performing Embodiable Topoi," 304).

75. Christa J. Olson, "Places to Stand: The Practices and Politics of Writing Histories," *Advances in the History of Rhetoric* 15, no. 1 (2012): 77–100, at 84–85. For a study that

places "peculiarity" centrally, see Bjørn Stillion Southard, *Peculiar Rhetoric: Slavery, Freedom, and the African Colonization Movement* (Jackson: University of Mississippi Press, 2019).

76. Jacqueline Jones Royster, "Disciplinary Landscaping, or Contemporary Challenges in the History of Rhetoric," *Philosophy and Rhetoric* 36, no. 2 (2003): 148–67, at 150.

77. Ibid.

Anostos

ANTHONY J. IRIZARRY

"Tell me about a complicated man. / Muse, tell me how he wandered and was lost / . . . / and where he went, and who he met, the pain / he suffered in the storms at sea, and how / he worked to save his life and bring his men / back home."[1] So begins Homer's *Odyssey*, a recurring tale of homecoming. For as long as the home has been conceptualized, songs of homecoming have occupied human speech. As the poetic genre of homecoming, *nostos* provided communities with the rhetorical means for communicating the home as the center of human desire. As wars and migrations over the millennia combined, separated, and altered populations, identity became contingent on home and one's ability to physically or mnemonically return there. In the Homeric tradition, *nostos* most readily meant a return home from Troy by sea.[2] The return signaled a return to safety and stability in identity for the Achaeans. Yet the rhetorical efficacy of *nostos* depended on figures like Odysseus, whose return home was never guaranteed. The pull of *nostos* was predicated on the risk of *anostos,* a place of no return.

The risk of no return motivated and moved Homeric heroes. Today, that same risk structures the very deliberative possibilities of those seeking asylum and refuge for self and others across geopolitical borders, as well as those actively working against them. In each instance, *anostos* marks the limits of homecoming's rhetorical and democratic potential. *Anostos,* therefore, can be explained in one of two ways. It can be the inability to realize home or return. It can also be the illusory feeling of being-at-home, which renders the act of returning or homecoming unnecessary. *Anostos* should be understood in either case as a place of rhetorical and mnemonic immobility, a place in which relations of geopolitical, cultural, economic, and historical powers restrict the ability for democratic communities to effectively deliberate, commemorate, and advocate for themselves and others.[3] Specifically, *anostos* signals the immobilization of communities by way of the erasure of indeterminacy, the reduction in multidirectionality of rhetorical invention, and the stifling of citizens' deliberative potential. While the risk of *anostos* may move and motivate communities toward deliberative action, the actualization of *anostos* immobilizes and forecloses the possibility for critique, deliberation, and civic health.

In a field concerned with affordances, capacities, and potentialities, *anostos* offers a useful vocabulary for conceptualizing the limits of memory and mobility within Rhetorical Studies. As I see it, *anostos* goes beyond moments of stasis to also encompass what Lisa Flores has conceptualized as "stoppage." Flores advocates for attention to be paid to rhetorical climates of stoppage, to moments and systems that "craft lives living in vulnerability, fear and shame. Lives stopped."[4] Stoppage is involuntary and forced, while stasis is not. Yet *anostos* inverts processes of mnemonic and rhetorical homecoming by way of both stoppage and stasis. It prompts rhetoricians to look at climates where immobility is forced unto others as well as climates where it is chosen, even wished for, by those who feel they are already safely at home. Furthermore, *anostos* allows us to analyze the costs that come from processes of return. In climates where communal stasis is overcome and *nostos* worked toward, *anostos* lends itself to the analysis of those racialized, gendered, and marginalized people who have effectively been stopped so that others' homecoming can be made into reality. At the borders of *anostos*, one can find the limits of civic community.

The remainder of this chapter is divided into five sections. The first section analyzes three *topoi* of *nostos*—indeterminacy, multidirectionality, and civic engagement—as a way to show how each *topos* is challenged and modulated by the alpha privative. The second section places Theopompus's description of Anostos, a mythical island on the edge of the world, alongside extant Homeric literature to construct relationships among *anostos*, mortality, and memory. The third section explores the concept of rhetorical death as an effect of *anostos*. The fourth section places *anostos* alongside home in order to nuance our understanding of home's rhetorical efficacy. This chapter briefly concludes with a discussion of navigating *anostos* in our everyday lives.

(A)NOSTOS

Both within and beyond the Homeric texts, *nostos* signifies a multifaceted and complex appeal of homecoming. The *nostos* within Homer's *Odyssey* "is a return to something old but also a new beginning," Jeffrey Perl argues; "it is a meeting of oldest and newest, yet it is in addition the seemly conclusion of an unbroken continuum."[5] Homecoming encompasses both old and new, both a return and a sense of natality. The tensive space between old and new, coming and going, return and natality, recreates *nostos* as an appeal for potentiality and mobility. The promise of return is not lost within this understanding of *nostos*, but that promise need not be actualized for *nostos* to retain its allure.

Nostos builds itself around three *topoi*: indeterminacy, multidirectionality, and civic engagement. These *topoi* can be understood temporally (i.e., in the form of mnemonic and commemorative acts), physically (i.e., migration or return from exile), or civically (i.e., acts of public ritual that return the citizen to a given community). While these three *topoi* encounter their rhetorical limits through *anostos*, the same limits help widen the path of their rhetorical wanderings. The remainder of this section gives attention to each *topos* in turn. Through indeterminacy, multidirectionality, and civic engagement, we may begin to view *nostos* as a rhetorical appeal whose employment allows for communities to safely navigate pivotal moments of their existence. Through these *topoi*, we may also witness what simultaneously gives *nostos* its rhetorical strength and limits: *anostos*.

Nostos is indeterminate. Sutured to the sea by way of poetic tradition, *nostos* is by nature an in-between state, a point situated somewhere between origin and destination. Its etymology suggests a sense of indeterminacy, since the term manifests through multiple, overlapping definitions. *Nostos* can denote coming back from Troy, having a safe journey, going toward, reaching successfully, homecoming, and saving oneself.[6] The valence of the word suggests a further indeterminacy. *Nostos* does not always reward its returners. The completion of Agamemnon's *nostos* following the fall of Troy resulted in his death.[7] *Nostos* can be translated as many things, but each definition provides a sense of the term's indeterminate position. To be in a state of return suggests that one is not quite home, yet not quite away from home. Caught in a perennial state of in-betweenness, *nostos* becomes potentiality.[8]

The indeterminacy of *nostos* travels beyond the Homeric tradition to suggest a relationship between home and identity predicated on instability and processes of becoming. As bodies in a perennial state of identity formation, we rely on constructed memories of home and its feelings of security, stability, and wholeness, so that we may understand who we are as individuals and as citizens of a larger civic community. The body within this process is "specific, pivotal, and subject to change," posits Diana Taylor, which "challenges the impression that the individual or group is somehow a stable entity, an unchanging conduit for receiving and transmitting the swirl of events around them."[9] The process of self-discovery and identification has no obtainable terminal point, for we can never truly reach a position of stable identity or memory within a larger civic community. Likewise, *nostos* may never be fully realized. The indeterminacy of the return journey, the simultaneous journey of recovery and discovery, marks the present condition of citizens and civic communities who look to the past in order to understand themselves and the world around them. *Nostos* can mean either going toward or coming back. In our desire to remember, to return to a place of safety and stability, we also go forward, creating ourselves anew. We exist in a state of indeterminacy between home and elsewhere, between past and future. *Nostos* carries us into a space of potentiality.

As an appeal for potentiality and mobility, *nostos* must be multidirectional. One's return home need not begin from a specific point of origin, nor does home's destination signify a fixed location. Instead, as Anna Bonifazi suggests, *nostos* denotes surviving lethal dangers.[10] Because home has historically been understood as a place of safety, the overlap between homecoming and surviving death makes perfect sense. Abstracting *nostos* to mean surviving death, however, provides the word with a degree of multidirectionality it otherwise lacks. Within tales of *nostos*, "speakers may refer to 'coming back home,' to 'going back home,' and also to 'reaching a land by sea that is not home (or not yet home).'"[11] *Nostos* becomes movement in the direction of a safe destination, any safe destination, when read in this way.

The multidirectionality of homecoming nurtures democratic processes of communal remembrance and civic engagement. The ability for a community to remember different fragments of the past and reassemble those fragments in a multitude of ways forms the very grounds on which public memory creates civic community and ensures its survival.[12] Home may never become a static object of remembrance for pluralistic communities, even if a community's *telos* is to safely navigate the seas of political and civic crisis toward a place of safety and stability. What "survival" looks like is always in flux. These communities rely on the multidirectional promise of homecoming, then, for their very survival. "Dictating how communities should remember, uniformly and authentically," argues Bradford Vivian, "promotes a culture of public memory that threatens the ability of marginal communities to sustain their unconventional memorial practices and to vie for public recognition of their professed heritage."[13] A unidirectional *nostos*, by definition, cannot be *nostos*, for the survival of democratic communities depends on a multidirectional understanding of what it means to return to a place of safety.[14]

The indeterminacy and multidirectionality of *nostos* make it a productive model for civic engagement. This may at first seem counterintuitive. Odysseus's *nostos* saw the death of his men as well as Penelope's suitors and enslaved women back in Ithaca. If *nostos* relies on the death of others for its fulfillment, it may not be a particularly strong mode of civic engagement. But civic engagement relies on a nonutopic reality abounding with exigence and crisis. Communities must navigate an imperfect and dangerous world; this navigation sometimes produces its casualties. Bonifazi writes, "The experience of *nostos* is inseparable from performing *nostos*, to the extent that every *nostos* tale retains memory of the successful experience of getting life again; it makes memory survive time and gives the hero afterlife."[15] *Nostos* becomes the memory of successful journeys home, and through that memory a *periplous* (a sailing-around) for future journeys. The construction of such *periploi* often rely on the failures, mistakes, and deaths of predecessors. For *nostos* to retain its rhetorical power, the risk and fulfillment of *anostos* must loom nearby.

Nostos is an appeal for potentiality and mobility that relies on indeterminacy, multidirectionality, and civic engagement for its rhetorical efficacy. *Nostos* becomes the model for communal survival and democratic potential, a perpetual state of indeterminacy and instability that frees identity and prompts deliberative action. Yet *nostos* cannot be understood in its totality without the risk of *anostos*. The following section explores how the alpha privative binds *nostos* while also expanding rhetorical understandings of potentiality and mobility as they relate to mnemonic and democratic expression.

THE DEADLY ISLAND OF *ANOSTOS*

Anostos is a place of no return, a place that erases indeterminacy, limits the directionality of mnemonic and rhetorical invention, and stifles the potential for civic engagement. The risk of its actualization lends strength to appeals for communal *nostos*, yet its fulfillment can signal the decay of civic health. *Anostos*, then, denotes either a state of immobilization for persecuted communities seeking to reach home or a state of concretization for hegemonic communities who feel they need not change the homes in which they comfortably rest. It is within these sites of *anostos*, these places where the potential for mobility appears most futile, where we can begin the process of critical diagnosis and communal rehabilitation.

One of the earliest mentions of *anostos* comes from a passage in Aelian's *Historical Miscellany*. He cites Theopompus's original description of Anostos, a mythical place at the edge of a massive continent that surrounds the outside of the world. This island is thought to be a parody of Plato's Atlantis. Theopompus describes:

> On the edge of their territory is a place named *Anostos*, which looks like a chasm and is filled neither by light nor darkness, but is overlaid by a haze of a murky red color. Two rivers run past this locality, one named Pleasure, the other Grief. Along the banks of both stand trees the size of a large plane. Those by the river Grief bear fruit, which has this quality: if someone tastes it he sheds so great a quantity of tears that he melts into laments for all the rest of his life and dies in this condition. The other trees, growing by the river Pleasure, produce a fruit that is quite the opposite. The person who tastes it loses all his previous desires; and if he had any love, he forgets it as well, and is slowly rejuvenated, recovering the previous stages of life that he has passed through. Casting off his old age he returns to his prime and finds his way back to the years of adolescence; then he becomes a child and an infant, after which he dies.[16]

This passage begins to highlight the rhetorical work done by the alpha privative to both illuminate and interrogate the limits of *nostos*. *Anostos* pivots on the *topoi* that help define *nostos* in several ways. We now have a fixed, stable, and identifiable place on land rather than a state of indeterminacy on the sea. This land is bound to two rivers, which flow in a single direction, reducing the multidirectional nature of return. Even the sky has changed in *Anostos*. Day and night, light and darkness, give way to a "haze of murky red color." Time in this land has effectively ceased. Past, present, and future lose their connective tissue under this murky red sky, rendering the didactic function of memory inert. Tales of *nostos*, of coming, going, or survival, go unheard. Only the dead can listen now.

The fruit that *Anostos* bears is lethal. The dwellers of *Anostos* are not long to live. How, then, do we reconcile the term's intimate entanglement with death? One could make an argument for the obvious role played by affective excess in the decay and erosion of the dwellers of *Anostos*. This same pattern of decay and erosion mirrors the work of those who have written about the effects of affective excess on a polity's health. Erika Doss has devoted time to the discussion of communal grief and the politics of mitigating such public affect. When public expressions of grief "[fixate] on exclusionary religious and political tenets," Doss argues, they risk becoming "the material and emotional testimonials of a nation grief stricken by violent death and yet seemingly disengaged from the social and political initiatives that might check such violence."[17] Public expressions of grief that focus singularly on an attempt at catharsis but fail to explore avenues for mitigating the root cause of grief may in fact lead to *anostos*. Expressions that focus on closure without a critical eye toward the larger political reasons for the public affect could lead to a prolonging of such affective states within a given community.

Likewise, it has been argued that an excess of uncritical and naïve pleasure may stunt the growth of a given polity. Marita Sturken writes about the proliferation of the teddy bear following moments of crisis as a way for communities in grief to momentarily forget their woes and find comfort in material objects. "The teddy bear doesn't promise to make things better," Sturken posits; instead, "it promises to make us feel better about the way things are."[18] Uncritical focus on such material objects of pleasure during national moments of crisis or war-mongering can draw attention away from civic engagement with the ongoing exigencies that help sell these objects in the first place. The proliferation of the teddy bear after the Oklahoma City bombing or 9/11 cultivates cultures of innocence and comfort, argues Sturken. These cultures may rhetorically distance a polity from retaliatory acts of aggression enacted by the nation-state as the focus on pleasure and innocence infantilizes the polity that is taken hold by this form of affective excess.[19] Affective excess can lead to *anostos*, a state of mnemonic and rhetorical immobilization. Yet the island of *Anostos* is a place of death, a permanent place of no return. Is death the sole limit of *nostos*'s rhetorical appeal?

The relationship between *anostos* and death receives a further nuance when we remember how *nostos* was contrasted in Homeric texts. *Nostos* was juxtaposed not with *anostos* but with *kleos*, immortality through fame and glory. Bounded on one side by death, *nostos* receives another threshold in the form of deathlessness. In the *Iliad*, Achilles is faced with a dilemma: die at Troy and achieve *kleos* or return home and live a long life but be forgotten.[20] *Kleos* proves to be the antithesis of *nostos* if *nostos* is understood here as "surviving lethal dangers"; Achilles must not survive battle if he is to live on in memory.

Kleos is not synonymous with *anostos*, but the unchanging and everlasting glorification of a hero can be. With ongoing debates over the *kleos* of such venerated yet controversial "heroes" of the former Confederate States of America, Robert E. Lee in particular, *kleos* can indeed lead to *anostos*. When a national community glorifies figures who symbolize treason and violence, it can lead to the silencing of voices whose continued marginality within the nation stems, in part, from the survival of these figures' memory. *Kleos* can lead to the fossilization of memory, the limiting of democratic mobility, and the erasure of many citizens' potentiality of claim-making and national belonging. Mnemonic and civic death are all but guaranteed for the polity that actively tries to keep certain memories alive through freezing them in place. Likewise, the polity that actively forgets its past and fails to work toward a better future takes a bite out of the fruit of *anostos*.

THE HOMELESS AND RHETORICAL DEATH

The centrality of death within the tale of *Anostos* cannot be dismissed when Theopompus's island is translated into contemporary places of no return. *Anostos* exists in the form of a rhetorical death for many who find themselves immobilized by interlocking geopolitical, cultural, economic, and historical oppressions. When these interlocking oppressions restrict the deliberative and civic potentiality of a particular community, the available rhetorical means for these communities perish. This particular framing of rhetorical death extends from existing work on social death, a concept with deep roots in critical theory and Afro-pessimism. Orlando Patterson conceives of social death as the conditions in which marginalized groups, enslaved people in particular, become deprived of rights and access to the body politic. This deprivation leads them to be culturally legible through their abject status.[21] Building on this theory, Lisa Marie Cacho argues that "any and every option is unthinkable" within spaces of social death, "not because of impracticality or the US public's reluctance to change but because of the threat and promise of state violence. We are disciplined to not think the unthinkable when we learn about the risk of incarceration or deportation or when our families are held hostage."[22] The conditions of social death structurally and discursively restrict marginalized communities' mobility within and between specific spaces. These conditions of immobilization coercively disallow the possibility for deliberative action and advocacy, perpetuating a drought of rhetorical means for escaping such conditions of death. Social death and rhetorical death are coterminous in their perpetuation of a place of no return, a place where home proves to be impossible.

The rhetorical death grip of *anostos* materializes in the context of immigration policy. In the midst of writing this chapter, employees of the US Immigration and Customs Enforcement (ICE) have conducted a nationwide raid of major cities in which thousands of migrants, most of whom have no criminal record, are being targeted for arrest and deportation. The potentiality of such actions precludes a social death for the targets of such raids, and the risk of their simultaneous rhetorical death extends beyond the raid targets to include anyone who might advocate on their behalf. In 2017, Texas suffered a series of ICE raids alongside a publicized and ongoing campaign to ban sanctuary cities within the state. Within this time, the number of Latinx people in Texas reporting rape and violent crimes went down significantly, while clinic visits in central Texas that served predominantly Latinx people dropped as well.[23] The geopolitical, juridical, cultural, and economic forces that allow for violent ICE raids to be conducted unencumbered produce the conditions for *anostos*. When fear of existence and a heightened risk of violence, incarceration, detainment, deportation, and disease become sutured to targeted bodies, the spaces they occupy cannot serve as home. By May 11, 2020, almost half of the 1,700 ICE detainees who had been tested for COVID-19 came back positive for the virus.[24] The stakes of rhetorical death, of the *anostos* that perpetuates the stoppage of alienized people, can and continue to be physical death.

Yet the rhetorical death of those who have been denied access to the body politic does not always doom them to a permanent *anostos*. The rhetorical death of some provides the very conditions for the rhetorical potential of others. For many, this potential is used to reinforce the foundations of hegemonic homes. For others, this potential can be used to locate the cities, communities, and detention centers where the stench of rhetorical death is most potent and make visible the thresholds that severely limit the potential of those stuck in *anostos*. The risk of rhetorical death, indeed the act of bearing witness to others' rhetorical death, may provide the potential to transgress the limits of *anostos* and begin processes for coalition building and public advocacy. Karma R. Chávez frames coalition as a "horizon that can reorganize our possibilities and the conditions of them. Coalition is a liminal space, necessarily precarious, and located within the intermeshed interstices of people's lives and politics."[25] The risk of maroon on *anostos* and the witnessing of others dwelling on *anostos* form the conditions for *nostos*. The journey is necessarily liminal and precarious, for those conditions of liminality and precarity are not just our own. The sea on which our *nostos* relies affects us all differently. The risk of *anostos* will always be greater for certain communities and bodies. However, the possibility for empathy, recognition of interlocking oppressions, and construction of coalitional movements may help inform an appeal for *nostos* that includes those most affected by *anostos*. The precarious sea we travel on forces us to rely on others, to recognize the intermeshed interstices of our lives and politics. On the sea of our journey home, we may begin to realize that our own homecoming requires the homecoming of others.

THE AT-HOME

Anostos marks the rhetorical limits of *nostos*. On one side of this place of no return, the limit may create a sense of homelessness and rhetorical death for marginalized communities who are denied the means of homecoming. On the other side, *anostos* marks a concretization of hegemonic homes through an illusory feeling of being-at-home. If the return in *nostos* is always toward home, then one need not return when one is already there.

Home is often perceived to be a place of safety and stability set apart from a dangerous and uncertain world.[26] It is a bordered locus that can provide a certain sovereignty over identity construction. Lisa Flores suggests home can be a space made from a rhetoric of difference. Such spaces allow communities to construct an identity that is separate and counter from identities created by hegemonic groups. Through this process, these communities can "begin the process of carving out a space for themselves where they can break down constraints imposed by other cultures and groups."[27] Home can provide a much-needed sense of communal or personal safety in an otherwise dangerous and violent political, mnemonic, or physical space.

There exists a danger for the space outside one's home, however, when a home is crafted from within a hegemonic space. Being at home is a rootedness, a dwelling that grounds and limits the development of someone's ethos. We judge from our homes, wherever they may be, but our political and mnemonic homes also limit the objects of our judgment as well as the expression that our judgment ultimately takes. When people find their home within a hegemonic space, a space that lacks indeterminacy and thus goes unchallenged by those who inhabit it, they risk inhabiting *anostos*. When this hegemonic home-space is abstracted to the nation-state, home may create a limited vision of hypernationalism. The effects of such home dwelling surface in violent acts of white supremacy against American citizens. These effects manifest in the form of communities dismissing the killing of Brown and Black people while simultaneously mourning the perceived destruction of property by those who seek to climb out of structurally embedded mechanisms of *anostos*. Meanwhile, geopolitical constructions of home allow for politicians and presidents to dwell comfortably within policies that maintain the internment of human beings in concentration camps along the border. The feeling of safety and stability for some stems from the stoppage and abjection of others.

Being-at-home forms the threshold of our potentiality as citizens. This is not inherently bad. However, we live in a time of hyperpartisanship. Homes crafted out of the content of Fox News and MSNBC provide ideological stability but democratic immobility. Democratic action relies on a political plurality, and that plurality can still exist when we are at home.[28] We just need to be willing to leave from time to time.

NAVIGATING *ANOSTOS*

Nostos is a rhetorical appeal that highlights potentiality and mobility for communities within pivotal moments. *Anostos* is not antithetical to *nostos* but instead illuminates the appeal's limits. If *nostos* provides the space for indeterminacy, multidirectionality, and civic engagement, *anostos* denotes the place where indeterminacy gives way to immobilization and concretization, multidirectionality to unchanging finality, and civic engagement to civic silence. *Anostos* can take the form of a community that has been stopped by rhetorical death through interlocking geopolitical, cultural, economic, and historical powers that deprive it of the ability to deliberate, commemorate, and advocate. *Anostos* can also be the illusory feeling of being-at-home, which shuts down the possibility of knocking down hegemonic and concretized homes.

In a discipline that privileges forms of intellectual wandering while still maintaining violent forms of disciplinary gatekeeping and terminological immobility, the politics of homecoming and their inversion survive in the journey of rhetoric's many (re)turns. Though the destination of home fueled Odysseus's journey, it was the journey itself that exposed him to the various elements of civic health. The search for safety and stability drives us, yet it is only in that journey of return that we encounter the plurality, the potentiality, and the indeterminacy that ensures a healthy democratic society and scholarly community. Ekaterina Haskins marks citizenship to be "a relationship among strangers that is modeled by discourses of public culture and embodied through performance."[29] To perform citizenship among strangers requires one to leave home from time to time. To perform good scholarship requires the same. In an ideal world, each return home would be followed by a return to sea, fulfilling *nostos* as both a coming and going, a multidirectional state of indeterminacy, mobility, and potential.

NOTES

1. Homer, *Odyssey* 1.1–5, trans. Emily Wilson (New York: W. W. Norton, 2018).

2. Anna Bonifazi, "Inquiring into *Nostos* and Its Cognates," *American Journal of Philology* 130 (2009): 481–510, at 481.

3. Mohan Jyoti Dutta and Raka Shome, "Mobilities, Communication, and Asia: Introduction," *International Journal of Communication* 12 (2018): 3960–78, at 3961. Dutta and Shome define mobility as movements that are situated in interlocking systems of power. Mobility, according to the authors, is an embodied practice that is not opposed but rather entangled with immobility. My own understanding of mobility draws from this framing.

4. Lisa A. Flores, "Stoppage and the Racialized Rhetorics of Mobility," *Western Journal of Communication* 84, no. 3 (2020): 247–63, at 251.

5. Jeffrey M. Perl, *The Tradition of Return: The Implicit History of Modern Literature* (Princeton: Princeton University Press, 2014), 18.

6. Bonifazi, "Inquiring into *Nostos* and Its *Cognates*," 492.

7. Homer, *Odyssey* 1.36.

8. Erin Rand forwards indeterminacy as a foundation through which rhetorical agency can be enacted. For Rand, this same foundation partly defines queerness. Erin Rand, *Reclaiming Queer: Activist and Academic Rhetorics of Resistance* (Tuscaloosa: University of Alabama Press, 2014), 22.

9. Diana Taylor, *The Archive and the Repertoire: Performing Cultural Memory in the Americas* (Durham: Duke University Press, 2003), 86.

10. Bonifazi, "Inquiring into *Nostos* and its Cognates," 492.

11. Ibid., 500.

12. Edward S. Casey, "Public Memory in Place and Time," in *Framing Public Memory*, ed. Kendall R. Phillips (Tuscaloosa: University of Alabama Press, 2004), 17–44, at 29.

13. Bradford Vivian, *Public Forgetting: The Rhetoric and Politics of Beginning Again* (University Park: Penn State University Press, 2010), 131.

14. Whitewashed appeals to *nostos* have been made evident by Reagan's and Trump's (Let's) Make America Great Again campaigns. Multidirectionality and democratic potential are lost when homecoming is promised to a very specific demographic of constituents.

15. Bonifazi, "Inquiring into *Nostos* and its Cognates," 507.

16. Aelian, *Historical Miscellany* 3.18, trans. N. G. Wilson (Cambridge: Harvard University Press, 1997).

17. Erika Doss, *Memorial Mania: Public Feeling in America* (Chicago: University of Chicago Press, 2010), 115.

18. Marita Sturken, *Tourists of History: Memory, Kitsch, and Consumerism from Oklahoma City to Ground Zero* (Durham: Duke University Press, 2007), 7.

19. Ibid., 8–9.

20. Homer, *Iliad* 9.412–16, trans. A. T. Murray, 2 vols. (Cambridge: Harvard University Press, 1924).

21. Gershun Avilez, "Staging Social Death: Alienation and Embodiment in Aishah Rahman's *Unfinished Women*," in *The Psychic Hold of Slavery: Legacies in American Expressive Culture*, ed. Soyica Diggs Colbert, Robert J. Patterson, and Aida Levy-Hussen (New Brunswick: Rutgers University Press, 2016), 107–24, at 108.

22. Lisa Marie Cacho, *Social Death: Racialized Rightlessness and the Criminalization of the Unprotected* (New York: New York University Press, 2012), 145.

23. Sen. Sylvia R. Garcia, "Reason for Vote," *Senate Journal: Eighty-Fifth Legislature—Regular Session* (Austin, Texas), May 3, 2017, 1617; Nancy Flores, "Area Nonprofit Fearful After 'Sanctuary Cities' Law's Passage," *Austin American-Statesman*, May 12, 2017, https://www.mystatesman.com/news/local/area-nonprofits-fearful-after-sanctuary-cities-law-passage/u3dwbKfiX6VDKYqMdNg5MK (site no longer available).

24. Tammy La Gorce, "'Everybody Was Sick': Inside an ICE Detention Center," *New York Times*, May 15, 2020, https://www.nytimes.com/2020/05/15/nyregion/coronavirus-ice-detainees-immigrants.html.

25. Karma R. Chávez, *Queer Migration Politics: Activist Rhetoric and Coalitional Possibilities* (Urbana: University of Illinois Press, 2013), 146.

26. See, e.g., Greg Dickinson, *Suburban Dreams: Imagining and Building the Good Life* (Tuscaloosa: University of Alabama Press, 2015).

27. Lisa A. Flores, "Creating Discursive Space Through a Rhetoric of Difference: Chicana Feminists Craft a Homeland," *Quarterly Journal of Speech* 82 (1996): 142–56, at 143.

28. Hannah Arendt, *The Human Condition* (Chicago: University of Chicago Press, 1998), 8.

29. Ekaterina Haskins, *Popular Memories: Commemoration, Participatory Culture, and Democratic Citizenship* (Columbia: University of South Carolina Press, 2015), 2.

Akairos

BESS R. H. MYERS

Whether delivered at an intimate gathering or on a national stage, eulogy engages with what characterizes a "good" death. This is a tall order, since death is not commonly seen as good, and it rarely comes at what is perceived as the right time. It is often a eulogistic necessity, then, to recast and reinterpret the untimeliness of death in order to console mourners.

The term *kairos* (καιρός) refers to an opportune moment, and in a rhetorical sense it is the moment during which something ought to be said to have the intended effect. In eulogy, we may explore *akairos*, its alpha-privative form, as an inherently paradoxical concept. Essentially, the eulogist is responsible for finding the kairic in the akairic to reframe death as timely, even and especially for deaths that are, by all accounts, untimely.[1] However, it is not simply timing that is a necessary condition for kairic speech. *Kairos*—possibly etymologically linked with the verbs *keirō*, "cut" or "cut down" (thus *kairos* is a "decisive moment") or *kurō*, "meet" or "meet accidentally," as in an arrow and a target—also suggests spatiality.[2] The homonymous word *kaīros* (καῖρος) is a weaving term referring to a row of thrums, the line of excess warp threads, which run vertically on a loom.[3] In order to weave, one must move the shuttle, which holds the weft thread, through the opening between warp threads. Analogously, according to Eric Charles White, *kairos* refers to "a passing instant when an opening appears which must be driven through with force if success is to be achieved."[4] In other words, kairic speech requires one to take advantage of the opportunity to say the right thing at the right time, and further, to do so in the right place.

Akairos, *kairos*'s alpha-privatived foil, refers to the unseasonable, ill-timed, and inopportune.[5] Though *akairos* and its variants are found much less frequently in ancient Greek texts than *kairos*, the uses of *akairos* range greatly. For example, in Theophrastus's *Characters*, a humorous exploration of thirty less-than-moral character types, we learn of *akairīa*, "unfitness" or "tactlessness." The tactless man, explains Theophrastus, engages in egregiously untimely behavior, such as offering to be a witness in a case that has already been judged, inviting for a walk someone who has just returned from a long journey, or attempting to dance with someone who is not yet sufficiently drunk.[6] In contrast to this humorous interpretation of *akairos* is its earlier use in Aeschylus's *Agamemnon*. Upon seeing Agamemnon's return home after the Trojan War, the chorus anticipates that the king will soon learn who has kept watch over the city lawfully and justly (*dikaiōs*), and who has done so *akairōs*.[7] Here, the force of the adverb *akairōs* goes well beyond "unfittingly" or "inopportunely," and suggests that Agamemnon's wife, Clytemnestra, has ruled in her husband's absence unlawfully (that is, outside of or beyond what it lawful) and not in accordance with the city's civilized customs. By this point in the play, the chorus has already been made aware of Clytemnestra's illicit machinations to murder her husband as retribution for sacrificing their daughter, Iphigenia. Here, *akairōs* as an antonym of *dikaiōs* implies not that Clytemnestra's rule is simply ill-timed, but that perhaps there is no conceivable time or place where her rule could be considered socially acceptable, lawful, or just.

We may initially render akairos in a rhetorical sense, as Philip Sipiora does, as a "time"—presumably, to speak—"that is without opportunity."[8] Collapsing the dichotomy of *kairos* and *akairos* is the presence of *kairos* itself, which implies that a "right time" to speak is possible, and that, in order to understand what speech qualifies as akairic, one must already have an understanding of *kairos*.[9] Just as *hamartia*, a "missing of the mark"—a term used by Aristotle to describe a character's actions in a tragedy that result in something other than what was planned or desired—is not solely an internal flaw but an external error resulting from that flaw, *kairos* and *akairos* do not speak to statements or events independent of context but are entirely situationally dependent.[10]

Unsurprisingly, *akairos* has not been examined with the same depth as its nonprivatived counterpart, and even *kairos* could do with further investigation, as Richard Crosby has argued.[11] Indeed, James Kinneavy and Catherine Eskin have stated that *kairos* is not a characteristic *of* rhetoric, but rather, is concomitant *with* rhetoric, as evidenced by Aristotle's *Rhetoric*, which, they maintain, entirely depends upon and engages with *kairos*.[12] By considering *akairos* outside of the binary of the "right time" and "not-right time," I aim to continue the work of rhetorical scholars who have begun investigating the complex ethical, political, and aesthetic dimensions of the term *kairos*.[13]

According to Aristotle, the *telos*, the ultimate purpose or overarching goal, of each genre of public speech corresponds to a particular time: forensic rhetoric concerns past events and seeks to accuse or defend; deliberative rhetoric is used to debate what action ought to be taken and therefore concerns the future; and epideictic rhetoric, speech that praises or blames, concerns the present state of affairs.[14] Pursuing *akairos* allows us to go a step further than *kairos*: while *kairos* urges us to consider the context of the speech delivered, *akairos* allows us to investigate world building that takes place *within* speeches themselves.

Victoria Wohl has explored the worlds created in Athenian forensic oratory, and how these worlds relate to, but do not replicate, the world outside of the speeches. For example, according to Wohl, the period of the Thirty Tyrants, a group of magistrates who took political control of Athens after its defeat by Sparta in 404 BCE, was a "traumatic episode" that "constituted a violent breach in the historical continuity of the polis" because it "disrupted the Athenians's relation to their own political past and their sense of the present as the extension of a single democratic moment."[15] After democracy was restored in 403, citizens—with the exception of the Thirty and a number of high-ranking magistrates—pledged an oath not to hold grudges against any other citizens, an oath that required a kind of civic amnesia that asked citizens to "forget before they forgave, and to forget that there was anything even to forgive."[16] In Lysias's speech *Against Agoratus*, in which Agoratus is charged with being an informant for the Thirty, the prosecutor asks the jurors to remember a period of time they have taken an oath to forget.[17] By examining forensic oratory and other oratorical genres through the lens of *akairos*, we may understand not only what was effective or ineffective in, say, Lysias's speech, but also how the world within the speech itself relates to and differs from that outside of the text, and how rhetorical world building can aim to heal an extratextual temporal rupture. In this way, *akairos* may be understood to mean "unfitting" precisely because the world within the text differs from the world that the text references but cannot and will not reproduce.[18]

While we may productively consider each genre of public speech through the lens of *akairos*, *akairos* has a unique relationship with epideictic in that they are both characterized by a suspension of time or a temporal pause. *Akairos,* when broken down into its discrete parts, is "without-*kairos.*" If *kairos* is a passing instant that presents itself and then disappears, then *akairos* may be thought of in this context not as a moment that passes, but as a suspension of that moment during which rhetorical activity can take place. Megan Foley has articulated how it is not the simple present ("I go"), the perfect ("I have gone"), or even the present progressive ("I am going") that fully encompasses the timing of epideictic; according to Aristotle, the realm of epideictic is *ho parōn* (ὁ παρών), from the verb *pareimi,* the temporality of which "is simultaneously progressive and perfect."[19] In essence, *pareimi* and, therefore, epideictic mark "a point of no return," and they hang "between the as-yet and the already."[20] In Cynthia Sheard's words, epideictic allows us to consider "both the real—what *is* or at least *appears to be*—and the fictive or imaginary—what *might be,*" which in turn "allows speaker and audience to envision possible new, or at least different worlds."[21] We may consider the timing of epideictic as one of suspended animation: many possible worlds may grow out of the present, and though epideictic marks a point of no return, the past is very much alive in its influence on the present. Epideictic is thus *akairic* in the sense that it is timeless, without the forward or backward movement of time, and it is not in spite of but rather *because* of its timelessness that rhetorical possibilities abound.

We can observe the relationship between epideictic and *akairos* in the impulse of the eulogist to create an ever-present world within the eulogy. This world building necessarily takes place on a grand scale when the eulogy is delivered to a national audience, and we are especially able to observe trends in this world building if we examine eulogies delivered by different people on the same occasion. Like the *epitaphioi logoi* of classical Athens, in which, according to Nicole Loraux, orators referenced the Athenian empire as "merely the *sign* of a deeper, more durable reality," contemporary eulogies take place during a suspension of time in which the deceased has always existed and will always exist, in body or in spirit.[22]

For example, at the funeral for Senator John McCain in September 2018, multiple speakers offered eulogies characterized by this type of world building, including former president Barack Obama and McCain's daughter, Meghan McCain. During his eulogy, Obama cited McCain's favorite book, Ernest Hemingway's *For Whom the Bell Tolls,* choosing a quote that spoke directly to this world-building impulse: "Today is only one day in all the days that will ever be. But what will happen in all the other days that ever come can depend on what you do today."[23] Obama explained how "each moment, each day, each choice, is a test. And John McCain passed that test again and again and again." Although Obama spoke of events that took place in the past, long before McCain's death, the choice of quotation reinforced the significance of the eternally present moment. It underscored the akairic nature of eulogy during which time itself was suspended, and the world of the eulogy existed in an interminable today. The present-tense sentiment that each day *is* a test had to be reconciled with the past-tense sentiment that McCain had *passed* that test "again and again." The two statements, of past and present, implied that he would continue to pass this test over and over again in the future. In this way, Obama consoled mourners by imagining that McCain, though deceased in the world outside of the eulogy, would continue to pass each day's moral test, as he had always done.

ENTERING INTO *(A)KAIROS*

To further pursue the boundaries of *akairos* in eulogistic speech, I focus my attention on two opposing readings of the relationship between *kairos* and rhetoric enumerated by Crosby.[24] We may read rhetorical texts either "for the way they import kairos *into rhetoric*," an approach that views *kairos* as a tool in the rhetorician's toolbox, or we may read texts "for the way their rhetoric enters *into kairos*."[25] If we take the former approach, then argumentation deteriorates into sophistry in the most disparaging sense of the word. Relating *kairos* to the sophistic notion of *dissoi logoi*, Ekaterina Haskins explains how, "Because the truth is multifaceted, the speaker temporarily resolves the tension between the many possible answers by thrusting forth the one most suitable for the moment."[26] Consider this sophistic understanding of *kairos* in the context of Socrates's statement in Plato's *Phaedrus* about the steps students of rhetoric must take to master their craft. According to Socrates, once the student has learned to discern which sort of person is persuaded by which types of speech and can recognize this sort of person in everyday life, and further, once the student has learned to choose among different types of speech for each occasion—specifically, from among the sorts of speech that are quite timely (*eukairian*) and untimely (*akairian*)—only then will the student's craft be whole and complete (*kalos te kai teleos*).[27] Of course, the *Phaedrus* traces Socrates's skepticism about rhetoric itself, so it is no surprise that the student of rhetoric would be tasked with choosing among different types of speech.[28] Socrates here implies that one must first learn what types of arguments appeal to certain sorts of people and to recognize these situations when they arise organically. Only after one has gained this understanding may the student *add* the knowledge of timeliness and untimeliness. According to this view, *kairos* is the pyramidion of rhetorical education: the pyramid is incomplete without *kairos*, but *kairos* bears no weight.

If we take the latter approach, that *kairos* is the foundation upon which the art of rhetoric is built, then the notion of timeliness becomes a keystone of the craft. Kinneavy and Eskin have argued that there are kairic elements in Aristotle's presentation of *ēthos*, *pathos*, and *logos*, and even his primary definition of rhetoric—that it is the ability to locate the available means of persuasion in any given case (*peri hekaston*)—speaks directly to that which is fitting (*to prepon*) for the occasion.[29] To put it simply, in Kinneavy and Eskin's view, Aristotle defines rhetoric as the ability to locate the right thing to say and the right time to say it. Cynthia Sheard has argued that, though "*kairos* can imply opportunism and manipulation (as it so often does in the context of sophistic)," it can also imply "appropriateness and propriety with respect to time and place"; in this way, the source of rhetoric's power is to "adapt to circumstances and to deceive (ethically or unethically) its users."[30] If we assume that there is no rhetorical art without *kairos*, then perhaps we may approach *akairos* with the same assumption: namely, that understanding untimeliness—or, in eulogy and epideictic generally, time*less*ness—is essential to the way we understand rhetoric itself.

To continue this logic, *akairos*, rather than *kairos*, may be the basis for how we conceive of time in eulogistic speech. But what if it were also the basis for how we conceive of rhetoric more broadly? This is not to say that *kairos* has lost its utility; rather, there is creative energy available in *akairos* that has not yet been realized. For example, how are rhetors to anticipate what arguments will resonate with whom and at what time without having spoken or written *akairically* first? Additionally, there are instances when saying the wrong thing, or saying the right thing at the wrong time, has turned out to be effective, perhaps even more effective than saying the right thing would have been. What if such instances were thought of as points of invention and creative exploration, and were thus the basis for thinking about argumentation? What if, by undermining argumentative expectations of what is timely and appropriate, we could locate and create productive rhetorical activity? It would be the case, then, that the realm of *akairos*—the realm of the inappropriate, the improper, the unfitting—would more readily allow for invention and possibility than the realm of *kairos*. *Akairos* offers us a generative and inventive paradox.

Creative flexibility itself is inherent in *akairos*. Indeed, in *Against the Sophists*, Isocrates criticized instructors who "overlook the fact that they bring to bear on poetic creation a model of an art with fixed rules."[31] He reinforced the fact that speechmaking and argumentation are creative endeavors rather than activities with a set list of formulas. In the *Panegyricus*, he argued that past events "are passed down to all of us in common, but to employ them at the right time [*en kairoi*] and to consider them in the appropriate way in each individual case and to express them well, these skills are particular to those who are especially astute."[32] As Sipiora has emphasized, for Isocrates, "an understanding of the principle of *kairos* means that the rhetor remains accommodative—unlike some other philosophers and Sophists, who are bound by rigid laws and systems."[33] Conceiving of rhetoric within a binary of timeliness and untimeliness can lead to the misconception that some rhetoric is objectively "right." *Kairos*, then, would be an imperative that requires us to wait for the right time during which we may say the right thing. It is more productive to reconsider *akairos* in the Isocratean sense, as a time that does not present the rhetor with obvious or easy opportunity, but instead requires creativity, ingenuity, and imagination. In eulogy, this creativity leads the orator to create an entirely different world, one that is defined by a timeless expectancy that only exists as long as the eulogist speaks.

AKAIRIC SUSPENSION AND EULOGISTIC SPEECH

To return to Senator McCain's funeral, Meghan McCain's eulogy for her father offers another site where we may investigate akairic timelessness and suspension within the world of eulogy. Meghan McCain's eulogistic task was to honor her father, but also, as Adrianne Kunkel and Michel Dennis argue regarding the purpose of eulogy, to positively reappraise a "distressing circumstance, so that its meaning becomes more acceptable to the distressed."[34] This "consolatory obligation," they maintain, is crucial to the eulogy's success, because "beyond honoring the deceased, all aspects of eulogies are subordinate to the eulogizer's major goal and responsibility," namely, to console the audience.[35] In this case, as with many eulogies, the speaker, too, is a member of the audience in need of consolation. In eulogy, consolation and didacticism are bound together: the rhetor fulfills the consolatory obligation by interpreting and retelling the deeds of the deceased in a didactic fashion. As Gerard Hauser notes, the subjects of epideictic are not the "teachers of society," but rather, the "moral of their acts emerges . . . in the storyteller's province of how their deeds are narrated."[36] Meghan McCain, like Obama, both consoled and educated her audience through akairic world building. In essence, she could not reconcile her father's death with her desire to comfort the living, so instead she reframed it as a not-death, and navigated her father's passing by creating a timeless world within her eulogy. Her speech is characterized by *akairos* in that she created a world in which Senator McCain's influence stretched into the past, existed in the present, and would endlessly endure in the future.

Meghan McCain stated early in her speech, "My father is gone."[37] Consider Foley's understanding of epideictic: it is simultaneously present ("he goes") and progressive ("he is going"). Her statement that her father "is gone" is akairically paradoxical: to be gone is a state of being, but Senator McCain, at least outside of the eulogy, was in a state of *not*-being. Within the eulogy itself the elder McCain lay in a casket at the front of the cathedral, draped with the United States flag, its occupant both present and absent. The world of eulogy is one of suspension: of not having left yet, being about to leave, and already having gone.

In retelling a childhood anecdote, in which Senator McCain encouraged his daughter to get back on her horse after she had fallen off, Meghan McCain explained how, "Now that I am a woman, I look back across that time and see the expression on his face when I climbed back up and rode again, and I see the pride and love in his eyes as he said, 'Nothing is going to break you.'" When she recalled his reassuring statement, it was as though she conjured her father and he spoke through her and to her. In the timeless world of the eulogy, she could see his expression, though he was, outside of the eulogy, no longer there. She continued, "For the rest of my life, whenever I fall down, I get back up. Whenever I am hurt, I drive on. Whenever I am brought low, I rise. That is not because I am uniquely virtuous or strong or resilient. It is simply because my father, John McCain, was." Note the tenses here. Her father spoke to her in the past, though his influence, she implied, would last for the rest of her life. As a result, "whenever I fall down, I rise." This is not a statement in the future—"I *will* rise"—but rather a statement made in the eternal present. She insisted that this ability to rise above adversity "is not because I am uniquely virtuous," but rather, "because my father, John McCain, was." Although she spoke of her father in the past tense, she also spoke in his voice as though he were present, and underscored how his influence would shape her future.

Like Obama, who consoled the audience by imagining an eternally present Senator McCain passing each day's moral test, Meghan McCain sought consolation through the repetition of eternal encouragement whenever she would be "brought low." The world of both eulogies is characterized by *akairos*: a timeless suspension that existed as long as the eulogist spoke. To offer a eulogy is to exist in the realm between the as-yet and the already. In this way, in eulogistic speech we may understand the timelessness, rather than the untimeliness, of *akairos*.

AKAIROS AND PEDAGOGICAL POSSIBILITY

Since *akairos* holds creative possibility, it is worth considering how this concept may be used in a pedagogical context to expand students' understanding of what rhetorical activity entails, contains, and effects. Notions of timeliness and untimeliness, of "right time" and "not-right time" or "without a right time" are genre specific, and potentially underproductive and unnecessarily constraining. Of course, I am not suggesting that every time is the right time to make a particular statement. Indeed, certain genres and arenas of speech exist with varying expectations, and there are more appropriate and less appropriate things to say to have the desired effect on an audience. Instead, I echo James Kinneavy, who argued for the consideration of the ethical, political, and aesthetic dimensions of *kairos*. He related the term not only to the notion of time, but also to the notion of measure, fitness, and proportion in a multidimensional sense.[38] *Akairos*, like *kairos*, must be understood not only in the context of time but in space as well.

Michael Harker has argued that introducing *kairos* in the writing classroom as simply saying the right thing at the right time neglects "the most critical facts of a fundamental component of rhetoric" and misses "the opportunity of providing students and instructors with an expression that identifies not only the temporal but the ethical influences that complicate how we navigate and understand the social context of argument."[39] He advocates for adding *kairos* to the formerly two-dimensional rhetorical triangle to show its connection to *ēthos, pathos,* and *logos*. This addition creates a pyramid "that presents . . . the significance and influence of the passage of time and the importance of identifying the ethical 'preferences' that inevitably inform our arguments and actions in the world."[40] These "preferences" ultimately relate to the *telos* of *kairos,* in that "the term expresses action that is directed to a particular end."[41] In this way, *kairos* contextualizes rhetorical activity.

In the classroom, *akairos* may be offered as a productive lens through which to examine rhetorical theory and practice. It is the time*less*ness, not the untimeliness, of *akairos* that suggests a creativity and flexibility that *kairos* cannot offer. Like eulogy, which takes place in a suspended world in which the deceased will never die, *akairos* implies an eternal present. Viewing rhetoric from an akairic perspective can encourage student writers to ask themselves what worlds they seek to build in their writing, and how time in their created worlds relates to the reality on which those worlds are based. The domain of the akairic—the tactless, the untimely, the unfitting, the inopportune, the inappropriate, and even the unlawful—is expansive and generative, if one only takes the time to pursue it.

NOTES

1. The adjective *kairotic* is equally grammatically sound, though I prefer *kairic* because of its similarity to the adjective "chronic," derived from *chronos*.

2. Robert Beekes, *Etymological Dictionary of Greek* (Boston: Brill, 2010), 617.

3. Ibid.

4. Eric Charles White, *Kaironomia: On the Will-to-Invent* (Ithaca: Cornell University Press, 1987), 13.

5. Henry George Liddell, Robert Scott, and Henry Stuart Jones, *A Greek-English Lexicon,* 9th ed. (Oxford: Clarendon Press, 1996), s.v. ἄκαιρος.

6. Theophrastus, *Characters,* ed. and trans. James Diggle, Cambridge Classical Texts and Commentaries 43 (Cambridge: Cambridge University Press, 2004), XII.

7. Aeschylus, *Oresteia: Agamemnon. Libation-Bearers. Eumenides,* trans. Alan H. Sommerstein, Loeb Classical Library 146 (Cambridge: Harvard University Press, 2009), lines 807–9.

8. Phillip Sipiora, Introduction to *Rhetoric and Kairos: Essays in History, Theory, and Praxis,* ed. Phillip Sipiora and James S. Baumlin (Albany: State University of New York Press, 2002), 2. While this volume was in copyedit stage, Matthew Houdek and Kendall Phillips coedited a special issue of *Women's Studies in Communication* on "rhetoric and the temporal turn" (2021, Online First), featuring an essay by Lee M. Pierce that explores akairic elements in narrative. See Lee M. Pierce, "For the Time(d) Being: The Form Hate Takes in *The Hate U Give*," *Women's Studies in Communication* (2021, Online First).

9. A note adjacent to my argument but related to the collapse of the alpha privative and its root: the Seleucid king Demetrius III of the first century BCE is currently known by the nickname "Eukairos"; however, as David Levenson and Thomas Martin have argued, this nickname is incorrect, and the correct nickname, transmitted by Josephus, is "Akairos." They argue that this change was possibly caused by a scribe confused by the attribution of a negative nickname to a royal figure, or the mistake was based on a now-lost manuscript. David B. Levenson and Thomas R. Martin, "Akairos or Eukairos? The Nickname of the Seleucid King Demetrius III in the Transmission of the Texts of Josephus' *War* and *Antiquities*," *Journal for the Study of Judaism* 40 (2009).

10. *Hamartia*, from the verb *hamartanō*, "miss the mark, fail one's purpose, go wrong." Liddell, Scott, and Jones, *Greek-English Lexicon*, s.v. ἁμαρτάνω. In *Poetics* 1453a, Aristotle explains that the plot of tragedy changes trajectory from good fortune to misfortune not on account of the main character's wickedness, but rather, on account of that character's internal flaw (*hamartia*). Crucially, this flaw must express itself through action. Indeed, for Aristotle, character (*ēthos*) is that which reveals or makes clear a choice (*proairesin*), and speeches in which no choices are made do not reveal character (*Poetics* 1450b). See Aristotelis, *De Arte Poetica Liber*, ed. Rudolphus Kassel (Oxford: Oxford University Press, 1965).

11. Richard Benjamin Crosby, "Kairos as God's Time in Martin Luther King Jr.'s Last Sunday Sermon," *Rhetoric Society Quarterly* 39, no. 3 (2009), 263.

12. James L. Kinneavy and Catherine R. Eskin, "*Kairos* in Aristotle's Rhetoric," *Written Communication* 17, no. 3 (2000).

13. Including, for example, William C. Trapani and Chandra A. Maldonado, "*Kairos*: On the Limits to Our (Rhetorical) Situation," *Rhetoric Society Quarterly* 48, no. 3 (2018); Cheryl Price-Mckell, "When Kairos Compels Composition: Women's Response to the 1924 Burpee Seed Company® Contest, 'What Burpee Seeds Have Done for Me,'" *Rhetoric Review* 38, no. 4 (2019); Alexandria Peary, "The Role of Mindfulness in *Kairos*," *Rhetoric Review* 35, no. 1 (2016).

14. Aristotle, *Rhetoric* 1358a (from Aristotelis, *Ars rhetorica*, ed. W. D. Ross (Oxford: Oxford University Press, 1959).

15. Victoria Wohl, *Law's Cosmos: Juridical Discourse in Athenian Forensic Oratory* (Cambridge: Cambridge University Press, 2010), 203.

16. Ibid., 204. Wohl points out that every Athenian swore, "I will not hold a grudge [*mnēsikakēsō*, literally "remember evils"]"; as such, the oath itself demanded this civic not-remembering, or amnesia, a term formed from the same root as amnesty (*a-mnēsteia*). Wohl, *Law's Cosmos*, 204.

17. Ibid., 217.

18. For further exploration of *akairic* tension, see Friedrich Nietzsche, "On the Uses and Disadvantages of History for Life," *Untimely Meditations*, trans. R. J. Hollingdale (Cambridge: Cambridge University Press, 1997), 57–123. Nietzsche admits that his essay itself "is untimely, because I am here attempting to look afresh at something of which our time is rightly proud—its cultivation of history—as being injurious to it, a defect and deficiency in it; because I believe, indeed, that we are all suffering from a consuming fever of history and ought at least to recognize that we are suffering from it" (60).

19. Megan Foley, "Time for Epideictic," *Quarterly Journal of Speech* 101, no. 1 (2015), 210.

20. Ibid., 209, 210.

21. Cynthia Miecznikowski Sheard, "The Public Value of Epideictic Rhetoric," *College English* 58, no. 7 (1996), 770.

22. Nicole Loraux, *The Invention of Athens: The Funeral Oration in the Classical City*, trans. Alan Sheridan (Cambridge: Harvard University Press, 1986), 85.

23. Quotes from Obama's speech from "Read the Full Text of Barack Obama's Speech at John McCain's Memorial Service," NBC News, September 1, 2018, https://www.nbcnews.com/politics/barack-obama/read-full-text-barack-obama-s-speech-john-mccain-s-n905721.

24. See also, for example, Eric Charles White, *Kaironomia*, Part One, "The Paradox of the Liar"; Ekaterina V. Haskins, *Logos and*

Power in Isocrates and Aristotle (Columbia: University of South Carolina Press, 2004), chapter 3, "Between Kairos and Genre"; Philip Sipiora's introduction to *Rhetoric and Kairos: Essays in History, Theory, and Praxis.*

25. Crosby, "Kairos as God's Time," 264.

26. Haskins, *Logos and Power*, 67.

27. Plato, *Phaedrus* 272a. All translations in this chapter are my own. Greek text of *Phaedrus* is from Plato, *Platonis Opera*, vol. 2, ed. John Burnet (Oxford: Oxford University Press, 1995).

28. Here, for the act of "choosing among," Plato uses *diagnonti*, from *diagignōscō*, "discern," as opposed to simply *gignōsco*, "perceive, know."

29. Kinneavy and Eskin, "*Kairos* in Aristotle's Rhetoric," 434.

30. Cynthia Miecznikowski Sheard, "Kairos and Kenneth Burke's Psychology of Political and Social Communication," *College English* 55, no. 3 (March 1993), 293.

31. Isocrates, *Against the Sophists*, in *Isocrates II*, ed. George Norlin (Cambridge: Harvard University Press, 1980), 12.

32. Ibid., IV.9.

33. Phillip Sipiora, "Introduction," 10.

34. Adrianne Dennis Kunkel and Michael Robert Dennis, "Grief Consolation in Eulogy Rhetoric: An Integrative Framework," *Death Studies* 27, no. 1 (January 2003), 2.

35. Kunkel and Dennis, "Grief Consolation," 2, 4.

36. Gerard A. Hauser, "Aristotle on Epideictic: The Formation of Public Morality," *Rhetoric Society Quarterly* 29, no. 1 (1999), 15.

37. Quotes of Meghan McCain's speech from "Meghan McCain Eulogy of John McCain: Celebrating Her Dad's Love and Influence While Criticizing Trump," *Arizona Republic*, September 1, 2018, https://www.azcentral.com/story/news/politics/arizona/2018/09/01/meghan-mccain-full-text-eulogy-john-mccain-trancript/1174328002.

38. Roger Thompson, "Kairos Revisited: An Interview with James Kinneavy," *Rhetoric Review* 19, nos. 1–2 (2000), 75–76.

39. Michael Harker, "The Ethics of Argument: Rereading Kairos and Making Sense in a Timely Fashion," *College Composition and Communication* 59, no. 1 (September 2007), 79.

40. Ibid., 93.

41. Ibid., 84.

(Not) Knowing for Sure

Adoxa

CADDIE ALFORD

> For if you are serious and these things you are saying happen to be true, wouldn't the life of us human beings have been turned upside down and don't we do, as it would appear, all the opposite things to what we ought?
>
> —PLATO, *Gorgias*

Some decades feel more upside down than others. The world feels upside down when common sense fractures into discordant extremes. Such extremes do not accord with one another, let alone with any cohesive, over-arching values and beliefs. Writing "Philosophy and Politics" in 1954, Hannah Arendt defined her own moment as upside-down: "We live today in a world in which not even common sense makes sense any longer."[1] Extreme systems like totalitarianism lead to bewilderment and feelings of chaos. When, for instance, the familiar appeal to "think of the children!" does not extend to children kept in cages on US borders, or when political rallies invoke Robert E. Lee to praise his leadership, the world has embraced a more upside-down way of life.

Arendt posits that problems with common sense are similarly problems with the breakdown of philosophy and politics. Such a breakdown signals a need for philosophers to build entry points into human affairs by making the plurality of perspectives the main object of their philosophical wonder. It just so happens that a natural bridge between philosophy and politics is exactly the fissure that began "their old conflict": opinions (*doxai* in ancient Greek), or what we might see as the very things at the heart of today's own divisiveness.[2] It is a pressing issue when those divisions are valued far above reliable—however evolving—political commonplaces. Dana L. Cloud, for instance, begins *Reality Bites: Rhetoric and the Circulation of Truth Claims in U.S. Political Culture* with an uncomfortable acknowledgment: "There are a number of claims circulating in political culture with no basis in reality that are persuasive nonetheless."[3] When opinions truly manifest as tyrannical, the state of opinions is upside-down.

Opinion and its intersections with knowledge, emotion, politics, selfhood, and mastery are troubling to philosophers and rhetoricians alike. The proliferation of opinions through digital circulation and the subsequent slippage between opinions, social facts, facts, and faith present urgent political problems. Martha Nussbaum's *The Monarchy of Fear* points to how what we hold dear can be exploited toward fractal partisanship.[4] Patricia Roberts-Miller's *Demagoguery and Democracy* argues conditions of demagoguery thrive when discourse becomes "identity as logic" all the way down.[5] Jia Tolentino's *New York Times* bestseller *Trick Mirror: Reflections on Self-Delusion* grapples with how "the internet collapses identity, opinion, and action."[6] Clearly, there are many cases to be made for rethinking opinion.

The current resonance of opinion is an issue because opinions are rhetoric's most fundamental materials. However much they have changed conceptually, opinions still function as shared and received knowledge, oriented to everyday matters of concern. Because *doxa* are common starting places that can hold communities together, some scholars have referred to *doxa* as the "medium"[7] of rhetors while others call doxa rhetoric's "province."[8] As Aristotle definitively puts it, "The whole business of rhetoric is with opinion."[9] What, then, can a rhetorician do when opinions increasingly become less a checks and balances of identification between the individual and a healthy collective and more an antimovement of asociality?[10] The apparent warping of opinions on a mass scale troubles the very foundations of rhetorical practice. While a theory of rhetoric *with* opinions is public facing, rhetoric *without* opinions is solipsistic. While rhetoric with opinions traffics in seemingness, rhetoric without opinions is almost too transparent. With opinions, rhetoric has available means; without opinions, rhetoric has empty pockets. Quite simply, rhetoric without public opinions degrades commonsense into nonsense, both in terms of contemporary political conditions and in terms of rhetorical studies as we know it.

But maybe that is precisely what an upside-down world needs right now: an approach that favors not the rhetorical ties that bind, but the rhetorical ties unbound. The problematic Arendt identifies as the severing of philosophy from politics is ongoing in opinion's current crisis: as April Flakne determines from Arendt's corpus, the "only truth of the human world is that it has as a condition the plurality" of those who compose it,[11] and yet when we say "opinion" now, what we really mean is something deeply personal. Mere "opinion," then, currently operates "within an epistemological tradition that takes opinions to be held by individuals, who can be thought to invent original or unique opinions."[12] Within this framework, opinions are just waiting to become silos. This asocial *telos* would have confused the ancient Greeks: to them, *doxa* were culturally interwoven and productive sources of energy. So, if everyone is entitled to his or her own opinion, everyone is entitled *not* to *doxa* in the classical sense, but to *adoxa*, which are opinions that lack sociality or commonsensical purchase. The current rhetorical symbol spectrum is segmented, as captured by user @joedct on an online *Fox News* thread about climate change: "What's great about our nation [is] you can have your opinions, and I can have mine."[13] *Asserting* individuality and actually *being* an island unto oneself are different, but some opinions feel, and are handled as, more discrete than others.

Increasingly, rhetoric's reason for being stems not so much from the friction between knowledge (*epistēmē*) and *doxa*, but from the relations among opinion, widespread values, and the decidedly improbable underbellies of each: the appearances and beliefs "obviously unworthy of praise," "being trivial, ugly, useless, ridiculous, dangerous, or vicious."[14] The word *adoxa* is not a common term of art in the so-called Western rhetorical tradition, but I want to argue that *adoxa* has been instrumental to rhetoric as we understand it.[15] I would hasten to say that all along, the story of rhetoric has been written by the panting need to run away from these "obviously unworthy" views. While *epistēmē* and truth mobilize rhetoric to an extent, I argue it is actually *adoxa*, or "generally rejected" positions, that most motivate rhetorical theory, activism, and criticism.[16]

Adopting Sharon Crowley's call for theories of rhetoric to "do more than revive ancient notions" and to actually "adapt old notions to address contemporary rhetorical situations," this chapter recuperates the alpha-privative *adoxa* in order to tell a different version of rhetoric's story, one that makes explicit a rhetorical kind of philosophical dialectic.[17] As I show, such a dialectic implies that divisions—the same divisions that we commonly bemoan as blockages—potentially lead to generative outputs while gesturing to an immanent trajectory for Rhetorical Studies.

Like many before us, we are emphatically living in an upside-down world, negotiating the anxieties that inhere in the legacy of "truthiness," and so, like many scholars, I am offering an ancient concept to address the puzzling effects of the "post-truth" era. As Donna Zuckerberg notes in "Make Comparisons Great Again," however, the ongoing impulse to turn to the ancient Greco-Roman world for answers is not always questioned as critically as it needs to be.[18] Letting her reminder inform my choices, I turn purposefully to Plato's *Gorgias* because it is the dialogue most invested in the tensions between *doxa* and *adoxa*—between believing, to use an example from our own time, that climate change is an urgent problem and believing, say, that climate change is a hoax perpetuated by scientists who stand to make a profit in the switch from fossil fuels to alternative energy. By building on both Aristotle and James Kastely's "In Defense of Plato's *Gorgias*," and treating Plato's *Gorgias* as a careful attempt to rethink rhetoric for the good of the polis, I find in *adoxa* a robust understanding of the self as it stands in relation to the community, the private as it laments the public, and the primordial suffering that lets us suffer together.

DOXA AND/OR RHETORIC

Typically thought of as an art of persuasion, rhetoric is indebted not to truth (and also not to lying), but to opinion, to drawing out and amplifying what things seem and appear to be, through greater and lesser degrees of probability. *Doxa* is therefore the coin of rhetoric's realm—both coin and realm. Generally, *doxa* is translated as "opinion" or "belief," but it harbors other meanings such as fame, conjecture, and expectation. Michele Kennerly elaborates that "concepts in the *dok-* family" etymologically revolve around "seemingness, opinion, reputation."[19] *Doxa* are forms of knowledge that fluctuate—the flighty tides of personal and communal opinion joining one's image to others' impressions. As such, doxastic materials can be difficult to notice, embedded as they are in what gets taken for granted: minutia of identity fluxes, inheritances of norms, tales of folk wisdom, and tried-and-true assumptions. It is rhetoric that enables practitioners to "observe the persuasive" of the doxastic, which means the practice of rhetoric has a long history of trying to "aim at commonly held opinions."[20] Alongside Raymie McKerrow and Dana Anderson, I want to stress that rhetoric is a doxastic art—you can't have one without the other.[21]

As a specifically *doxastic* art, rhetoric is an ethic of sociality, a discerning method of invention, and a prescient embrace of indeterminacy. To bring *doxa* into focus as rhetoric's main substance is, as Kennerly claims, to render knowledge social: *doxastic* critique "returns knowing to the realm of the social, to the 'seems to *us*.'"[22] In their ancient conception, opinions formed through bonds. Eric Havelock spells out that both *doxa*'s noun and verb form denote "both the 'seeming' that goes on in myself, the 'subject,' namely my 'personal impressions,' and the 'seeming' that links me as an 'object' to other people looking at me—the 'impression' I make on them."[23] These social impressions compose a logic of connectivity that details rhetoric's groundwork.

Doxa's sociality suggests that the ancient treatment of opinions encompassed more of an ethic than what we grant opinions today. More than indicating the individual's uniqueness, and more, even, than indicating "mere intersubjectivity," Flakne posits that *doxa* indicate "a co-primordiality and interrelation at the origin of self, world, and fellows."[24] This is a complex that seals the fate and flourishing of what might emerge as one with what might emerge as many. *Doxa*, therefore, are always igniting a preexisting responsibility for others similarly entangled in their meshwork. Perhaps the most enduring ethical system is rhetoric's doxastic cooperative.

The ancient conception of *doxa* shows how opinions can create vectors across difference, which is why the concept of *endoxa*, or the most commonly held opinions, makes sense: some opinions' vectors are stronger than others. Perhaps Aristotle recognized this ethic when he wrote the *Rhetoric* as more or less a systematic schema of *endoxa*. In most cases, *endoxa* contain "at least a partial grasp of the truth," so "any serious inquiry into moral or political subjects must start from them."[25] Putting it in terms of Aristotelian proofs, *doxa* and *endoxa* are both artistic *and* inartistic: they objectively are that community's lived reality (the raw data points waiting to be made into sense), but at the same time they are constructed and adjusted in accordance with that lived reality. *Doxa*'s gradations from better to worse offer rhetoric an ethic of sociality whose principles rest on the *mostly*—the commonly—reputable: as long as the rhetorician adheres to *doxa* and *endoxa*, they will probably avoid *adoxa*, or the least realistic premises. The ethical and moral stakes of using *doxa* and *endoxa* are high.

Relying on *doxa* or *endoxa* can potentially shape or even constitute the very possibility for persuasion as such, signaling a fundamental connection between *doxa* and rhetorical invention. The Aristotelian "capacity" for rhetoric really lies in the moment invention responds to the interplay between *endoxa, doxa,* and, sometimes, *adoxa*: "It belongs to the same capacity both to see the truth and [to see] what resembles the true, and at the same time humans have a natural disposition for the true and to a large extent hit on the truth; thus an ability to aim at commonly held opinions [*endoxa*] is a characteristic of one who also has a similar ability to regard the truth."[26] We are accustomed to thinking about invention as the creative processing of rhetorical means, but perhaps that processing is really a mode of ranking; perhaps, as Aristotle implies above, an act of rhetorical invention is one that tests and ranks the repute of various *doxa*. *Doxa* are naturally invention's building blocks, but considering them, weighing them, is just as inventive as hastily leaning on or interfacing through them. As Sharon Crowley posits, the resonances of expectation in *doxa* lend "a temporal cast to doxa, implying something previously constructed that can, in an event, *be met or thwarted*."[27] Meeting and thwarting *doxa* activates a specifically discerning kind of invention.

Circulating, becoming buried, resurfacing, *doxa* are repetitive, networked social lineages that can be ranked toward invention. The Aristotelian "given," *doxa* are literally things given and passed down from communities to individuals and back again, orchestrating a generative gift economy that thrives on indeterminacy.[28] Such indeterminacy is inherent in what it means to conjecture, to throw something out there that makes sense to you, to yours, to you and yours, even to you and yours and most everyone else. We hope that it will land.

But that is precisely what rhetoric *with doxa* requires: a social and implicitly ethical form of invention that operates by publicly assessing the repute of *doxa*. Without *doxa* and *endoxa*, rhetoric is truly lost, lacking orientation to any social good, receptive creativity, or quality control. That is to say, with as much irony as possible, rhetoric *without* doxa is actually the rhetoric Plato was skeptical of.

ADOXA AND/OR RHETORIC

The business of rhetoric, then, is a business of the always social, resourceful, and provisional ebb and flow of *doxastic* elements both within and outside of our control. From antiquity onward, however, rhetoric-with-*doxa* has been juxtaposed to stable knowledge, located in a version of Plato's *epistēmē*.[29] A distraction from the painstaking work of soul-betterment, *doxa* received a notorious and enduring reputation. As unstable appearances that propel toward variety, *doxa* began to represent, terminologically, the predicament that tends to cast rhetoric as marginalized. When scholars perpetuate the notion that "Plato was rhetoric's most ardent critic," they are also perpetuating the implication that rhetoric only deals with a kind of belief and set of appearances that are completely separate from and inferior to knowledge. In this story, rhetoric becomes "*mere* rhetoric."[30]

Focusing on this tension, with Plato in the thick of it, is the most obvious—even *doxastic*—way to tell rhetoric's story; as Robin Reames stresses, this narrative reduces rhetoric to "the lesser counterpart of philosophy, useful only for speaking to ignorant masses for whom more rational methods are ineffectual."[31] Rereading Plato's works, however, illustrates just how much nuance we obscure when we continue to accept this narrative about rhetoric's origins and its marginalization at the hands of Plato. With the figure of Socrates, Plato implies that there are hierarchical shades of opinion, from outlandish to appropriate. In the *Meno*, for example, Socrates claims, "*True* opinion is as good a guide to rightness of action as knowledge."[32] In fact, Socrates suggests the only thing differentiating opinion's flight from knowledge's stability "is the tether" you can use to capture and then improve an opinion's utility.[33] While the idea of transforming *doxa* into better *doxa* suggests an eventual rigidity to *doxa*, John Muckelbauer interprets Socrates here as "claiming that the capturing itself fosters a certain kind of value," *not* that *doxa*'s freedom of movement can ever be stopped.[34] Plato actually recognized both the mobility of opinion and the importance of teasing opinion toward philosophical ends. Plato, in other words, has a lot to teach rhetoricians about both *doxa*'s complexity and its place in rhetoric's ancient origin story.

If it hasn't seemed like that, it's because rhetoricians have focused too much on Plato's explicit conflations of rhetoric with *doxa*. I want to argue, however, that what Plato really objected to wasn't *doxa* per se, but rather a rhetoric without *doxa*: an adoxastic rhetoric. According to Aristotle, there are a few sure-fire ways to identify *adoxa*: "Care must be taken not to uphold a hypothesis which is generally unacceptable [ἄδοξον]. There are two ways in which it may be unacceptable. It may be one which leads to the making of absurd statements, for example, if one were to say that everything or nothing is in motion; on the other hand, it may be one of those which a bad character would choose or which are contrary to our wishes, for example, that pleasure is the good and that to commit injustice is better than to suffer it."[35] *Adoxa* are often unsubstantiated and nonsensical in their radicality. They are the opposite of collaborative because, as absurd statements cultivated in private, they have not been matured and tested by others in public. *Adoxa* are thus like shadowy figures, insulated from and even dismissive of difference. With the emphasis on "bad character," Aristotle renders *adoxa*'s antisocial manner suspect. As Arendt makes clear, the ancients considered *doxa* in terms of fame and splendor: "To assert one's own opinion belonged to being able to show oneself, to be seen and heard by others."[36] Therefore, "in private life one is hidden and can neither appear nor shine, and consequently no *doxa* is possible there."[37] *Adoxa* spawn in solitude, products of an indecorous hush.

Even so, *adoxa* are sometimes released into the wild, and when they are they stand apart, resonating as bizarre takes on a world many wouldn't recognize. To return to the previously mentioned Fox News climate change piece, at issue is whether Elizabeth Warren's analogy between environmental catastrophe and World War II makes sense or is an overblown indication of leftist hysteria. In response, user @MARTUS attempts to throw climate change into question altogether: "If humans are causing global warming, Mars would not be getting warmer too. But it is. Photos of disappearing polar ice caps over the generations prove it." One of the top commenters, @MARTUS has gained "leader" status. Other users have grown frustrated with @MARTUS, calling them a troll, dismissing them outright, and making inside jokes out of their previous comments and arguments.

Beyond being slightly undeveloped, the opinion of @MARTUS is without repute, without relevance, without substantiation, and without status: it gives pause to most, if not immediately causing laughter or bewilderment. To rhetoricians, the fallacious false equivalence of this opinion sends up red flags. And while @MARTUS appears to be drawing on evidence of sorts, Jenny Rice's work on anomalous claims demonstrates repeatedly that "evidence that seems to exist 'out there' in the world may, in some cases, be our own feelings we identify as being "out there."[38] This is the two-edged, both subjective and objective sword of all forms of *doxa*.

While *doxa* can act as constraints, they can also be mobilized as pathways that work between beings. *Adoxa* simply halt, too idiosyncratic to keep things moving. In traditional rhetorical terms, such *adoxa* are clear constraints on deliberation, consensus, and exchange. Following Arendt's logic, no *doxa* can exist in private, which means that the *dokei moi*, or "of what appears to me,"[39] that we each possess is often, in fact, *adoxa*. In private, opinions form that we tend to keep to ourselves—ill-formed, nascent traces of naïve realist tendencies.

Because *adoxa* can get in the way of interlocutors reaching any kind of stasis or commonplace, they have to be troubled by refutation. Looking at refutation through the lens of *adoxa* reveals just how intertwined rhetoric has always been with philosophical dialectic. As a relentless "contravening of expectations,"[40] Plato's *Gorgias* is the dialogue perhaps most informed by opinion's shadow, which means it is an essential text to engage in the construction of a spectrum of *doxa*. We are used to thinking of *Gorgias* as the dialogue that best crystallizes philosophy's charges against rhetoric: what does a rhetorician even need to know to do rhetoric? Can rhetoric actually help people better themselves? Can rhetoric improve the health of the polis? Socrates hits the nail on the head when he questions whether rhetoric is a genuine *epistemic* art: "Does the rhetorician happen to be in this same situation in regard to the just and the unjust, the shameful and the noble, and good and bad, as he is in regard to the healthy and the other things belonging to the other arts: not knowing the things themselves—what is good or what bad or what noble or what shameful or just or unjust—but having devised persuasion about them so as, though not knowing, to seem to know more than the one who knows, among those who don't know?"[41] Is it seeming all the way down or is the rhetor actually responsible for uncovering and shaping certainties? It would be easy to see *doxa* as the essential ingredient in all this cookery, but I contend it is actually *adoxa* that the dialogue is troubled by.

The *Gorgias*, it is safe to say, has long been understood as Plato's attempt to yoke rhetoric to seeming as opposed to being. This project can be distilled to the famous analogy between sophistry and "cosmetics." Reames, however, argues that the translation of "cosmetics" is not quite accurate. Rather, she demonstrates that Plato was probably, as he was wont to do, creating a neologism that brought questions of consumption and foreign influence into the equation, thereby critiquing "specific practices of particular sophists who whetted Athens's appetite for acquisitive luxuries and in so doing lured them into a disastrous campaign for regional domination."[42] Through the technology of writing, language could be analyzed as such, giving rhetoric its enduring architectonic role. The *Gorgias* was influential in fleshing out and experimenting with that role, however inadvertently. That is, the *Gorgias* offers a "critique that passes *through* the rhetoric of the sophist Gorgias and arrives ultimately at its true object: the use of power for acquisitive gain. In other words, rhetoric and sophistry serve as a medium for the critique; they are not the target of the critique."[43] As such, Reames claims that the dialogue has "more to do with gluttony and excess than with sophistry and rhetoric as such."[44] I agree, but rather than explore further the historical conditions that gave way to those exigencies, I am more interested in unpacking the implication that the dialogue is concerned with that which is too much, with that which exceeds the mean.

Tracing opinion to its salience in the seventeenth and eighteenth centuries, Donald R. Kelly explores its emergence at that point with connotations of probability, approval, and demonstrable principles. Citing the French *Encyclopédie* entry for "science," Kelly shows a balance forming between science and doubt, with opinion forming as a kind of "'mean' between perfect science and absolute doubt."[45] In that sense, *doxa*, what are and are not generally agreed upon and what are and are not generally rejected, functions as the mean not just of rhetoric's range, but also of other formulations of knowledge types, whether inflected by science or religious faith. The *Gorgias* is in no way a dialogue that is interested in the mean. Through a variety of directions, the dialogue cares most about what sandwiches the mean—when *doxa* are *just* seemingness as self-evidence. It strikes me that many engagements with opinion—particularly now—do not recognize how "opinions" could and do occasion a mean. Muckelbauer admits that like "tradition," opinions can be "unreasoned beliefs whose force actively prevents an engagement with reason."[46] That fixity, though, is opinion's surplus, only one extreme of opinion's intricate inclinations.

Among other things, the *Gorgias* wants to theorize opinion's excesses, rendering *adoxa* in turn a crucial contribution to rhetorical theory. Kastely's "In Defense of Plato's *Gorgias*" is significant to this interpretation of the *Gorgias* because Kastely makes the case that the dialogue is an exploration of rhetoric's importance to philosophical matters. Kastely underscores that the *Gorgias* offers an "alternative way to write the history of rhetoric, a way that values rhetoric for its role in refutation."[47] What Kastely means by this is that philosophical dialectic cannot work without rhetoric because philosophical dialectic is not something that most people will enjoy.[48] The refutation involved in dialectic is daunting work: it asks us to zero in on one of our most raw notions, extract it from our beings, look at it from uglier vantages, and remold it before accepting it back into the fold. Rhetoric helps that medicine go down by readying us to give up those secret predilections and naïve perceptions. Indeed, the first demanding question Socrates asks in the *Gorgias* is not about justice or rhetoric or virtue, but actually about disposition: turning to Callicles, he asks if Gorgias would "be willing to talk with us?"[49] That willingness is essential because it equips the interlocutors to relate differently to themselves.

After all, at stake in philosophical dialectic is identity; through refutation, rhetoric finds dialectic's available means *within us*: "Rhetoric needs to undertake the more difficult task of making *us* available for dialectical refutation."[50] When a dialectic is going well, those involved "cannot rest content in an unreconstructed understanding of who they are but will take a risk and find out what they can become."[51] Each interlocutor has to become available because each interlocutor hosts *adoxa*, or dialectic's starting points.

The *Gorgias* is a dialogue that confirms how dialectic starts not with opinions, but with those juvenile and somewhat private opinions. The first task Socrates undertakes is getting Gorgias—an accomplished rhetorician, no less—to revise the unproductive opinion that rhetoric is just "about speeches."[52] With forceful conviction, Socrates identifies *adoxa* as the ultimate enemy: "For I think that nothing is so great an evil for a human being as false opinion about the things that our argument now happens to be about."[53] The "false opinion" is parasitic; the "love of the people" that makes Callicles resistant to Socrates, for instance, is "present in [his] soul,"[54] lodged so deep, with such intensity, that Callicles will not question a single adoxastic belief. Bringing Socrates palpable sorrow, Callicles fades from the dialogue unchanged, still believing that the strong few naturally overcome the weak masses. And after his heated exchange with Socrates, he definitely still believes that philosophy is "the corruption of human beings."[55] To be fair to Callicles and Polus, refuting *adoxa* requires being insincere, to a point, about who you are. Such insincerity takes vulnerability because it is unclear who you will be when all is said and done.[56]

Dialectic must start by refuting *adoxa*. Callicles cannot move forward until dealing in some way with what his argumentative disposition lacks: a readiness when necessary to contradict a beloved notion or even what has become the Athenian status quo.[57] This is a readiness that embraces dialectic's rhetoricity: "To be addressed and affected, to be able to respond, and to be able to become a rhetorical subject, we must somehow be vulnerable, exposed, or open to the affection of address from outside ourselves."[58] Spiraling within that rhetoricity, within the very constitution of relationality, the movement of dialectic is from the private and the individual to the public and the communal. Philosophical refutation works from our personal commitments to build shared commitments. Refutation, that is, tries to get us to meet in *doxa*, to meet in social accordance with the slightly reputable common. If Plato's dialogues end inconclusively, Arendt notes, it is because talking something through often "seemed result enough"—dislodging and nudging *adoxa* into doxastic territory is result enough, however vague or slight the shift is.[59] To find oneself more in synch with *doxa* and even *endoxa* is to have reached a set of acceptable parameters, occupied by fellow humble interlocutors who have similarly unburdened themselves of falsehoods.

I say "humble" because I want to honor the role *adoxa* plays in this more rhetorical conception of philosophical dialectic. In the process of being refuted, *adoxa* activate a more ethical positionality. As private opinions, *adoxa* are the original kindling for shame, the suffering-to-come that will, eventually, render us more empathetic, more social, and more *doxastic*. Refuting *adoxa*, unleashing it for public scrutiny, is the ultimate embarrassment that accompanies the accretions of a faulty worldview.

It is no wonder, then, that the *Gorgias* is a dialogue charged with shame: Callicles believes Polus was shamed into silence; Gorgias has to endure witnessing his pupils' inadequacies,[60] Callicles accuses Socrates of shameful argumentation, and at the end, Socrates sheepishly picks up the pieces of his failures.[61] Thematically and structurally, it is Socrates's final speech that ultimately crafts a connection between *adoxa*, refutation, and shame. Like the private perceptions we inevitably form over time, Socrates's myth, as Marina Berzins McCoy articulates, "begins with the idea that human woundedness, or openness to wound, is one of the most basic facts or truths about our own existence."[62] A foundational truth, the adoxastic scars of a life are found written on souls, creating a disagreement between the soul and the person's doxastic appearance. "Base souls," that is, can be "clothed in fine bodies, ancestry, and wealth."[63] McCoy notes that the myth demonstrates the meaning of *alētheia* (truth) as "an 'uncovering,' in the soul's being uncovered for judgment."[64] Removing the trappings of sociality exposes what lies underneath—or does it?

When *adoxa* are purged during refutation, they are not wholly dispelled. Rather, the *adoxa* that we courageously offer up leave in their wake a shame that transforms the individual's embarrassment and regret into its upside-down: humility. It is the shame *adoxa* leave us with that instills the interpersonal disposition of humility, bending us toward both recognizing and suffering shame with others. Just as humility is kindred with shame, so are *adoxa* not *doxa*'s polar opposite: *adoxa* cannot be *doxa*'s flipside when they both operate via logics of regard and connectivity.

So in this way, *adoxa* are the pathways back into *doxa* not only in terms of refutation, but also in terms of the grounded humility that *adoxa* impart. Giving public expression to *adoxa* captures us in regard's disregard, holding us chastened in the eyes of others. *Adoxa*, then, can be thought of as the rhetorical mechanisms by which we feel and appreciate shame in common. In this way, Plato's "justification for rhetoric" truly is, as Kastely articulates, that "it is the one intellectual practice that allows us to live responsibly in a world in which we are inadvertent origins of others' suffering."[65] With that responsibility, Plato has given rhetoricians our most important mission to date: we need to attend to *adoxa* in ways that enact care not only for a world bubbling over with filter bubbles of doxastic socialities turned adoxastic internalities, but also for the participants involved in that world's dialectic, whose *adoxa* form in a solitude not unlike my own solitude or your own solitude. Even though *adoxa* are problematic resources and evidence, humans still require pathways to reveal the common world through speech, through "the medium" of *doxa* "*to, for*," and, yes, "*against* others." Voicing *adoxa* are one such way "both a common world and an individual come into appearance, into view."[66]

DOXA, *ADOXA*, AND/OR RHETORICAL STUDIES

Aristotle attaches a perverse sincerity to the act of using *adoxa*: "For men hate him who makes such assertions, regarding him not as maintaining them for the sake of argument but as saying what he really thinks."[67] When people use *adoxa*, we sense they are being indecorously honest about what they think. Of course, such honesty runs counter to rhetoric's principle of concealment. As Carolyn R. Miller elucidates, through toggling between constructing a relative artifice of sincerity and concealing that artifice, rhetoric shrouds and dissembles more than it lays bare.[68] And therein lies the main criticism thrown at rhetoric: "That's just rhetoric!" is synonymous with a pervasive suspicion of insincerity, and yet ultimate sincerity is at the root of "obviously" ignoble opinions.

Although we can see that the concept of *adoxa* is at odds with how rhetoric is typically practiced and understood, it is easy to see that the *doxa about* rhetoric—the through-lines of deception, flattery, and mere fluff that have given it a bad name—are really products of a conflation over time between *doxa* and *adoxa*. *Doxa* is not the devil term we have long made it out to be. It's *adoxa* that weakly correspond to truth. It is *adoxa* that bespeak a lack of concern with the good of the polis. It is *adoxa* that do not trust expertise. And it is rhetoric's associations with *adoxa* that have been the problem all along.

If Robert Hariman is right that Rhetorical Studies will "always have to answer to Plato's questioning of its merit," then let rhetoricians acknowledge *adoxa* as not-quite-*doxa* so that we can definitively, finally, and commonly accept our worthwhile and affirmative contribution to meaning making.[69] Rhetoric-with-*doxa* need no longer cause shame.

NOTES

1. Hannah Arendt, "Philosophy and Politics," *Social Research* 57, no. 1 (1990): 102.

2. Ibid., 103. *Doxai* is the correct pluralization of *doxa* in ancient Greek, but, in my building with and theorizing *doxa*, I treat the word as plural because I am using it as a concept that constellates many meanings and that I am forwarding to different purposes (an apparatus of sorts).

3. Dana L. Cloud, *Reality Bites: Rhetoric and the Circulation of Truth Claims in U.S. Political Culture* (Columbus: Ohio State University Press, 2018), 1.

4. Martha C. Nussbaum, *Monarchy of Fear: A Philosopher Looks at Our Political Crisis* (New York: Simon & Schuster, 2018).

5. Patricia Roberts-Miller, *Demagoguery and Democracy* (New York: The Experiment, 2017), 49.

6. Jia Tolentino, *Trick Mirror: Reflections on Self-Delusion* (New York: Random, 2019), 19.

7. Bernard A. Miller, "Retrieving a Sophistic Sense of Doxa," in *Rhetoric in the Vortex of Cultural Studies: Proceedings of the Fifth Biennial Conference*, ed. Arthur Walzer (Minneapolis: University of Minnesota Press, 1992), 32.

8. Raymie McKerrow, "Critical Rhetoric: Theory and Praxis," *Communication Monographs* 56 (1989): 104.

9. Aristotle, *On Rhetoric: A Theory of Civic Discourse*, trans. George A. Kennedy (New York: Oxford University Press, 1991), 1404a.

10. John Muckelbauer, *The Future of Invention: Rhetoric, Postmodernism, and the Problem of Change* (Albany: State University of New York Press, 2008), 159.

11. April Flakne, "'No Longer and Not Yet': From Doxa to Judgment," *Graduate Faculty Philosophy* 21, no. 2 (1999): 160.

12. Sharon Crowley, *Toward a Civil Discourse: Rhetoric and Fundamentalism* (Pittsburgh: University of Pittsburgh Press, 2006), 47.

13. Greg Gutfeld. "Gutfeld on Elizabeth Warren's Apocalyptic Climate Change Rhetoric," Fox News, June 5, 2019, https://www

.foxnews.com/opinion/gutfeld-on-elizabeth-warrens-apocalyptic-climate-change-rhetoric.

14. Arthur Stanley Pease, "Things Without Honor," *Classical Philology* 21, no. 1 (1926), 29.

15. Another technical note: Though *adoxa* looks like it would be *doxa* in its alpha-privative noun form, it is actually its alpha-privative adjectival form. *Adoxia* is the noun form, and, in ancient texts, it often has the force of "obscurity" or "insignificance" (see Liddell and Scott entries). I use *adoxa*, in keeping with the use of *endoxa* as a noun in rhetorical theory (especially Aristotle's).

16. Aristotle, *Topics* 159b, trans. Hugh Tredennick (Cambridge: Harvard University Press, 1960).

17. Crowley, *Civil*, 47.

18. Donna Zuckerberg, "Make Comparisons Great Again," EIDOLON, accessed May 20, 2019, https://eidolon.pub/make-comparisons-great-again-f778e953e691.

19. Michele Kennerly, "On Being and Seeming (Good)," EIDOLON, accessed June 15, 2019, https://eidolon.pub/on-being-and-seeming-good-8f779ab34342.

20. Aristotle, *Rhetoric* 1355b and 1355a.

21. McKerrow, "Critical Rhetoric"; Dana Anderson, *Identity's Strategy: Rhetorical Selves in Conversion* (Columbia: University of South Carolina Press, 2007).

22. Kennerly, "On Being."

23. Eric Havelock, *Preface to Plato* (Cambridge: Harvard University Press, 1963), 250.

24. Flakne, "No Longer," 160.

25. Larry Arnhart, *Aristotle on Political Reasoning: A Commentary on the Rhetoric* (DeKalb: Northern Illinois University Press, 1981), 7.

26. Aristotle, *Rhetoric* 1355b (1.1.11).

27. Crowley, *Civil*, 47, emphasis mine.

28. Aristotle, *Rhetoric* 1355b.

29. On the heels of the twentieth-century conception of rhetoric's epistemic capacities, we now appreciate that appearances and reality are not so much layered as they are mutually informing: *doxa* and *episteme* are not polar extremes, but understood instead as engaged in a kinetic tug-of-war. Therefore, the pioneering attempts of, e.g., Robert Scott to reject a "prior and enabling truth" (12) to recuperate a robust sense of rhetoric's inventional capacities has certainly been valuable in complicating our tradition's origin story, however much that project can still be problematized for the ways it continues to subjugate *doxa* beneath *epistēmē*. See Robert Scott, "On Viewing Rhetoric as Epistemic," *Central States Speech Journal* 18 (1967): 9–17.

In calling rhetoric "epistemic," Scott aligns rhetoric's worth with knowledge-production. And as James Jasinski glosses, Scott revisits "epistemic rhetoric" with a degree of regret: "in so doing, Scott realized in 1993, he had allowed Plato—and the objectivist tradition—to dictate the terms of the debate. Reflection on rhetoric's epistemic status is problematic, Scott suggested, because it is an effort to play Plato's game" (226–27). See James Jasinski, "Epistemic, Rhetoric as," in *Sourcebook on Rhetoric: Key Concepts in Contemporary Rhetorical Studies*, 219–29 (Thousand Oaks, CA: Sage, 2001).

30. Robin Reames, *Seeming and Being in Plato's Rhetorical Theory* (Chicago: University of Chicago Press, 2018), 2.

31. Ibid.

32. Plato, *Meno* 97b, trans. W. R. M. Lamb (Cambridge: Harvard University Press, 1924), emphasis mine.

33. Ibid., 98a.

34. Muckelbauer, *Invention*, 178.

35. Aristotle, *Topics* 160b.

36. Arendt, "Philosophy," 80.

37. Ibid., 81.

38. Jenny Rice, *Awful Archives: Conspiracy Theory, Rhetoric, and Acts of Evidence* (Columbus: Ohio State University Press, 2020), 115.

39. Ibid., 80.

40. James Kastely, "In Defense of Plato's *Gorgias*," *PMLA* 106, no. 1 (1991): 90.

41. Plato, *Gorgias* 459d–e, trans. James H. Nichols (Ithaca: Cornell University Press, 1998).

42. Reames, *Being*, 16.

43. Ibid., 45.

44. Ibid., 43.

45. Donald R. Kelly, "Philodoxy: Mere Opinion and the Question of History," *Journal of the History of Philosophy* 106, no.1 (1991): 127.

46. Muckelbauer, *Invention*, 154.

47. Kastely, "Defense," 97.

48. Moreover, as Kastely points out, most people don't really see the value of philosophical dialectic: "The world agrees with Callicles that philosophical reflection is irrelevant to practical affairs" (106).

49. Plato, *Gorgias* 447b–c.

50. Kastely, "Defense," 106, emphasis mine.

51. Ibid., 108.

52. Plato, *Gorgias* 449e.

53. Plato, *Gorgias* 458a–b.

54. Plato, *Gorgias* 513c.

55. Plato, *Gorgias* 484c.

56. For a recent treatment of Socratic (in) sincerity, see Elizabeth Markovits, *The Politics of Sincerity: Plato, Frank Speech, and Democratic Engagement* (University Park: Penn State University Press, 2008).

57. Plato, *Gorgias* 481d–e.

58. Kendall Gerdes, "Trauma, Trigger Warnings, and the Rhetoric of Sensitivity," *Rhetoric Society Quarterly* 49 (2019): 14.

59. Arendt, "Philosophy," 82.

60. Kastely, "Defense," 99.

61. Plato, *Gorgias* 494e.

62. Marina Berzins McCoy, *Wounded Heroes: Vulnerability as a Virtue in Ancient Greek Literature and Philosophy* (Oxford: Oxford University Press, 2013), 104.

63. Plato, *Gorgias* 523c.

64. McCoy, *Heroes*, 101.

65. Kastely, "Defense," 105.

66. Flakne, "No Longer," 164.

67. Aristotle, *Topics* 160b.

68. Carolyn R. Miller, "Should We Name the Tools? Concealing and Revealing the Art of Rhetoric," in *The Public Work of Rhetoric*, ed. David Coogan and John Ackerman (Columbia: University of South Carolina Press, 2010), 19–38.

69. Robert Hariman, "Status, Marginality, and Rhetorical Theory," *Quarterly Journal of Speech* 72 (1986): 39.

Aporia

DAMIEN SMITH PFISTER

Aporia is usually understood as an insoluble puzzle. In conventional usage, the alpha privative "a" is often taken to mean "not"; paired with the root word of *poros,* meaning "path or passage," an *aporia* refers to a problem that presents no obvious way out. Zeno's many *aporiai* are quintessential examples, and the most famous of these is indicative of the form: in order to cross the finish line, one must get halfway there, which requires getting halfway to halfway, which, infinitely regressing, means that final destinations are always just out of reach. Logically, this rings true; phenomenologically, few things are demonstrably more false. The resulting paradox presents an *aporia* that either cannot be reconciled or requires much inventional labor for reconciliation. This is the sense of *aporia* that Derrida refers to as "the impossible, the antinomy, or the contradiction . . . a nonpassage because its elementary milieu does not allow for something that could be called passage, step, walk, gait, displacement, or replacement, a kinesis in general. There is no more path (*odos, methodos, Weg,* or *Holzweg*)."[1] An *aporia,* in this understanding, is an existential contradiction. Although more famous as a philosophical term, *aporia* is also a rhetorical figure. Brooke Rollins explains the lexical patterning of *aporia* as "the rhetorical figure in which a speaker expresses doubt about how to approach a subject."[2] The rhetor who acknowledges the apparent contradictions, paradoxes, or confusions surrounding a specific issue concedes complexity—until, that is, they articulate a path out of what previously had appeared impassable.

In this chapter, I propose a reading of *aporia* that does not have vexation or impassability at its core. To interpret *aporia* in the spirit of this volume as "without a path," rather than "no path," is to situate *aporia* less as an existential philosophical contradiction and more as a pragmatic rhetorical challenge. This more open concept of *aporia* can be used to generate two concepts needed to steer digital culture in less panoptic directions: the *aporia* of the glance and hyperporization. "The *aporia* of the glance" refers to looking practices that are without a defined path; that is, to the visual focusing of an analogical body occurring without a stable, discrete, trackable pathway of looking that is objectified and commodified. When a person glances around, the object of their visual focus is always somewhat ambiguous. Humans' visual fields are so wide that we can never be certain of what another is really looking at. Crucially, for the purposes of my argument, glances leave few traces. A human body's glance leaves little to no external record of a visual pathway. Fleeting glances are not typically preserved, aggregated, and made available for analysis. By contrast, technology companies are rapidly improving the granular tracking of visual pathways as a way to monetize attention in augmented reality (AR) and virtual reality (VR). Building on decades of eye-tracking research and enabled by headset apparatus resting right before the eyes, these efforts to track glancing promise to *hyperporize* looking, laying down pathways to advertisers and other attention merchants. Using the start-up cryptocurrency Gaze Coin as a case study in how gaze measurement and gaze control enable this hyperporization of vision, I develop the "*aporia* of the glance" as a way to theorize the advantages of untracked visual perception. While Gaze Coin is a marginal cryptocurrency that may never have the influence that its founders hope for, it is representative of efforts to use eye-tracking technologies to exert ever-more-granular data collection and control in budding AR/VR media ecologies. Indeed, the Gaze Coin team's robust vision of how to monetize looking promises to be imitated in some form as the virtual reality imaginary congeals within advertiser-driven consumer cultures.

Gaze Coin offers itself as the solution to an apparent *aporia* in the traditional sense of the term: the seemingly insoluble problem of monetizing virtual reality. As a proof-of-concept white paper authored by the Gaze Coin team articulates, conventional ad-supported business models do not quite work in AR/VR contexts: making users "stop and watch an ad makes immersion unworkable," there is "a lack of an ad metric/data layer" to track user engagement, and there is no agreed-upon standard to measure user attention to advertisements in the platforms now being developed.[3] Of course, these three problematics for monetizing AR/VR obtain to various degrees in other media ecologies, but, according to the white paper, the specificities of AR/VR interfaces require the development of native modes of interaction and new grammars for measurement. Indeed, the opportunities for advertising in virtual and augmented reality are enticing, the authors note, "because literally everywhere you go, look, or touch in VR and AR can be monetized."[4] Their articulation of Gaze Coin's potential is worth quoting at length:

> Using patent-registered technology, Gaze Coin is the only VR/AR blockchain token (unit of exchange) measured by gaze control/eye tracking. By measuring "gaze," Gaze Coin creates a model for advertising in VR/AR environments (from short-form experiences and simple digital objects all the way to fully-rendered virtual worlds) at the heart of how mixed reality is created and consumed through the eyes of the beholder. Brands can use eye-tracking in a myriad of ways: to evaluate their packaging designs, advertising, and online shopping behavior, in order to optimize the customer experience. Metrics include engagement (number of fixations, dwell time, % of time in an area), ease of processing (fixation duration), findability (time to first fixation and number of fixations prior to first fixation), order of processing (gaze path), comprehension (repeat fixations) and excitement (pupil dilation).[5]

By using eye-tracking methods conducive to AR/VR interfaces, Gaze Coin creates a medium-specific way of navigation that tracks the direction of the eye's movement to activate content. In a demonstration video that serves as a proof-of-concept enticement to potential investors, a user's eyes fixate on a digital sign, which generates the beginning of a circle that, over the course of a couple of seconds, progresses to close the loop and then "transports" the user to the enclosed content.[6]

Gaze Coin's ability to use practices of looking as a navigation tool is an impressive demonstration of a long-time dream of virtual reality innovators. However, it is the grammar that they have developed around this navigation tool that promises to be more consequential. Mirroring the grammar that has evolved in the context of clicking links (sessions, session duration, click throughs, bounce rate, etc.), Gaze Coin develops metrics appropriate to the gaze that promise more granular data about visual attention. Currently, web analytics firms can offer only the loosest of assurances that internet users are paying attention to advertisements. This is, in part, why advertising on websites and social networking platforms is so cheap—there's no guarantee that a user will actually look at a banner ad or engage with it in more than a cursory way. By contrast, Gaze Coin's efforts to track visual attention at a more granular level is ostensibly more assuring to advertisers. By tracking the gaze, Gaze Coin can credibly claim to capture pathways of visual attention more precisely, creating a heat map of what people looked at and for how long. "Fixation," the act of focusing on a discrete piece of what digital entrepreneurs call "content," becomes the unit of gaze measurement with a number of corollary metrics like duration, gaze path, and repetition, which is taken as a sign of comprehension. Indeed, the authors of the white paper suggest that they can assess even emotions like excitement by gauging pupil dilation, part of the larger goal of affective computing proponents to dynamically automate sentiment analysis so that (advertising) content can be adapted to suit or modulate the mood of the viewer.

What happens when a gaze is turned into a "unit of exchange"?[7] For the proprietors of Gaze Coin, "accurately calculated and accessible engagement-based transactional data, together with precise monetization calculations, is the VR/AR business model holy grail; an engine that funds the expansion of content and elevates the synergy between stakeholders."[8] The religious metaphor of the holy grail reflects the messianic impulses that often accompany new digital technologies. Indeed, Gaze Coin zealously aims for nothing less than the ultimate goal of converting the world toward a unified vision of the good life in virtual reality. For Gaze Coin dreamers, the "vision is to connect the real world and the immersive world as seamless environments where all interactions are measured and monetized through gaze."[9] The world projected in Gaze Coin's white paper is one in which a subject's looking is always tracked, producing a constant whirlwind of micropayments between businesses, advertisers, and users. Gaze Coin aims to actualize the logical endpoint of the attention economy, converting the selectivity of perception into never-ending revenue-generating opportunities. While tracking of gazes is now sporadic and clunky, Gaze Coin's hope to track all gazes at all times through a combination of AR/VR technology puts the "hyper-" (literally, over, above, beyond, with connotations of excessiveness) in hyperporization. This kind of hyperporization of the gaze is hinted at by a range of science fiction texts, perhaps most ambitiously in Stephen Spielberg's *Minority Report*. In one famous scene, John Anderton, played by Tom Cruise, walks through a mall corridor that personalizes advertisements to him based on a retinal scan. "John Anderton! You could use a Guinness right about now," shouts a Guinness ad as he walks by.[10] The novel and film *Ready Player One* similarly envisions a potential virtual world of hyperporization, with the conniving Innovative Online Industries seeking to take over ownership of the ad-free virtual reality platform OASIS in order to colonize the visual field with ads.[11] This is not just the stuff of science fiction. As platforms like Instagram evidence, the attention economy attempts to turn glances into gazes as a way of, in Diana Zulli's felicitous phrase, "capitalizing on the look."[12]

In universalizing the gaze as a preferred practice of looking, Gaze Coin partisans extend the hegemony of the gaze associated with painting, film, and television into a new medium. As Edward S. Casey writes, "indulging in these omnipresent media nonstop encourages a recourse to a mesmerized gaze as the main organ of an oculocentric culture. This is a gaze that is at once narcissistic (we see what we want to see) and stultifying (we see only what predominant channels of culture allow us to see)."[13] Casey's critique of the gaze and defense of the glance offers clues as to what is lost when the *aporia* of the glance is eclipsed by the hyperporization of looking. For Casey, gazing and glancing are "two ends of an entire axis that extends from steady, continuous looking to darting and discontinuous seeing."[14] The gaze, long-prized by philosophers and scientists, aims to stabilize that which is gazed at. Casey, drawing from Sartre's notion of *le regard*, argues that a studied gaze is an act of objectification: "My own outgoing consciousness is spontaneous and free from any such petrification, but when it gazes at another human being—who as-for-herself is just as free as I—it endows that other with a carapace of characteristics, a scletorized presence that is foreign to freedom."[15] Gazing can thus be a gateway to essentialism. If I've gazed at a person for a while, I may come to think I know something fundamental about them. Casey warns that this assumption is erroneous. First, any act of gazing is premised on selective perception (which implies, following Kenneth Burke, both reflection and deflection). Thus, gazing does not guarantee objective knowledge. Second, gazing is an act always already prejudiced by one's life history. What one is habituated to accept as credible evidence of an essence is steered by the largely unknowable weave of one's own past. Third, the gaze is always subjected to interpretation, often nonconsciously. To assume that one can seamlessly translate a gaze into objective knowledge assumes that affect, ideology, the un/nonconscious, and other intermediaries between perception and knowing do not intervene.[16] These inherent limitations of the gaze should give us pause when crediting this kind of looking with elevated epistemic powers. These limits to the gaze should also give pause to Gaze Coin–style business models: the relationship between gazing, attention, affect, cognition, and action are far more complicated than is convenient for digital entrepreneurs to admit.

"The sobriety of the gaze," in Casey's formulation, is premised on a depth hermeneutic: "It presumes that these same contents (things, ideas, and so on) have depths worth plumbing, holding that in these depths the truth of what is gazed-at resides."[17] Acts of sober gazing are characterized by a concern for "incorrigible evidence," a "passion for objectivity," and "consistency in procedure."[18] The glance is associated with revelry, play, and fancy, whereas the gaze is associated with seriousness, calculation, and the real. Gaze Coin's pursuit of reliable metrics reflects Casey's diagnosis of the sober gaze: they will be able to monetize AR/VR more consistently by objectively measuring eye tracking as evidence of attention. Of course, defenses of gazing as a mechanism to acquire more evidenced, objective, consistent knowledge are at least as old as Plato's Theory of the Forms, and the modern history of gazing is just as consequential. One of Michel Foucault's cardinal achievements was to decipher how the gaze worked as disciplinary power in nineteenth-century carceral, medical, and pedagogical contexts. The gaze "records and totalizes," ultimately aiming to identify and normalize particular ways of living.[19] Similarly, Laura Mulvey's study of the male gaze in twentieth-century film documents how the totalizing force of the gaze reproduces patriarchal social relations.[20]

The normativity of the gaze is underlined by the various social axes that are highlighted in concepts like the male gaze, the white gaze, the colonial gaze, and the various other oppositional gazes that emerge in response to dominant modes of looking.[21] Although Gaze Coin imagines itself to be an all-purpose AR/VR advertising intermediary, a specific VR project the coin supports suggests that virtual reality gazing is largely yoked to cishet, white, masculine fantasies of sexuality (pornography, of course, is often the avant-garde of digital technology). Gaze Coin powers a virtual world called FANTASY, set on Mars and modeled after Amsterdam's Red Light District. FANTASY has different districts with names like "Disciplinarian" for fetishes, a racialized "Booty Sector" for "hip hop and booty," and "Cherry Bomb," the gay district.[22] Gaze Coin hopes to sell virtual space—apartments, streets, billboards—to users who can then monetize the space through the gaze. "Land Sale Walkthrough," a promotional video intended to gin up support for selling real estate, called "Dreamspaces," showcases what this FANTASY world looks like.[23] The video, shot from a first-person perspective, whisks the viewer down an impressively rendered digital street. Powered by the gaze navigational interface, the viewer is led first into a DJ space, where a woman is dancing to the tunes being spun, before being transported to the heart of the red light district. There, women call out from behind red-light windows, prompting the viewer to ultimately focus on "Sinderella," who dances provocatively in black lingerie. The Fantasy Coin white paper explains that these Dreamspaces should be attractive to adult pornography actors: "The key USP [unique selling proposition] for adult stars is that VR content gives adult stars the ability to re-use a scene over and over while giving the appearance of being live 24/7. An adult star on average has to have sex 5 times to make the maximum amount of money from an [*sic*] porno movie—after which they can no longer make money from it. Using Fxxx [Fantasy Coin] they only have to have sex once, and scene [*sic*] can make money for them 1000 x over."[24] The pornographic gaze, a term emerging from Sut Jhally's study of music videos in the critically acclaimed documentary series *Dreamworlds*, now has new terrain to colonize in the Dreamspaces of virtual reality.[25]

Gaze Coin's model of eye tracking is both susceptible to and intensifies many critiques of the gaze by turning the gaze itself into an object to be gazed at. While gazing can have panoptic and normalizing effects outside of the orbit of digital technology, once enclosed by digital technology the very act of looking itself can be captured, quantified, measured, and compared to provide granular data that can then be used to nudge users in preferred ways.[26] Much like the modern gaze produced populations that could be worked on by the state, hyperporized gazing captured by virtual reality technology produces aggregate data about looking that can be exploited by corporate actors. Data about gaze patterns can be used to improve advertising strategies, reconfigure virtual architectures, and otherwise exploit visual attention in service of monetization. If the development of virtual reality follows the pathway of the world wide web and wearables, then a panoply of "attention merchants" will emerge as intermediaries trying to craft user attention patterns in ways that privilege profit-oriented motives.[27]

The hyperporization represented by Gaze Coin offers, by contrast, an appreciation of the *aporia* of the glance. The *aporia* of the glance indexes, first and foremost, the pathlessness of glancing. Glancing is so furtive an act that it resists stabilization. If a gaze fixes a pathway, a glance merely flirts with paths. Glances in non-AR/VR contexts are not tracked—at least not from the internal perspective of the viewer (a surveillance camera can catch a glance, but not with the level of granularity proposed by Gaze Coin.) "The radical democracy (if not the anarchy) of the glance," Casey explains, "is such that in a thrice it can look away—and thus abolish from view—what one is *supposed* to admire."[28] In contrast to the gaze, which is defined by duration, the glance is too fleeting to capture, measure, and study. Moreover, the glance, again following Casey, contains "a significant quotient of ambiguity, making it difficult to say *just what* a given glance signifies, whether by its intention or my interpretation."[29] This is what makes glancing subversive instead of sober—a glance doesn't last long enough to be studied, to be searched for meaning, to be probed for what it *really* implies. The historical indeterminacy of the glance makes it resistant to the analytics posited by Gaze Coin. This does not make glancing a lesser act. Indeed, glances map worlds by scanning the surfaces of things. In a glance, a body can sense a room: if it is hostile or hospitable, familiar or strange. In a glance, a body can acknowledge or dismiss others. "The direction of our glance," Michael Warner writes, "can constitute our social world."[30] If one's looking is tracked not just in virtual worlds but also through augmented reality lenses, then every world-making glance is potentially stabilized and monetized through digital capture. Hyperporization means every glance is made a gaze.

What distinctive powers of glancing are eroded with hyperporization? What is lost when the *aporia* of the glance is shrunk, when the pathlessness that characterizes much looking becomes captured, ordered, and systematized?

First, hyperporization weakens the power of the glance to democratically organize social worlds. As Casey explains, "A glance does not single out a designated item for *others*, that is, as having a definite meaning in the social domain. Instead, it tends to keep this domain open and flowing in such a way as to create a circuit of shared sense: I glance at you glancing at me while someone else is glancing at us both glancing at each other."[31] It is this loose network of glances that allows people to apprise situations quickly, to check things out and get one's bearings without the visual commitment implied by the gaze. At the bar after a day of conferencing, academics glance around to see who is there: old friends and colleagues, a panelist who gave a riveting talk earlier, the creepy dude or the bore bro who is best avoided. That context thrives on the glance, as people come and go, as moments of recognition light up faces or connect interlocutors for a moment—as a glance leads to an interruption leads to another glance leads to another conversation. Gaze Coin, or some other more advanced eye-tracking system, instrumentalizes these glances. In a virtual reality conference of the future, such glancing around at the digital bar might be accompanied by metadata about participants, histories of past interactions, advertisers suggesting their wares as a way into a conversation. The orienting propensities of the glance are attenuated when they are objectivated and made to serve the values of engagement or profit.

Second, hyperporization reduces the ability of the glance to usher us into surprising situations. For Casey, "The glance surprises us by its openness to surprise itself. Its very inconspicuousness gives it the advantage of the entering wedge, allowing it to be all the more effectively infiltrative of the most recalcitrant regions of the place-world."[32] No one thinks much of a glance, which gives it a certain kind of freedom in visually exploring the world in a way that produces serendipitous encounters and surprises. Chris Ingraham's account of glancing while on a road trip underlines the exploratory value of pathless glancing.[33] As he explains, a glance out the car window in the middle of the Navajo Nation yielded a glimpse of a large artwork of a Navajo person pasted onto the side of a trailer. A momentary glance led to intrigue, but the car kept moving. Attuned to the visual style of this work, Ingraham later stumbles upon another mural in Telluride done by the same artist, Chip Thomas, who signs his work "jetsonorama." Ingraham leaves the glance world to go into the gaze world, scrutinizing jetsonorama's art and profile. The glance thus wedges open space for the gaze, thus suggesting that gazing is not always bad. The deleterious consequences of gazing emerge when it is seen as the only or optimal way of looking. Ingraham's openness to serendipity, to surprise encounter, was only possible because he lives first and foremost in a world composed by glances. The serendipities of virtual worlds, which have been programmed from the ground up, are comparatively limited. Indeed, the virtual worlds that Gaze Coin supports, like FANTASY, still seem to reflect the basic limitations of early VR programming. Although one can imagine a more diverse and serendipitous virtual reality world emerging, it will likely do so in lockstep with the hyperporization of the gaze. Every visual interaction will be tracked, so a moment of serendipity—seeing virtual street art posted on a wall in FANTASY—will immediately be looped into the logic of the gaze, documented and archived for future commercial use.[34]

Third, hyperporization reads the epistemology of the gaze onto the practice of the glance. To relentlessly read greater meaning onto a glance is to assume that underneath the glance is some other, animating force that can be understood if mined thoroughly enough. But sometimes a glance is just a glance. As Sarah Jane Cervenak notes, "The visible and ostensibly public movements of the body aren't necessarily articulating a readable story."[35] While the power to gaze has always been articulated to social power, the glance is comparatively democratic, even as the power to glance is striated by social location. For Cervenak, freely moving one's body in space is a privilege of the privileged. Historically marginalized groups have largely had to wander not in the exterior promenades and town squares, but in their own minds. This kind of interior wandering "resists decryption" because "people move in ways that are invisible, along the grooves of their own mind, in the motion of a rambling tongue, outside the range of an administrative and purportedly enlightened gaze."[36] Cervenak's account is sympathetic to Casey's glance worlds—the glance is the way we wander, but our interiorities are not so transparent as to be deciphered or decrypted through an analysis of a look. Not even the administrative gaze of Gaze Coin proprietors can claim to definitively know the link between a glance and an affect or thought, despite their claims to. By turning a glance into a gaze that can be known, hyperporization may exacerbate the social inequities involved with gazing and glancing. Interiority is no longer a safe space for wandering by those made precarious or vulnerable, but a reserve that can—and must be—tapped by the forces of commercialism.

Rereading *aporia* through the frame of inversion, where the *a-* signals not a negation of but the absence of paths, orients us to a more expansive sense of how *aporia* might be conceptualized as rhetorical theory is revisioned for a rapidly changing digital media ecology. This reinterpretation offers two terms that may be of service as the virtual reality imaginary congeals: the *aporia* of the glance and the hyperporization of the gaze. The latter identifies the risks of a virtual reality that is founded on the bedrock of commercial eye tracking, while the former identifies the continuing value of untracked glancing. Leveraging both terms in the context of theorizing virtual and augmented reality might help produce immersive environments where interiority and dignity are more important than surveillance and profit.

NOTES

1. Jacques Derrida, *Aporias*, trans. Thomas Dutoit (Palo Alto: Stanford University Press, 1993): 20–1.

2. Brooke Rollins, "The Ethics of Epideictic Rhetoric: Addressing the Problem of Presence Through Derrida's Funeral Orations," *Rhetoric Society Quarterly* 35, no. 1 (2005): 5–23, at 21n6.

3. *Gaze Coin Whitepaper*, October 2017, https://media.gazecoin.io/whitepaper, 5 (and on file with the author).

4. Ibid.

5. Ibid., 6.

6. Kgrind Jonny, "Dream Channel POV," Vimeo, September 25, 2018, https://vimeo.com/291645610.

7. *Gaze Coin Whitepaper*, 7.

8. Ibid., 8.

9. Ibid., 32.

10. *Minority Report*, directed by Steven Spielberg (2002, Universal City, CA: DreamWorks).

11. Ernest Cline, *Ready Player One* (New York: Broadway Books, 2012) and *Ready Player One*, directed by Steven Spielberg (2018, Universal City, CA: DreamWorks).

12. Diana Zulli, "Capitalizing on the Look: Insights into the Glance, Attention Economy, and Instagram," *Critical Studies in Media Communication* 2, no. 35 (2018): 137–50.

13. Edward S. Casey, *The World at a Glance* (Bloomington: Indiana University Press, 2007), xiii.

14. Ibid., 132. Kevin DeLuca makes a similar distinction between the gaze and the glance, more keyed to the shifting media ecology; see "The Speed of Immanent Images: The Dangers of Reading Photographs," in *Visual Communication: Perception, Rhetoric, and Technology*, ed. Diane S. Hope (New York: Hampton, 2006), 76–90. For DeLuca, the gaze is associated with print literacy and the glance is associated with a world of speeding images. In my view, DeLuca overdetermines the form of mediation and underplays habits of engagement. The gaze/glance tension maps onto all media ecologies; after all, we often glance through a table of contents or index in a book, and gazing at a riveting video on the screen is not an alien proposition. Nonetheless, DeLuca's point about how scholars problematically adopt the framework of the gaze—studious contemplation of stable objects—when interpreting fleeting visual rhetorics is similar to Casey's point about how the gaze is often seen as the normatively preferred way of looking.

15. Casey, *World at a Glance*, 136.

16. Ibid., 137–8.

17. Ibid., 143.

18. Ibid.

19. Michel Foucault, *The Birth of the Clinic*, trans. A. Sheridan (New York: Random House, 1975), 121; Casey, *World at a Glance*, 205.

20. Laura Mulvey, "Visual Pleasure and Narrative Cinema," *Screen* 16, no. 3 (1975): 6–18.

21. Homi K. Bhabha, *The Location of Culture* (New York: Routledge, 1994); bell hooks, *Black Looks: Race and Representation* (Cambridge: South End Press, 1992).

22. *Fantasy Coin Whitepaper*, October 2018, https://www.fxxx.io/staticv/FXXX_White_Paper_300919B.pdf, 6 (and on file with the author).

23. Kgrind Jonny, "Land Sale Walkthrough," Vimeo, September 27, 2018, https://vimeo.com/292059222. A more built-out virtual city is viewable in a trailer made a year later, which showcases a number of women calling out sexually salacious invitations from behind red light district–style windows; see Dream Channel VR, "Dream Channel Trailer," YouTube,

December 9, 2019, https://www.youtube.com/watch?v=OKtcyjk2sZA&feature=youtu.be.

24. *Fantasy Coin Whitepaper*, 11.

25. *Dreamworlds 3—Desire, Sex, and Power in Music Videos*, directed by Sut Jhally (2007, Northampton, MA: Media Education Foundation).

26. Shoshana Zuboff, *The Age of Surveillance Capitalism: The Fight for a Human Future at the New Frontier of Power* (New York: PublicAffairs, 2018); Mark Andrejevic, "Surveillance in the Digital Enclosure," *Communication Review* 10, no. 4 (2007): 295–317.

27. Tim Wu, *The Attention Merchants: The Epic Scramble to Get Inside Our Heads* (New York: Random House, 2016).

28. Casey, *World at a Glance*, 145.

29. Ibid., 34.

30. Michael Warner, *Publics and Counterpublics* (New York: Zone, 2002), 62.

31. Casey, *World at a Glance*, 36.

32. Ibid., 168.

33. Chris Ingraham, "Serendipity as a Cultural Technique," *Culture, Theory, and Critique* 60, no. 2 (2018): 107–22.

34. J. Macgregor Wise describes this phenomenon as the "Clickable World," in which the world is perceived as a storehouse of information that can be made available through digital technology; see "Towards a Minor Assemblage: An Introduction to the Clickable World," in *Theorizing Digital Rhetoric*, ed. Aaron Hess and Amber Davisson (New York: Routledge, 2017), 68–82.

35. Sarah Jane Cervenak, *Wandering: Philosophical Performances of Racial and Sexual Freedom* (Durham: Duke University Press, 2014), 4.

36. Ibid., 4, 6.

Agnostic

CORY GERATHS

To his death, Socrates obeyed the oracular injunction to "know yourself [*gnōthi seauton*]."[1] The first word of this instruction is a form of the verb *ginōskō* (come to know, perceive). Several ancient Greek words are related to this verb, including the noun *gnōsis* (knowing, knowledge) and its adjectival form, *gnōstos* (known, knowable). Centuries after Socrates, *gnōsis* oriented the ideas, practices, and experiences of coming to know and understand God among early Christian communities throughout the Mediterranean and North Africa.[2] Though studied far less in Rhetorical Studies than *epistēmē* (secure, scientific-type knowledge), cognates of the Greek root *gnō-* have been used from antiquity to today to describe a mode of knowing oneself, others, and the surrounding world.

Likely more familiar than *gnostic* is its alpha privative form: *agnostic*. In the United States, the concept is usually understood to refer to being without knowledge that God exists and thus merits one's faith and works. According to a 2014 Pew Research Center survey of over thirty-five thousand people living in the United States, 4.0 percent of respondents claimed to be "agnostic," which is listed alongside "atheist" (3.1%) and "nothing in particular" (15.8%) under the broader heading of "Unaffiliated (religious "nones")."[3] Whereas an atheist, also an alpha-privative word, is literally "without God," an agnostic is "without knowledge" about God.[4]

Within ancient texts, bards, rhetoricians, historians, and missionaries pointed to that which was "unknown" or "unknowable," showing the word to have an application to general situations of knowledge-lack. For example, Homer uses *agnōston* to describe Odysseus when he arrives home in Ithaca after twenty years of warring and wandering.[5] Aristotle refers to syllogisms with unknown premises.[6] Thucydides classifies a language that is utterly unknown to Greek people as "exceedingly difficult to understand" (*agnōstotatoi*).[7] Notable is the use of the term by the apostle Paul in his first-century CE speech to the Athenians recorded in *Acts of the Apostles*. Speaking atop the Areopagus, Paul begins his address by praising the Athenian steadfastness in worshipping their pantheon of gods and, as he does, he also acknowledges that they praise an "unknown god" (*agnōstō theō*).[8] Paul metamorphizes this unknown god into his known God—the inverted *agnōstos* reverts back to *gnōstos*. The Athenians have indirectly been praying to Paul's God all along (or so he argued).

Agnostic continues to make meaning today in contexts other than the religious. In medicine, for instance, *visual agnosia* refers to the inability of the brain to correctly perceive objects and to readily identify or recreate them through handwriting or drawing.[9] Further, within the nomenclature of digital technologies, *platform agnostic* refers to a piece of software (e.g., Linux) that can be run across platforms and hardware.[10] And marketing and communications firms invoke phrases such as *media agnostic* and *channel agnostic* when describing advertising and other content that is deployed across a range of media, with no one medium favored.[11] With these latter few examples, we see *agnostic* meaning something like "noncommittal or nonpreferential," which loosens the relationship to knowledge that *agnostic* enjoys historically.

This chapter reactivates the potential of *agnostic* to mark an attitude toward aspects of life that resist attempts at knowing. Though, as I showed, *agnostic* has been applied to digital software and user experience, amplifying its connection to being without knowledge equips the concept for interpretive work with other features of digitality, such as the corporeal and relational complexities of virtual reality (VR). This chapter employs an agnostic orientation to follow the unknowable nature of hypermediated *erōs* (sexual desire, love) in a 2019 episode of the Netflix series *Black Mirror* titled "Striking Vipers." The episode's depiction of VR invites both its characters and audience to consider the sorts of unknowing wrought by coded *erōs*, simulated touch, and the difficulty of fully understanding these mediated sensations once the game (or episode) is turned off and "real life" returns.[12] Given that another definition of *ginōskō* is "to know carnally," *agnōstos erōs* (unknowable love) becomes part of a vocabulary for talking about the relationships among embodiment, sex, sexuality, knowing oneself, and knowing others when the bodies in question are VR avatars.[13]

"FUCKING TRANSCENDENT. YOU KNOW IT WAS": VIRTUAL REALITY AND *AGNŌSTOS ERŌS* IN *BLACK MIRROR*

Black Mirror has been widely studied by screen scholars, its very title prompting reflection.[14] David Kyle Johnson, Leander P. Marquez, and Sergio Urueña highlight its provocative nature: "Every time you touch the screen of your phone to make Netflix play an episode of *Black Mirror*, you see a reflection of yourself looking back. The title sequence . . . turns the screen into a mirror. . . . When you watch *Black Mirror*, you're watching a dark reflection of society—one that is just slightly cracked—that depicts our flaws, our fears, and our possible future."[15] Building from this attention to the reflective power of both the series's titular wordplay and its depictions of technology, I explore the gendered, sexual, and interpersonal complexities of *agnōstos erōs* (unknowable love) in "Striking Vipers."

"Striking Vipers" invites audiences into a not-too-distant future. The key difference is the widespread availability of fully immersive VR technologies for playing video games, such as *Striking Vipers X*, a fighting game in the vein of *Mortal Kombat* or *Street Fighter*. This VR technology enables the two main characters, longtime friends Danny and Karl, not only to fight each other through the bodies of their chosen avatars, Lance and Roxette, but to fuck each other, too.[16] Through this VR-enabled sex, Danny, Karl, and viewers at home are made to reckon with the *agnōstos erōs* sparked by coded pleasure.[17] This technology is, as explained by Karl/Roxette, completely immersive: "The game emulates all physical sensations."[18] Accordingly, the game enables users to not just embody an avatar of their choice but, in so doing, to feel everything that comes with this virtual body.[19] The episode revolves around both the real and in-game experiences of Danny and Karl, two seemingly heterosexual and middle-to-upper-class Black men. Both are cast in relationships with women from the outset of the episode: Danny with his girlfriend and later wife, Theo, and Karl with multiple women partners as the story progresses. Danny, in particular, does not seem fully content with the mundanity of his late thirty-something life. His disinterest is especially palpable in the episode's opening scenes, set at a barbeque for his thirty-eighth birthday. It is here that Karl arrives (they have grown distant over recent years) with a gift: the VR-enabled edition of their longtime favorite series, *Striking Vipers X*.

Later that night Danny is shown playing a solitary game of something like *Tetris*. A notification appears alerting him that Karl is online and has invited him to play *Striking Vipers X*. Karl briefly explains to the unfamiliar Danny how to use the VR technology. Here, through Karl's explanation of the "craziness" of the emulated experience to come, the audience encounters the first substantial agnostic attitude in the episode. After mocking Danny for presumably playing "something goddamn boring" (like *Tetris*), Karl informs him that the VR version of *Striking Vipers* is comparably "insane"; "you're gonna freak . . . [and] shit your pelvis through your asshole."[20] Karl's invocation of the adjective "insane" alongside the medically impossible (and hyperbolically vulgar) description that follows illustrates his difficulty in adequately explaining the experience of being fully embodied in one of the game's avatars.

After connecting the VR disc to his temple, Danny enters the game as Lance and appears alongside Karl/Roxette. As he gazes upon the game's "level" come to life, Danny/Lance marvels, "This is crazy. What the fuck?"[21] Looking down at his muscular pecs, Danny/Lance comes to a conclusion about his new body: "I feel solid."[22] His description is telling for both its reference to the physicality of Lance's body and the strange realness of the VR emulation itself. Both his chest and coded body feel, however improbably, solid. Karl/Roxette shares in this moment of self-discovery while feeling her breasts: "You think your chest is impressive? Check this shit out."[23] Immediately upon entering the game, "Striking Vipers" thus emphasizes the knowledge-bending nature of the game's VR technology. While far from the first piece of popular culture to depict counterfactuals concerning gendered, sexual, and raced bodies, "Striking Vipers" adds to this lineage by offering an alluring and affecting exploration of the sorts of unknowing wrought by VR-emulated *erōs*.[24]

Danny/Lance and Karl/Roxette spend far more time desiring each other and having sex than they do fighting. "Striking Vipers" depicts several of their sexual interactions, with many others implied, over what becomes a lengthy affair. The first of these occurs after Danny and Karl's initial entrance into the game. The two friends, embodied as Lance and Roxette, begin to fight using the game's heavily augmented mechanics, feeling everything as they do. After two introductory rounds of fighting, Danny/Lance and Karl/Roxette end up in an embrace as they wrestle, one that quickly takes on an unexpectedly erotic tenor. As Karl/Roxette lays on top of Danny/Lance, the two friends kiss. After several seconds Danny/Lance appears distraught and, recoiling from Karl/Roxette, exits the game.

In the following scenes, both Danny and Karl appear overwhelmed by what seems to be more than just confusion. Both appear unable to fully process, understand, and ultimately *know* what occurred. Complicating matters is a strange and unfamiliar link between the two bodies of each character—real and avatar. This is evident when Theo, reaching over to embrace Danny in bed later that night, is surprised by his erection; "Where did he come from?" she questions with a flourish of excitement after Danny's recent disinterest.[25] And, while the two do have sex, we are left to wonder who Danny was thinking about. Danny's implied sexual response to the memories of his time as Lance and with Karl/Roxette highlights the aftermath of their encounter. A kiss, made possible by the code of a game and the futuristic technology of a VR-disc, has left unfamiliar mental, physiological, and emotional impacts. *Agnōstos* is an apt description for coded kiss and confusing erection alike.

Danny and Karl try to make sense of what happened when they next speak. This conversation is punctuated by Danny's attempt to excuse their actions as Lance and Roxette: "Look, last time we played, I was drunk, man, from the party."[26] Karl agrees and the two decide to play "a serious game" of *Striking Vipers X*.[27] Their rhetorical turn to the effects of narcotics is familiar as a *topos* frequently invoked by straight men for excusing romantic and sexual encounters that veer into the unfamiliar realm of the queer.[28] And, as the two friends enter the game once more as Lance and Roxette, their mutual attempt at reckoning with the unfamiliarity of their earlier encounter proves ineffective as they immediately come together to kiss and, this time, have sex. In the afterglow Karl/Roxette jokes, "So, guess [that makes] us gay now" to which Danny/Lance responds without complete conviction, "It don't feel like a gay thing."[29] This attempt at reidentifying their sexualities and categorizing their affair according to their known, yet limited, scripts of sexual identity is likewise unsatisfactory for explaining the increasingly potent *agnōstos* of their *erōs* in *Striking Vipers X*.

This potency is further illustrated when post-sex conversation turns, in a later encounter, to Karl's experience of orgasm in his avatar, Roxette. In an attempt to better understand the complex sensations within their avatars, Danny/Lance asks, "How does it feel? I mean, like for you, being in a woman's body?"[30] Karl/Roxette responds: "Crazy. It's *crazy*. I mean, it's different. Like . . . the physical feeling of it is more sort of . . . satisfying. *I can't really explain it.* Like, one's a guitar solo, the other's a whole fucking orchestra. But, the tune is basically the same. Different tempos though."[31] Here, it is not rhetorics of narcotics or identification that are invoked to try to explain the *agnōstos* of the friends' *erōs* but, rather, one of comparison. And, while the invocation of an acoustic figure of speech is helpful as an explanation, it falls short. Indeed, Danny/Lance's retort that Karl/Roxette "ran that analogy into the ground" reminds the audience that even a maximally stretched metaphor is still insufficient for fully reckoning with the sensations of their VR-emulated sex.[32]

Following a confrontation with his wife, Danny proceeds to cut off the relationship with Karl. Roughly a year later, however, the two friends meet face-to-face after Theo—who is still unaware of the details of her husband's VR affair—invites Karl to dinner. Karl lambasts his friend's chilly demeanor: "What am I? Your ex-wife or something?"[33] Danny's reply, "Look, it's too strange . . . it's just too fucking strange," is laced with *agnōstos*.[34] As is Karl's weighty response: "I'll tell you what's strange. Nothing matches it. . . . I tried replacing it, man. I tried. I tried fucking the computer-controlled characters. . . . I tried it with real players. . . . I tried everything. I've gone in there as guy players, girl players, multi-player gang bangs . . . and I still couldn't get you out of my mind. . . . The best sex of my life. Best of yours too. *Fucking transcendent. You know it was.*"[35] Karl tries recreating his experience through a diverse, and, at times, troublingly phrased (e.g., "multi-player gang bangs"), series of sexual encounters and, through his failure to do so, invokes the sublime nature of his affair with Danny/Lance. His *agnōstos erōs* with Danny/Lance is, we discover, more than just code. Karl pleadingly draws upon both the embodied nature of their sex and the need for both of them to continue their mental and emotional work to better understand the seemingly unknowable, yet nevertheless transcendent, passion they have found. And, perhaps most revealingly, Karl invokes the commonplace English phrase, "you know." Karl believes that Danny knows, in a still unknown place inside himself, that he feels the same.

Karl concludes his plea to Danny with an invitation for the two to meet inside *Striking Vipers X* at midnight. They do and, after they again have sex, Karl/Roxette admits that s/he loves Danny/Lance and what they have within the game. This proves too much of an admission for Danny/Lance. He directs Karl to meet him outside of the game. They kiss in an attempt to see if "there are fireworks"—that is, *erōs*—in the real world; both men, according to Danny, "gotta know" what is real and what is not.[36] Their kiss pales in comparison to those enjoyed within *Striking Vipers X*. Karl's response, "*You know* it's different in the game, man," falls flat, and the two end up in a fistfight and then jail.[37] A rhetoric of knowing is once again invoked by both characters in their final attempt to come to terms with what has, throughout the episode, proved unknowable.

The episode concludes by revealing that Danny and Karl continue to meet in *Striking Vipers X* once a year as part of an agreement with Theo who, after learning of the affair, has agreed to sparingly open their relationship (she, too, is permitted to annually venture beyond her marriage). Thus, the ineffable nature of Danny and Karl's erotic connection, coded as it is with unfamiliar technology and the strange sexual sensations it makes possible, continues to elude complete explanation. Despite diverse rhetorical attempts (narcotics, identity, metaphor, knowing, fighting) to explain the *erōs* at the center of this episode, everyone remains in a state of unknowing about it when the episode ends and the screen fades to a reflective, mirrored black.

UNKNOWING IN OLD EROS AND NEW MEDIA

Together, through *Striking Vipers X*, Danny and Karl experience an *erōs* whose intensity exceeds that which they get from relationships with others in the game—and out of it, too. In their failure to account for their mutual pleasure when they have sex in the game as well as the longing they suffer when they cannot join together in the game, even though they are not sexually attracted to each other outside of the game, we have examples of how we are still developing language for sensations and experiences new media make possible. But here we should be careful about what is new and what is not. Notoriously, *erōs* operates outside of categorizing logics, especially ones that grant centrality to certain knowledge. In his entry on "The Unknowable" in his book *A Lover's Discourse*, Roland Barthes writes, "It is not true that the more you love, the better you understand; all that the action of love obtains from me is merely this wisdom: that the other is not to be known; his opacity is not the screen around a secret, but, instead, a kind of evidence in which the game of reality and appearance is done away with. I am then seized with that exhilaration of loving *someone unknown*, someone who will remain so forever: a mythic impulse: I know what I do not know."[38] And so we return again to Socrates's unceasing, never-satisfied, self-searching impulse, only this time turned toward the person one loves. Love never grants us knowledge of the loved one: love and knowledge repel one another. What Danny and Karl work through over the course of the episode is an old erotic challenge. It is a new technology, however, that pitches them into the place where "the game of reality and appearance is done away with," as Barthes puts it.[39] By the end of the episode, they no longer panic, stress, or even wonder about whether what they have in the game is real. It simply is.

While the fully immersive sex of *Striking Vipers X* does not exist in 2020, there are ongoing conversations about the changes that have already and might yet be initiated by VR and haptic technologies.[40] After all, currently available VR devices such as the Oculus Rift and Quest, the PlayStation VR, and the HTC Vive allow users to virtually interact with video games and other players within these virtual worlds. An orientation toward unknowing, this chapter suggests, can be fruitful for theorizing the corporeal and relational impacts of technologies that push us toward old and new forms of the agnostic.

NOTES

1. For more on Socrates and self-knowledge, see Christopher Moore, *Socrates and Self-Knowledge* (Cambridge: Cambridge University Press, 2015). All Greek translations come from the Perseus online edition of Liddell, Scott, and Jones's *A Greek-English Lexicon*, 9th ed. (Oxford: Clarendon Press, 1996).

2. Primary among such professors of *gnōsis* are the Gnostics (a disparate group of faith communities that professed "secret wisdom" from the divine). For one of the first full-length studies of Gnosticism in English, see Elaine Pagels, *The Gnostic Gospels* (New York: Vintage, 1979).

3. Pew Research Center, "Religious Landscape Study," https://www.pewforum.org/religious-landscape-study.

4. Notably, the Christian theology of "via negativa" (the way of the negative) uses alpha privatives to show respect for the limits of human knowledge where the divine is concerned. For the basics, see Raoul Mortley, "The Fundamentals of the Via Negativa," *American Journal of Philology* 103, no. 4 (Winter 1982): 429–39. Credit for coining "agnostic/ism" tends to go to Thomas H. Huxley, in 1869; see Bernard Lightman, *The Origins of Agnosticism: Victorian Unbelief and the Limits Knowledge* (Baltimore: Johns Hopkins University Press, 1987), especially chapter 1.

5. See Homer, *Odyssey*, vol. 1, trans. A. T. Murray (Cambridge: Harvard University Press, 1984), 2.175, on Odysseus's unfamiliarity (*agnōston*) upon returning to Ithaca after twenty years away.

6. See Aristotle, *Rhetoric* 2.24.10 on unknown (*agnōston*) premises in syllogisms (in Aristotelis, *Ars rhetorica*, ed. W. D. Ross [Oxford: Oxford University Press, 1959]).

7. Thucydides, *The Peloponnesian War* 3.94.5, trans. E. P. Dutton (London: J. M. Dent, 1910).

8. *Acts of the Apostles* 17:23.

9. See Martha J. Farah, *Visual Agnosia* (Cambridge: MIT Press, 2004).

10. See Tom McGeveran, "The New Media Religion: 'Platform Agnostic,'" *Observer*, August 4, 2008.

11. E.g., Louise Story, "A Media-Agnostic, Judging Campaigns of Others," *New York Times*, April 10, 2008; Katie Deighton, "Hims Is Bolstering Its Internal Marketing Team as Media Plan of 'Experimentation' Pays Off," *Drum*, June 11, 2019.

12. Fictional depictions of the future, while often hyperbolic and wondrous, nevertheless reflect for audiences the possibilities and dangers of not-yet-known technologies. For more, see Darren M. Slade, "*Striking Vipers* and Closed Doors: How Meaningful Are Sexual Fantasies?," in *Black Mirror and Philosophy: Dark Reflections*, ed. David Kyle Johnson (Boston: Wiley Blackwell, 2019), 241–50.

13. For more on this kind of knowledge, see Margaret R. Miles, *Carnal Knowing: Female Nakedness and Religious Meaning in the Christian West* (Boston: Beacon Press, 1989). For more on *erōs*, see Anne Carson, *Eros the Bittersweet: An Essay* (Washington, DC: Center for Hellenic Studies, 1986).

14. See, among other texts, Angela Cirucci and Barry Vacker, *Black Mirror and Critical Media Theory* (Lanham: Lexington, 2018); David Kyle Johnson, *Black Mirror and Philosophy*.

15. David Kyle Johnson, Leander P. Marquez, and Sergio Urueña, "*Black Mirror*: What Science Fiction Does Best," in *Black Mirror and Philosophy*, 3.

16. Rhetoric and media scholars have studied depictions of virtually mediated sex; see, for example, Robert Alan Brookey and Kristopher L. Cannon, "Sex Lives in Second Life," *Critical Studies in Media Communication* 26, no. 2 (2009): 145–64. See, also, work on virtual reality and posthumanism, including David J. Gunkel, *Hacking Cyberspace* (New York: Westview Press, 2001), 97–118 on VR; N. Katherine Hayles, *How We Became Posthuman: Virtual Bodies in Cybernetics, Literature, and Informatics* (Chicago: University of Chicago Press, 1999), 1–49, on the posthuman body, and 247–92 on its representations in literature. For a study of what they call "sexual rhetorics," see Jonathan Alexander and Jacqueline Rhodes, *Sexual Rhetorics: Methods, Identities, Publics* (New York: Routledge, 2015).

17. The question of the characters' "love" in the game is similarly raised by Slade, though without an attention to the ancient Greek ("*Striking Vipers* and Closed Doors," 246). See also Robert Grant Price, "Love in *Black Mirror*: Who Do We Really Love?," in *Black Mirror and Philosophy*, 301–10, particularly the section, "Knowing What Love Is," 308–9.

18. "Striking Vipers," *Black Mirror*, directed by Owen Harris, season 5, episode 1, June 5, 2019.

19. Danny's avatar, Lance, is a trim, muscular Asian man, and Karl's avatar, Roxette, is a toned, bleached-blonde, Asian woman. See Slade, "*Striking Vipers* and Closed Doors," 242.

20. "Striking Vipers."

21. Ibid.

22. Ibid.

23. Ibid.

24. See films such as James Cameron, dir. *Avatar* (Los Angeles: 20th Century Fox, 2009); Alexandra-Therese Keining, dir. *Girls Lost* (originally released in Sweden as *Pojkarna* [The Boys] (n.p.: Saffron Hill, 2015), and Martin Curland, dir. *Zerophilia* (n.p.: TLA Releasing, 2006); as well as novels like A. Igoni Barrett's *Black Ass: A Novel* (Minneapolis: Graywolf Press, 2015) and Andrea Lawlor's *Paul Takes the Form of a Mortal Girl* (New York: Vintage, 2019).

25. "Striking Vipers."

26. Ibid.

27. Ibid.

28. See Slade, "*Striking Vipers*," 242; also C. Riley Snorton, *Nobody Is Supposed to Know: Black Sexuality on the Down Low* (Minneapolis: University of Minnesota Press, 2014). My classification of Danny and Karl's encounter as "queer" is somewhat complicated by their male- and female-gendered avatars, Lance and Roxette. Nevertheless, there is a definite thread of transgression undergirding their encounter. Sexuality, in both *Striking Vipers X* and the real world, is fluid and can inspire moments of unexpected and queer unknowing.

29. "Striking Vipers."

30. Ibid.

31. Ibid., emphasis added.
32. Ibid.
33. Ibid.
34. Ibid.
35. Ibid., emphasis added.
36. Ibid.
37. Ibid., emphasis added.
38. Roland Barthes, *A Lover's Discourse: Fragments*, trans. Richard Howard (New York: Hill and Wang, 2010 [1977]), 135.
39. Ibid.
40. See Peter Rubin, *Future Presence: How Virtual Reality Is Changing Human Connection, Intimacy, and the Limits of Ordinary Life* (New York: Harper Collins, 2018); on VR's mediation of friendship (149–64); touch and tactility (165–94); and pornography (195–220).

(Not) Seeing
It That Way

Apathy

NATHANIEL A. RIVERS

> What the hell kind of deal is it here anyway?
> How much does it cost and how long can you stay?
> Should we dance? should we sing? should we curse? should we pray?
> Do I have to hang on every single word that you say?
> Every hour, every minute, every second of the day
> Hey, hey, hey, hey, hey, hey, hey.
>
> —THE MOUNTAIN GOATS,
> "ONE WINTER AT POINT ALPHA PRIVATIVE"

> Apathy takes work to produce.
>
> —NINA ELIASOPH, *Avoiding Politics*

A PATHETIC PROBLEM

In a tiny, locked room underground, a gun is leveled at a man's head. Two men, just minutes before, had been discussing bodhisattva (a merciful being in Buddhism) and sinsemilla (a particularly potent variety of cannabis). Now, the junior officer insists:

"Sir, we are at launch. Turn your key!"

"I'm sorry. I'm so sorry."

"Turn your key, sir!"

The Air Force captain does not turn his key. The nuclear missiles under his command do not launch. Not that they were ever going to. The launch was a test run—a war game—designed to ascertain the commitment of all flight officers to their mission. The captain was not alone: nearly one fourth of all officers involved in the test refused to turn their key. Their refusal is a problem for those military personnel and government officials tasked with maintaining readiness for thermonuclear war with the former Soviet Union. It's a problem of *pathos*, of (shared) feeling within the United States' defense forces. Whatever happens, the stakes themselves must be maintained.

The key-turning operation, which opens the 1983 film *WarGames*, is a pathetic situation contingent upon a human hand and heart working in sympathy with others.[1] Commitment must in some way be ensured. The possibility of refusing to turn the key must be controlled for. These opening scenes set up a strange pathetic problem: a certain pathos must be secured in the face of *a*pathetic humans who could refuse it. Those *without this* particular feeling, and not some generalized pathos, but a particular pathetic formation within and holding together a particular rhetorical dynamic.

"In a nuclear war we can't afford to have our missiles lying dormant in those silos because those men refuse to turn the keys!"[2]

At first blush, apathy (from ἀπάθεια) appears antithetical to rhetorical action. Persuasion moves people; the apathetic are immobile. Apathy seemingly marks a lack of energy, engagement, and a shared sense of exigence. In public discourse, apathy is styled in a more reactionary way. Apathy is trouble and troubling, either spoiling democracy's full potential or actively undermining its very possibility; so-called "voter apathy" may be the most well-known form of apathy these days. Daniel Gross, attending to the unique, alpha-privative qualities of apathy, writes, "Apathy is . . . the inverse of enthusiasm, when one's social value is systematically underestimated, with equally devastating consequences for the smooth operation of civil society."[3] Gross traces the conceptual relations of apathy, such as "acedia, melancholy, indifference, boredom, ennui, and 'spleen.'"[4] This litany should spell trouble for rhetoric.

To be without feeling is to be outside a rhetorical situation composed, we suppose, by a common feeling that something is going on to which we must respond. "Pick a side!" the sympathetic demand. "How much longer do we have to be here?" the apathetic respond. Rhetoric has fiercely debated what makes a rhetorical situation. Apathy has us ask, "How can we get out of one?" The pathetic rhetor wants, needs really, to be within a rhetorical situation defined by a meaningful exigence; the apathetic rhetor just wants to get without. Like pathos, apathy is always in relation to something. The Air Force captain, it is important to note, apologizes. This apology signals a felt failure: his inability to commit to the urgency and purpose of the situation he finds himself in. It is perhaps strange to describe the Air Force captain as apathetic, but apathy is a unique relationship to caring that allows one to dwell, forcefully, in the context of arrestive antagonisms.

In this chapter, I recast apathy as a rhetorical capacity—a disposition—to disengage from the often-arresting confines of an exigence terminally shaped by shared feeling. I take "disposition" from the work of Keller Easterling: "Disposition remains as a potential or tendency until activated, but it is present even in the absence of an event."[5] Disposition here resonates with the alpha-privative quality of apathy. Apathy is a pathetic tendency, present even while absent. Apathy isn't simply a negation of pathos, but an often-necessary redirection of pathos that unbinds rhetorical situations. Pathos is not the only way to feel and so not the only motivating force. Furthermore, apathy isn't a measure of pathos: apathy isn't simply *less* pathos. There's nothing contradictory about a state of fervent apathy, for instance. "For in the *a* that signifies a marked nonpresence of emotion," Gross intones, "we intuitively read not an arithmetic zero point but rather a node of special density in a dynamic social field, where the very possibility of emotion is at issue."[6] Apathy remains folded into *pathos*.

I stage this treatment of apathy through a reading of *WarGames*. In brief, *WarGames*, with its video-game-playing, slacker protagonists, offers up apathy as a legitimate political affect. Sympathy, being within feeling, locks the combatants (the United States and the USSR respectively) into an exigence leading them to annihilation. The disaffected teenager, without the feeling of annihilating fervor, interrupts the exigence of this doomed game. In the face of global thermonuclear war, "a strange game," these apathetic rhetors conclude, "The only winning move is not to play." They don't not care, but their caring moves against the feeling-within that powers an exigence that is the end of the world.

THE PROBLEM OF APATHY

One of the chief problems of apathy is ascertaining its location. If one wants to root it out, one has to know from where it comes. Is apathy a feature of (apathetic) individuals or is apathy a (reasonable) response to certain (disenfranchising) conditions? We can here turn to Nina Eliasoph's book-length study of how Americans produce apathy in everyday life. "Common sense and much social research direct our attention to two common ways of understanding apathy and engagement: one focuses on structural power, the other on beliefs. Examinations of structural forces typically focus on the seemingly 'outer,' seemingly impersonal, objective, and automatic systems of money and power. Examinations of beliefs focus on the seemingly 'inner' seemingly personal, subjective, and active realm of feelings, meanings, and experience."[7] To describe someone as apathetic is typically, then, to either judge them as an individual or to comment upon the scene in which they find themselves. However, to reduce apathy to individuals is to leave unaddressed the when and where of their being without feeling. To trace apathy to external conditions is to strip individuals of agency or political purpose. "Cynicism, distrust of politics, even apathy," Susan Wells argues, "are neither moral failings nor signs of a romantic (or postmodern) political innocence."[8] Eliasoph herself continues, "Neither the 'inner' nor the 'outer' approach pays enough attention to the 'in-between.'"[9] This more relational approach to apathy pays dividends in its capacity to mark not the singular source of apathy but to trace its contingent emergence.

Once apathy is handled as neither an individual motive nor a force exerted from the outside, apathy resounds as its own kind of political relationship. Jenny Rice, writing that "emotions are all relational," argues, "Apathy or withdrawal is not an empty cipher. Feeling a relation is the very beginning of public orientation. To connect publicness with a feeling about one's relation to crisis leaves open the possibility that feeling nothing is how one kind of public subject comes into being. Feeling subjects always already are public subjects."[10] The specificity of the phrase "I don't feel it" provides a telling example of this. It marks the particularity of apathy. We would be wrong to hear apathy as "I don't feel." The alpha privative, as this collection's introduction makes plain, is a particular sort of negation. Apathy isn't *not feeling* but a not feeling *toward a* feeling. The speaker of the phrase marks that they are feeling but feeling unlike the de facto *pathos* of the moment. There's then a relational quality: feeling always in relation to something. Rice is interested in how feeling shapes publics and so how even feeling bored and disengaged is still a public feeling—the apathetic are still, by definition, public subjects. Not feeling as one should in relation to something is apathy, which emerges as a relation between particularly disposed individuals and specific situations. Apathy isn't active everywhere and all the time. It emerges kairotically.

Treating apathy as a contingent, political relation opens up a space in which we can ask what it might do rhetorically rather than what it might prevent. Gross asks, "Under what historical conditions . . . can we consider apathy a productive force in shaping public life."[11] Apathy, a potentially powerful rhetorical force, has been circumscribed by the thesaurus. My wager is that apathy is a particularly affective, political relation with the potential to hack and reconfigure well-worn affective dynamics to still other possibilities: other ways (out or through).[12] Reengaging apathy's alpha-privative roots makes more tangible the rhetorical work it does and can perhaps accomplish. Keep the sympathetic close; keep the apathetic closer. For any given rhetorical event, there must be people who won't participate. An outside that's still inside. But a capacity for apathy is relational. The apathetic aren't always the same. Apathy moves around, inhabiting and (de)motivating bodies in motion. Apathy is in-between.

DISPOSITIONAL APATHY

Apathy is a disposition within rhetoric. Treating apathy as such opens it up to a more productive reading in the way that Gross outlines. I am here drawing from Easterling's work on disposition alongside what she calls "medium design." She describes a disposition as the "unfolding relationship between potentials."[13] Medium design as an attunement to tendencies—which are not unlike dispositions—is the work of "adjust[ing] stories and organizational potentials."[14] Activating dispositions, for Easterling, becomes another way of enacting change—not by directly engaging but by subtly shifting attachments. Easterling is thus drawn to disposition and medium design because of the rhetorical work they can do. They are different than something like dissent, which "adopting a binary, exists in a world of enemies and innocents. Since the world's big bullies and bulletproof forms of power thrive on this oscillation between loop and binary, it is as if there is nothing to counter them—only more ways of fighting and being right and providing the rancor that nourishes their violence."[15] Apathy is thus not dissent, as we sometimes imagine it. Apathy nudges rather than negates. Easterling asks, "How do you drop through a trapdoor and engage the flip side of these logics?"[16]

Easterling introduces medium design in our particular political moment of seemingly intractable antagonisms wherein the only viable option seems to be doubling down: to assert rightness and correctness in ways that only fuel the dynamic, which is itself the trouble. This is decidedly not Easterling trying to carve out a middle path between supposedly "extreme" viewpoints: there's nothing centrist about her position. Her position is that the world is in trouble—beset by financial, humanitarian, and environmental crises—and that nothing seems to be working. "So, armed only with rationality or a desire to win the argument, it is nearly impossible to derail or interrupt this seduction or oppression."[17] Easterling seeks a way through these binaries, not via dissent but via manipulations of the political dynamic itself as a medium. There is a strongly alpha-privative quality to her argument: not outright negation but a being toward something otherwise. It is productive to see her as advocating something akin to apathy as I am articulating it: another relation toward feeling that generates still other, differing ways of feeling. Not antipathy but apathy.[18]

Easterling provides a compelling and domestic example of medium design. Two children are fighting with one another over something or other. "The parent does not try to parse the content of the argument but swiftly changes the disposition of the context. They lower the temperature of the room, move a chair into the light, increase the blood sugar of one child, or introduce a pet into the arms of another so that the chemistry of the room no longer induces or supports violence."[19] In the terms of this chapter, there is a certain apathy in parents' actions here. Picking sides will do nothing to make the dynamic stop: it's parental apathy that conjures the trapdoor that brings the child's tantrum to an end. This work of medium design, it is crucial to note, draws upon the dispositions of the experienced and skilled parent. What Easterling means by disposition is another mode of engagement possible in practices, places, and individuals. These dispositions, it must be noted, emerge over time: they are cultivated as well as constituted relationally. "Disposition requires more than a single encounter."[20] Dispositions aren't automatically present and so always available. They are sneaky, shadow skills honed over time. "In the medium, some unanticipated means to counter violence or encourage productivity may have the capacity to engage mysterious or stubborn problems."[21] Dispositions are shadow skills that, like any skill, must be practiced through iterative, serial engagement.[22]

Easterling wants to pursue "techniques for a stealthier form of activism that, without being tagged as an opponent, make systematic changes that are under the radar."[23] This work "is dispositional and essentially indeterminate because it requires the deployment of practical skills unfolding over time and the ability to react to a changing sequence of cues."[24] Apathy is never simply marking a set of dispositions ready to be activated. Apathy isn't a tendency that one can easily and deliberately toggle on and off. "Apathy is productive," Gross argues, but it is produced "with great social effort."[25] Easterling's articulation of disposition attends, then, to how such a productive apathy might emerge. "These skills ["discrepancy or trickery"] are 'picked up' by those sensitive to active forms and in the process of enacting them." Easterling argues that "[disposition] does not describe a constant, but rather a changing set of actions."[26] Dispositions are detected as they are practiced. "As a continuum of values dispositional expressions cannot be controlled, only inflected, conditioned or tutored."[27] Dispositions don't wholly preexist their cultivation.

"WOULD YOU LIKE TO PLAY A GAME?"

WarGames allows me to tease out how apathy as a disposition can operate as an "auxiliary activism." The various empathetic, sympathetic, and antipathetic engagements that constitute the rhetorical ecology of the film: the pressing end of the world as two nuclear superpowers face off. Long story short, a young slacker named David Lightman (played by Matthew Broderick), looking for a new computer game to play, accidentally hacks the United States' War Operations Plan Response (WOPR) computer through a long forgotten "backdoor." David is portrayed as the classic apathetic teenage slacker: deeply interested in video games, disrespectful of authority, smart but uninterested and unmotivated by the world around him. We learn later in the film that David's (hastily assembled) FBI profile describes him in stereotypically apathetic terms: "intelligent, but an underachiever, alienated from his parents, few friends," and later "the little prick." David is wasted (political) potential that annoys the dominant pathetic paradigm.[28]

Early in the film, David befriends his classmate Jennifer Mack (Ally Sheedy), who is intrigued by David's slacker ethos. David attempts to win her favor by hacking into the school's computer in order to change one of her grades. It is here we start to see David's dispositions emerge through multiple encounters. Curious, Jennifer wants to know more, and so she is there when David finally finds what he is looking for: the backdoor into the computer he is trying to hack. Unfortunately, it remains password protected. Following a serpentine research endeavor, wherein he learns a great deal about the computer's creator whom he will soon meet, David hits upon the password he needs to get in. Hacking is here portrayed as both a digital and analog activity that includes flipping through library card catalogs. David looks anything but apathetic as he attempts to access what he assumes is a treasure trove of computer games.

But, of course, David hacks WOPR just after the powers-that-be have handed it the keys to the missiles, which had previously been in the uncertain hands of humans ambivalent in their commitment to their mission. The brass needed a way to secure mission commitment.[29] "The men must be taken out of the loop," a serious man in a suit passionately argues. Perhaps counterintuitively, the computer guarantees pathos. A machine that cannot (seemingly) help but care about the stakes of the present antagonism. Surprisingly, apathy emerges as a problem only a machine can solve: the cold machine is a pathetic guarantee. All WOPR can do is care about nuclear warfare. All *pathos* all of the time: a closed loop of feeling toward war. The computer maintains the pathetic commitment that ensures the rhetorical situation that is the Cold War.

This sets up what can be read as the crucial moment of and for apathy in the movie: choosing sides. Now interfaced with WOPR and having chosen "Global Thermonuclear Warfare" from a list of both mundane- and malicious-sounding games, David and Jennifer are prompted with "Which side do you want?" Thinking it is nothing but a game, they choose "the Russians" in a cheeky act of rebellion. The power now vested in WOPR thus raises the stakes of David's exploit: he has hacked a computer holding the keys to the end of the world. It's picking *a* side—*this* side—that sets in motion the crisis around which the film turns. Their choosing of a side locks them and everyone else into a war game threatening to become an actual world-ending conflict. Not knowing that WOPR is running a simulation with David, NORAD responds as if it's real, which then prompts WOPR to do the same. By virtue of the unwavering pathetic dynamic, the situation quickly escalates. Unchoosing sides, as it were, becomes the quest, unrecognized as such until the last possible moment. It is in the unwinding of his cheeky choice that we see the activating of David's dispositional apathy. The hacking he has done in other contexts becomes redeployable to other ends by virtue of multiple encounters. The apathy that David practices becomes otherwise productive.

Alongside his hacking disposition, it is equally instructive to trace David's movements throughout the film. They too are alpha privative. He is in the rhetorical situation but in its untraveled pathetic channels. David hacks doors, locks, and phones. He hides and travels through ducts. He escapes and returns, first brought to NORAD unwillingly (after being exposed as the hacker), and then later by the skin of his teeth (rushing back in to save the world) as the blast doors seal everyone inside. NORAD becomes the pathetic center of the film: a place of intense feeling toward, and it is in and out of this location that David sneaks. Apathy is an interruption emerging from within rather than without an intensely bounded rhetorical situation—apathy creeps within. "Apathy, in other words, is a shadow phenomenon that refers at each point to the emotional economy writ large," in the estimation of Gross.[30] This sneaking in and out, David's capacity to move around, can be juxtaposed with the opening scene's characters, who are locked into their situation by a mechanical door not unlike that which seals in NORAD. Indeed, at the critical moment, the captain tries to place a call out but the line is dead. Apathy moves through the ducts in and out of an over- and already determined *pathos*. Apathy isn't an external intervention (from some "outside"): apathy is the phone call coming from inside the house.

Jenny Odell, in her recent *How to Do Nothing*, helps to mark this work of apathy. She describes doing nothing as "escaping laterally."[31] Her elaboration of this resonates with the alpha privative. Her version of doing nothing "is to take the view of the outsider without leaving, always oriented toward what it is you would have left."[32] "I will participate, but not as asked."[33] She calls this to "resist in place," which "means refusing the frame of reference."[34] Odell's use of standing apart does just this work—to be outside while inside. I think this captures something of apathy: the way that, in *WarGames*, David stands apart—"oriented toward 'what it is' he 'would have left.'"[35] The apathetic stands apart but never completely away from—always drawn, tending toward what they might leave. Apathy is still a species of *with-ness*. It prefixes itself to *pathos*—it is literally feeling but differently. Apart from is still a part of.

As part of his quest, David must locate Dr. Stephen Falken (John Wood), the computer scientist who built what became WOPR. David needs Dr. Falken's help in convincing NORAD that Russian threat is unfounded—that WOPR is simply stuck in a simulation. Finding Falken is hard because the doctor has taken himself off the grid, and he is living under an assumed name. It is in his meeting with Dr. Falken where the distinctiveness of apathy crystalizes. Dr. Falken has, simply put, given up. Dr. Falken performs a slide show for teenagers about the lesson of "futility" (in a somewhat bizarre scene in the film where he turns on a projector and lectures to the high school students about the end of the world): "Extinction is part of the natural order," he concludes. What is coming cannot be stopped. "Bullshit!" David responds. Dr. Falken's nihilism is perhaps too easily or too quickly rendered as (mistaken for) apathy. However, his feeling is something more akin to antipathy. He coolly awaits the apocalypse. In the logic of the film, *pathos* and *antipathos* lead to the same place: the end of the world. His is a negation that misses the possibilities of the alpha privative.

Juxtaposing apathy ("without feeling") with antipathy ("opposed in feeling") is instructive. Falken describes "the horror of survival." David asks him about "the last thing he cared about," which recalls apathy's complex relationship to pathos. "A person who lacked feeling or concern for politics would not be moved to voice these expressions whatsoever. The non-feeling person would feel indifferent to the matter at hand and would feel no need to justify why he or she is not taking any particular action in this case."[36] This helps to further differentiate David from Falken. Falken is a Bartleby, Herman Melville's infamously obstinate character. David is a better Bartleby: "I'd rather not" becomes "I'd rather do something else." Apathy isn't a refusal as such—it's a mitigation rather than negation. David is Easterling's Bartleby, we could say. Falken, because of his antipathy, is trapped, bound within (literally and figuratively) this pathetic dynamic: he is literally in too deep. He refuses and can offer nothing else other than his righteousness. David and Jennifer must bring antipathy into an apathetic relation to a troubling *pathos*.

They do just that, of course: Falken is remotivated to lend a hand in saving the world. They return together to NORAD, renewed in their apathy. Running unsuccessfully through a number of direct approaches to getting WOPR to stop, David and Dr. Falken hit upon an auxiliary approach. In the penultimate scene, the computer is instructed to play tic-tac-toe. Telling here is that tic-tac-toe is not immediately available as a game to play. That is, it isn't present on the list of games from which a user can choose. The game is present in the computer even while it's absent. Tic-tac-toe is a disposition redeployed rhetorically to undo the pathetic commitment to war. The *pathos* machine cannot be confronted head-on, as Easterling argues with respect to contemporary political life. WOPR is asked to play tic-tac-toe with "0" as the number of players. While technically this is done so that the computer can play itself, the choice is instructive for us as well. Apathy doesn't introduce a new side, a third player, but zeroes out the game, which, nevertheless, must still be played. David has to cultivate and then activate apathy as a disposition. The computer must encounter the futility of tic-tac-toe over and over and over again. Apathy emerges this way. David alters the medium this way. Like a sage parent, he gives WOPR something else to do in order to defuse the situation.[37]

Compelling is the fact that getting WOPR to release its hold on the missiles strangely resonates with a real-life hypothetical designed to forestall nuclear war: the Fisher protocol, composed by Roger Fisher in 1981 (two-years before the release of *WarGames*).[38] Fisher describes the protocol this way:

> My suggestion was quite simple: Put that needed [missile] code number in a little capsule, and then implant that capsule right next to the heart of a volunteer. The volunteer would carry with him a big, heavy butcher knife as he accompanied the President. If ever the President wanted to fire nuclear weapons, the only way he could do so would be for him first, with his own hands, to kill one human being. The President says, "George, I'm sorry but tens of millions must die." He has to look at someone and realize what death is—what an innocent death is. Blood on the White House carpet. It's reality brought home.
>
> When I suggested this to friends in the Pentagon they said, "My God, that's terrible. Having to kill someone would distort the President's judgment. He might never push the button."[39]

Fisher introduced the protocol (or what would later be minted as a protocol) in a speech delivered at a symposium hosted by the Physicians for Social Responsibility and organized around the theme of "the medical consequences of nuclear weapons and nuclear war." Although, one could just as easily imagine it being pitched in the writers' room of *Dr. Strangelove*. In fact, the protocol was dramatized in season three of HBO's *The Leftovers*. Its timely recirculation began just as President Trump decided to escalate tensions with North Korea. Disappointingly, a Cold War idea had to be reheated. Fisher prefaces the protocol in ways that resonate with Easterling's medium design. Speaking to a room full of physicians focused on the medical fallout of nuclear fallout, Fisher worries, "If all we do is deliver bad news and say that there's nothing we can do about it, the bad news does not become operational."[40] This echoes Easterling's treatment of the dead end of "only more ways of . . . being right": "Armed only with rationality . . . it is nearly impossible to derail or interrupt this seduction or oppression." Fisher himself proposes, "We have to turn that news into something we can do."[41] At this point there is a weird jump in his remarks; I have to imagine there was a pause when Fisher delivered them. He next says, "My favorite activity is inventing."[42] This is how Fisher moves from his stated desire for the operative to what becomes the strange protocol named after him. This room full of concerned physicians has to stop simply delivering the (bad) news hoping that it will be enough—that being right will win the day. They need to invent (other) ways of doing things—of making things happen. It's critical to note, then, that the protocol is not some standalone suggestion—a one-off thought experiment as it is often described—but a compelling example of the type of inventive thinking we should all be participating in.

Fisher's protocol is medium design. Hack the system so that launching nuclear missiles becomes a little less likely and even less desirable. The protocol thus plays with feeling as well. There's clearly a strong pathetic element. Fisher reminds us that at many points in the launch operation there is an attempt to distance any commander in chief from the full affective impact of a launch order. The president's judgment, as the Pentagon official's response to Fisher's protocol gestures toward, is predicated upon this distance. The protocol thus distorts the pathetic dynamic normally at work in such a scenario. I wouldn't say the protocol is exactly like the work of apathy in *WarGames*, but then it doesn't exactly have to be; resonant with *WarGames*, it introduces another way of feeling toward feeling. The protocol introduces a trapdoor into a truly apocalyptic rhetorical situation.

Apathy is a tendency in the medium and so it is by tweaking the medium that apathy might emerge and get something (else) done. One cannot be compelled to choose apathy. In line with the language of hacking that we find throughout Easterling and the film, apathy is a backdoor in(to) a pathetic machine. It is a backdoor that David accesses incidental to the WOPR's purpose; David just wants to play and not take out the trash. Apathy must be snuck in and out of everywhere it might work. Apathy tricks and cons us out of that in which we are invested. David's hack stops the game, saves the world, but also, it goes unsaid, renders the current operation enfeebled. Apathy has been activated. The computer, newly disposed, calls off the war game: it has grown bored of global thermonuclear war. "The only winning move is not to play," WOPR remarks. This is a compelling conclusion in the context of apathy's relationship to feeling, to *pathos*. It suggests not a lack of commitment, a disinterest in the outcome of something like politics, but another relation to the *pathos* of politics: a decidedly invested "fuck it," as it were. "Fuck it" still performs feeling, but it is a feeling about a particular pathetic orientation. WOPR's conclusion is akin to what Jenny Rice calls "a kind of rhetorical shrug."[43] "We have already seen that this rhetorical shrug is less of a turn away from the public, and more of an 'alternative' mode of public orientation."[44] And this orientation could prove productive of alternative rhetorical dynamics that we find less arrestive. *WarGames* doesn't collapse into an easy binary. If my wager is right, then the movie succeeds in performing apathy not as yet another side, but as an effacing of the sides as they are presently arranged.

APATHY'S REPERTOIRE

Now, our seemingly endless *now*, feels like an inopportune time to write on behalf of *apathy*. There is still a risk, even here at the end, of mistaking apathy as the negation of *pathos*—that what apathy always and ever recommends is *not caring*. This is to misunderstand the alpha privative. Apathy isn't *the* end of *pathos* but instead *a* refiguring of particular pathetic ends. Even grasping the potential of apathy, there remains a risk in eschewing sides, which seems like a dangerous move in a moment when the absence of pathetic engagement feels like complicity. Indeed, there may never be an opportune moment to *recommend* apathy; *apathy* itself is not commendable. Apathy may not be that which someone can offer and someone else can take up. Like *pathos*, apathy does not (if ever) answer to *logos*. Apathy is a crack in the rhetorical situation through which something or someone renders the situation otherwise. Or, in more temporal terms, apathy is always *meanwhile* to *pathos*.

Apathy is the emergence of something else: dispositions that can unbind particular affective formations in ways we might find ameliorating. It is another way of feeling rather than a rejection of feeling as such. With apathy "a new articulation of desire" emerges.[45] Herein lies its potential. Apathy eschews binaries that only serve to reinforce a dynamic that is itself the problem. Borrowing from Benjamin J. Robertson, we could describe apathy as a "liquidation of antagonism."[46] Apathy intervenes not in the existing rhetorical situation, but instead alters the ground from which the situation becomes possible.

Apathy promises another activist repertoire, to turn again to Easterling. She attends to the political capacity and necessity of *apathy* in our particular political moment of seemingly intractable antagonisms wherein the only viable option seems to be doubling down: to assert rightness and correctness in ways that only fuel the dynamic, which is itself the trouble. "It's not going to do me any good to come up against Donald Trump with a placard saying 'you are not being fair'—that's not going to work. And there is so much power that is operating in this other undeclared, dispositional layer. Of course we still march in the street; but I'm trying to expand our activist repertoire beyond declarations to include some other kind of subterfuge. I'm trying to outwit the superbugs and soften the ground."[47] Easterling seeks a way under these binaries, not via resistance but via manipulations of the political dynamic itself as a medium. She writes, "It is a repertoire of activism that many purists might not consider to be 'right.' Many people desperately need to be right all the time. That is fine. I don't want to be right, and being right often exacerbates a violent temperament."[48] The desire to be right, the drive to win, can lock one into an unwinnable situation. Not to play the game is to recognize that playing the game is but one form of engagement. Apathy is an indefinite rather than definite disposition.

Rhetoric should, of course, remain committed to pathetic maintenance, to keeping the fire stoked because it might burn out. But fires of *pathos* can exceed our control. Rhetoric should also attend to the stray ember, floating away, trying desperately to do something other than reduce everything to ash.

NOTES

1. John Badham, dir. *WarGames* (Beverly Hills, CA: MGM, 1983).

2. Ibid.

3. Daniel Gross, *The Secret History of Emotion: From Aristotle's Rhetoric to Modern Brain Science* (Chicago: University of Chicago Press, 2006), 81.

4. Ibid.

5. Keller Easterling, "Disposition," in *Cognitive Architecture: From Biopolitics to Noopolitics*, ed. Deborah Hauptmann and Warren Neidich (Rotterdam: 010 Publishers, 2010), 253.

6. Gross, *Secret History*, 54.

7. Nina Eliasoph, *Avoiding Politics: How Americans Produce Apathy in Everyday Life* (London: Cambridge University Press, 1998), 230–31. This is echoed by Zachary Davis, who writes, "Apathy is defined either as a particular state of mind wherein there is a lack of feeling, passion or interest, or as a type of behavior indicating the lack of participation and lack of action." Davis continues, "In the studies of mass apathy, it has been further assumed that the apathetic state of mind is the cause of apathetic behavior. That is, the apathetic person fails to act because this person lacks any feeling for or interest in the matter at hand." In this vein, apathy is thus frequently treated as a personal, moral failing, or even just a state of mind that must be overcome. Zachary Davis, "A Phenomenology of Political Apathy; Scheler and the Origins of Mass Violence," *Continental Philosophy Review* 42 (2009), 152.

8. Susan Wells, "Rogue Cops and Health Care: What Do We Want from Public Writing?," *CCC* 47, no. 3 (1996): 333.

9. Eliasoph, *Avoiding Politics*, 231.

10. Jenny Rice, *Distant Publics: Development Rhetoric and the Subject of Crisis* (Pittsburgh: University of Pittsburgh Press, 2012), 61.

11. Gross, *Secret History*, 53.

12. It is perhaps useful to think of apathy as interrupting what we could call *groupfeel*, which is akin to *groupthink* wherein one mode of thinking inheres across a group, blocking out any alternate modes of thought. My thanks to Michele Kennerly for suggesting this analogy.

13. Easterling, "Disposition," 251.

14. Keller Easterling, *Medium Design* (Moscow: Strelka Press, 2018).

15. Keller Easterling, "No You're Not," *e-flux*, September 26, 2016, https://www.e-flux.com/architecture/superhumanity/66720/no-you-re-not.

16. Ibid.

17. Ibid.

18. I will return to the antipathy/apathy distinction below.

19. Easterling, *Medium Design*.

20. Easterling, "Disposition," 254.

21. Easterling, *Medium Design*.

22. See Boyle's discussion of seriality in Casey Andrew Boyle, *Rhetoric as a Posthuman Practice* (Columbia: Ohio State University Press, 2018), 48–55.

23. Easterling, "No You're Not."

24. Easterling, *Medium Design*.

25. Gross, *Secret History*, 52.

26. Easterling, "Disposition," 254.

27. Ibid.

28. It is necessary to mark the white, male, cis, and upper-middle-class qualities of David's apathy. His apathy emerges from what is mostly a safe, privileged existence. We cannot ignore that his apathy is uniquely activated by his situation. He can afford and so maintain his apathy. Given the light touch and family-friendly vibe (and PG rating) of the film, the danger, legal and mortal, to David never overwhelms. *WarGames* might then be a performance of apathy on the cheap: one not dearly bought and paid for. In other words, apathy, as an emergent political affect, entails risks not explored here.

29. The problem faced by the brass in *WarGames* is a perennial one, particularly on the precipice of a war. In a 1918 newspaper item titled "Apathy Disappearing," the anonymous author responds to the claim that "America is too apathetic about [WWI]." The author responds, "Apathy is dangerous . . . but apathy of the kind that now exists loses its dangerous possibilities when we consider that it is but temporary." Once the "first casualty lists" provide a "true perspective," things will change. "Apathetic we are, perhaps, but give us time. What time will bring in lieu of apathy is

the thing the Kaiser must fear most." "Apathy Disappearing," in *The North American Review* (New York: North America Review Corporation, 1918), 154.

30. Gross, *Secret History*, 71.

31. Jenny Odell, *How to Do Nothing: Resisting the Attention Economy* (New York: Penguin Random House, 2019), xvii.

32. Ibid., 61.

33. Ibid., 68.

34. Ibid., xvii.

35. Ibid., 61.

36. Davis, "Phenomenology," 153.

37. It must be noted here that Dr. Falken named the computer "Benjamin" after his departed son, and that both David and Dr. Falken call it as such.

38. My thanks to Casey Boyle for alerting me to this protocol.

39. Roger Fisher, "Preventing Nuclear War," *Bulletin of the Atomic Scientists* 37, no. 3 (1981), 16.

40. Ibid., 15.

41. Ibid.

42. Ibid.

43. Rice, *Distant Publics*, 95.

44. Ibid.

45. Keller Easterling, *Extrastatecraft: The Power of Infrastructure Space* (New York: Verso, 2016), 228.

46. Benjamin J. Robertson, *None of This Is Normal: The Fiction of Jeff VanderMeer* (Minneapolis: University of Minnesota Press, 2018), 121.

47. George Papamattheakis and Keller Easterling, "Inside Keller Easterling's Personal Medium Design," *Strelka Mag*, September 18, 2019.

48. Ibid.

Aphantasia

BENJAMIN FIRGENS

On an icy morning in February 1892, Elizabeth Cady Stanton told the House Judiciary Committee of the unimaginable solitude of their souls. Why deny women the right to vote, she argued, when every woman, like everyone else, lives "in a world of her own"?[1] This "solitude of self" speech remains famous for its eloquent defense of each woman's right to be "arbiter of her own destiny."[2] Its fame may also derive from how it called upon some truths of the human condition: that, as Stanton said, life is "a little speck of light shut in by a tremendous darkness," and that the measure of our lives might therefore be nothing but the range of our responses to the unknown within ourselves and others.[3]

Bleak, but not wrong. Stanton's words performed *aphantasia,* which I understand as the experience, reached through the inversion of commonplace imaginations, of the pervasive influence of the unimagined. By "the unimagined" I mean neither an internal dimension of mind unavailable to self-consciousness nor aspects of the material world that consciousness cannot access. The phrase instead encompasses what we have not yet imagined, but could, and what we cannot imagine, but can know insofar as we know we cannot imagine it. *Phantasia* involves relationships among sensation, memory, and meaning; *aphantasia* inverts all three in a gesture to their reliance on what they lack. We may be tempted to label these inversions as failures of imagination: the illustration of lost sensation, faulty knowledge, or incomplete meaning. My argument in this chapter is that the only failure in such a diagnosis would be our own. Imagination's inversion looks like failure when we presume *a priori* the ethical status of *phantasia* or *aphantasia* as such. In contrast, I think we should forego the idea that imagination in general, or any particular modality thereof, is innately good or bad and instead learn to parse, in any given case, the practical and ethical implications of the unimagined.

This chapter clarifies these claims through consideration of received rhetorical traditions and modern psychology. I first survey anxieties regarding imagination's shortcomings voiced by scholars and teachers in ancient Greece and Rome to show how imagination has always prompted concern about things left unimagined. I then read modern psychological discourses about *aphantasia* to give the term some definitional weight while learning to avoid the implication that the absence of a "normal" imagination is the fault of an individual's deficient mind. I conclude reflecting on how and why scholars of rhetoric might pay more attention to the mutability and finitude of every mind's eye. Typical approaches to *phantasia* assume that different people visualize similarly. My goal is to use *aphantasia* to escape such normative assumptions and move toward a more neurodiverse way of conceptualizing imagination.

This chapter joins a revival of interest in imagination among rhetoricians. Imagination and its cognates have always been central concerns of rhetorical practice and theory, not to mention *foci* for philosophical questions about the limits of epistemology and the dangers of appearances.[4] It typically enters contemporary Rhetorical Studies from one of two directions. In the first, scholars return to past practices and theorizations of imagination to enrich our sense of rhetoric's history and nuance our understanding of how imagination works—or at least has been thought to work—in rhetorical practice.[5] In the second, imagination offers vocabulary and means to think and act outside hegemonic norms and social structures.[6] This chapter contributes to the first kind of study by exploring historical anxieties about imagination and the second by highlighting the present lack of neurodiversity in discussions of the concept. At issue is how we imagine imagination and how the alpha privative aids us in theorizing it consistently and rigorously while allowing room for the full diversity of its occurrences.

ANCIENT PHANTASMAL ANXIETIES

Phantasia does not directly translate to "imagination." Whereas imagination today signifies some combination of idle fantasy, artistic creativity, and mental imagery, *phantasia* referenced a specific understanding of the relationship among sensation, memory, cognition, and language. The word's meanings were flexible. As Dorthea Frede puts it, *phantasia* could name "the capacity, the activity or process, and the product or result" of retaining "sensory appearances" in memory and then reexperiencing those appearances later.[7]

The word's flexibility resulted not from imprecision but its status as a commonplace. Ruth Webb notes that ancient discussions of *phantasia* look vague to modern readers because the discussions presumed familiarity with long-forgotten assumptions about how language and sensation function; specifically, that vivid imagery imprints the soul and that those imprints contain the latent possibility to be activated by experience or language, which resulted in the reappearance of the original sense.[8] To describe this process in terms of representation and imagery is to use modern ideas alien to the original context. More accurate, as Webb writes, is to understand *phantasia* as the creation of "effects in the audience's mind that mimic the act of seeing," resulting in "immediate" bodily responsiveness that only reached "intellectual judgment" after the fact.[9]

The term *aphantasia* appeared briefly in ancient sources in the variant *aphantasiōtos* to describe a being "unable to imagine a thing."[10] This usage surfaced surrounding the question of whether nonhuman forms of life could imagine at all. Plutarch, for example, argued on behalf of the "cleverness of animals" and called "ridiculous" the idea that "living things" be either "imaginative or unimaginative." His view was that "it is the nature of every creature with a soul to be sentient and imaginative from the hour of its birth."[11] In this example, *aphantasiōtos* simply named the absence of a mind that could imagine.

Outside these few uses of *aphantasiōtos*, plenty of precedent existed for thinking imagination's inverse. It existed because of fears stoked by the idea of imagination itself, which often came up in philosophical discussion of the dangers of inaccurate judgment based on incomplete knowledge. In the *Sophist*, Plato complained that sophists could fool inexperienced minds with the mere appearance of the truth, just as a shoddy painter might dupe onlookers with brushstrokes that look artful at a distance and clumsy up-close.[12] Aristotle put similar concerns in a more abstract register in *De Anima*, where he defined *phantasia* as "a movement that comes about as a result of the activity of perception," a definition chosen to reinforce imagination's connection with pain and pleasure (since he used it to explain why bodies feel the need to move toward some things and away from others) and to emphasize that the possibility of error is intrinsic to imagination (since it results from perception, not belief, understanding, or knowledge).[13] From such perspectives, any performance or invocation of *phantasia* was inherently dubious.

Rhetoricians shared awareness of *phantasia's* slippery veracity, if not the philosophers' disdain for it. The question of how to make imagination persuasive in oratory led to some consistent answers: that an orator should themselves imagine the events they describe so as to embody the emotional and physical experience of witnessing alongside their audience,[14] and that detail and repetition succeed as specific stylistic devices for conveying vivid sights.[15] Such advice assumed that orators must speak *phantasia* in identifiable terms. For shared *phantasia* to work, audiences must relate to what orators ask them to feel and see. Audiences have to hold in their collective memory some precedent for why specific details and stylistic devices would invoke commonplace *phantasia*.[16] In this way, epistemological questions about *phantasia*'s trustworthiness led not only to practical questions about when techniques to mobilize imagination succeed and fail, but also to ethical questions about which of its uses result in prosocial ends, and which antisocial.[17]

Aphantasic experiences of the unimagined, I have been arguing, were well known to ancient sources insofar as they took any experience of *phantasia* to be inherently questionable, and therefore consisting of limits, absences, or errors.[18] To call an instance of *phantasia* complete or true was to commit a category error since assurance of completion and/or truth were the very factors that distinguished knowledge from *phantasia*.[19] *Phantasia* clearly had its uses; "There can be no thinking without" it, as Frede summarizes.[20] But if *phantasia* performed a necessary function by translating between sensation and cognition, it also, in so doing, enabled all manner of mistranslation. This mutability allowed for possibilities and perils simultaneously. Suffice it to say that ancient scholars and teachers were acutely aware of how unimagined things held determinative influence on imagination's effects and ethical status. A longer piece of scholarship should trace the history of how those anxieties changed across time and context; for its part, this chapter takes the point that *aphantasia* was implicitly present in fearful theorizations of *phantasia*, and moves to more modern and explicit discussions of the term.

PSYCHOLOGY'S *APHANTASIA*, WITTING AND UNWITTING

Psychologists only recently coined the term *aphantasia* but have theorized the condition it attempts to diagnose for centuries. The motivation for this ongoing theorization, as Rebecca Keogh and Joel Pearson put it, is "the large range of subjective reports in the vividness of an individual's imagery."[21] Different people self-report their capacity to imagine sensory details in intensities that range from detailed recreations to the inability to "picture" anything. Psychologists disagree over how to interpret that fact. More importantly, they disagree over how, considering this variation, to understand the nature of mental images in the first place.[22] What does it mean to have an image "in mind"? Conversely, what does it mean to be unable to "see" anything mentally?

The origin of *aphantasia* in psychology was diagnostic. In 2015, Adam Zeman, Michaela Dewar, and Sergio Della Sala published a paper about "lives without imagery," the lives of people afflicted with what they termed "congenital aphantasia," or the inability to imagine sensory details.[23] The paper was simple: they offered a questionnaire to self-selected participants (who had contacted the authors because they reported a "lifelong reduction of mental imagery") and relayed the answers, hoping to inspire further research.[24] Notably, in this, the apparent introduction of *aphantasia* into the literature, the term labels an "impairment" that is to some degree intrinsic and immutable in the lives of those it afflicts.

The studies that followed Zeman et al. demonstrate that people do seem to possess quite different capacities to mentally simulate sensations. Treating *aphantasia* as the inability "to experience the sensory qualities of objects that are not physically presented," Christianne Jacobs and coauthors gave a list of imaginatively demanding cognitive tasks to a single person who reported being *aphantasic*. Based on the results, the authors concluded that the condition indeed made that task-ridden person's performance "significantly worse" than control tests.[25] Working with a larger sample size and more sophisticated research design, Keogh and Peterson agreed that *aphantasia* names "a condition involving a lack of sensory and phenomenal imagery," and went further to rule out other possible explanations for why some people describe themselves as unable to draw up mental images.[26]

Demonstrating that people visualize differently is not the same as clarifying the meaning of those differences. The authors of these studies acknowledge this explicitly. Jacobs et al., for example, point out that "for many tasks supposedly involving mental imagery there are alternative cognitive strategies that lead to equally successful behavior."[27] The inability to picture something in the mind does not necessarily prevent a person from finding equally or even more productive ways to think that thing. On a similar note, Keogh and Peterson conclude their paper with the hope that their research illuminates "the vastly different abilities and experiences of our internal worlds."[28] These researchers are quite aware of the mind's complexity. Why, then, refer to *aphantasia* as a "condition" that besets "otherwise healthy" people? Why pathologize this particular aspect of the mind's variety?

There is no immediate reason to think images or sensations are the only, or even most important, components of imagination. As Keogh and Peterson put it, an inability to "see" images of "what" the mind conceptualizes does not equate with an inability to conceptualize "where" things relate to each other in space.[29] This is a point for which we could find support outside psychology. Edward Casey, for example, makes fundamental to his phenomenological account of imagination a tripartite distinction between imaginative acts that "image" something sensory, those that "imagine-that" certain relationships and situations exist in the world, and those that "imagine-how" one's sense of self would project forward or backward in time.[30] We do not have to accede to his particular categories to take the general point that imagination is not about sense alone. The question returns: Why assume the lack of a sensation-rich imagination is unhealthy?

Part of the answer involves the rhetorical nature of diagnosis. M. Remi Yergeau observes that when a person gets diagnosed with a putatively abnormal mental attribute, that person's "fullness or realness is always up for debate," because it is always possible to explain their actions, beliefs, arguments, and so on as mere effects of the attribute and not movements of a life worth taking seriously. To be caught in this "demi-rhetorical" loop of always having your intentionality potentially explained away as the "residue" of your mind's imperfections is to be rendered "non-rhetorical."[31] Yergeau makes this point with regard to autism diagnoses and in the midst of a wider argument on behalf of rethinking rhetorical norms by considering autism's neuroqueer rhetorics. *Aphantasia* seems like a comparatively low-stakes example of diagnosis causing harm. But the impulse to label the "vastly different" capacities of imagination as simple successes or failures is an example of the broader habit held by modern cognitive sciences, and by the subfield of "abnormal psychology" in particular, of explaining differences in behavior as mere symptoms of mental faults.[32]

Another explanation for *aphantasia*'s assumptive afflictiveness concerns the wider contexts of how we imagine imagination. Matthew MacKisack notes that "not only are metaphors for and theories about the operation of the mind informed by the wider culture's configurations of pictorial and linguistic signs, they are *part of* that culture."[33] In the case of *aphantasia*, the assumption that the inability to mentally visualize is an inherent fault highlights the ungrounded but popular assumption that imagination is roughly synonymous with lively visualization. But the most vivid expressions of imaginative activity are hardly the only ways such activity shapes our lives. The other ways—involving the imagination of situations and relationships, how people and things tend to relate to one another—are attention-shy by nature. Charles Taylor argues that social imaginaries circulate not just in images but in "stories and legends," or really any medium that can convey a "common understanding" of social practices, that can provide a "background" sense, "unstructured and inarticulate," of the meanings behind daily life.[34] Social imaginaries form the texture of daily assumptions that allow us to live by habit and taken-for-granted procedure. Small wonder scholars sometimes assume vivid sensation is all there is to it. Viewed as a social phenomenon, imagination's location and meaning are difficult to track down precisely because imagination sets the stage, as it were, for any possible shared sense of location and meaning.

For these reasons, we can see why *aphantasia* so plausibly names a mental failure or abnormality, which is all the more reason to think carefully about the alpha privative's ability to invert instead of invalidate. Instead of using *aphantasia* to signify the absence of images in a "blind mind," we should rely on the concept to elucidate differences in imaginative technique, not in terms of normalcy and abnormality but those of the movements of normative expectation and their inversion.[35] Doing so would, following MacKisack, move away from the universalizing "models of mind" that so often typify attitudes about cognition and toward the ability to see and understand many different "cognitive strategies"[36] for living in the world. The final section of this chapter explores the possibilities and implications of such a move.

ETHICS APHANTASIC

When imagination does not meet expectations, a kind of conceptual short-circuiting tends to occur. We arc, without noticing, from questions about what imagination gives us to know to questions about success and failure, good and bad. This chapter has shown how, in ancient and modern contexts alike, epistemological questions posed by imagination are never only that. Instead, the topic of imagination has been vexed in such different situations as ancient rhetorical pedagogy and modern psychological research because it poses unavoidable implications for what does and does not count as productive and ethically sound ways to conceptualize community.

This should not surprise us. Imagination and communal life are coconstitutive. After all, it is now commonplace in political, sociological, and anthropological literature to assert that imaginaries are the cognitive glue, so to speak, that holds communal bonds together against vicissitudes of space and time.[37] Community and imagination are inconceivable without each other. All of which is to explain why the stakes are high for finding better ways to think about differences in imagination, for to reject a specific variety of imaginative practice is to reject the possibilities of sociality it contained and foreclose space in communal life for neurodiversity.

Topoi of loss, meaninglessness, and failure typify how we talk about nonnormative imaginations. At best, these constitute lazy tropes that mask difference with cliché. At worst, they do literal violence. Lest these judgments seem to fall on psychologists alone, let me be clear that rhetoricians also lack literacy regarding—or even vocabulary involving—neurodiversity. This is clear in most attempts to theorize *phantasia* to date. We have so far collectively failed to ask serious and detailed questions about how *phantasia* works between different audiences, much less within the range of a single audience's cognitive diversity. More importantly, we have failed to consider what it would even mean to practice *phantasia* by invoking imaginations outside imagery or sensation, or to interrogate our own views of what counts as effective and ethical *phantasia*. Seen in this light, our traditions' and disciplines' treatments of *phantasia* and imagination amount to so many dangerous assumptions about what counts as a normal, effective, and good mind.

The underlying motivation of this chapter has been to get beyond the assumption that imagination's supposed failure is inherently bad and success innately good. This has involved reframing descriptions of imagination's failures into explorations of its inversions. Moving forward, we might coach our studies of imagination by an insight already won regarding memory. If forgetting, as Bradford Vivian argues, can mean not the oblivion of social life but its reinvention in reconstituted norms and memories, then *aphantasia* can reference not the thoughtless failure of moral perception but the lapse of otherwise rigid social imaginaries.[38] We should be less concerned with failures to imagine than with failures to imagine otherwise.

Contemporary examples for this last claim are too abundant to cite. Social imaginaries can cause harm when they work too well and succeed too often. Oftentimes, violently narrow boundaries of imagination exist not because of unconscious failures to imagine a different world but due to conscious refusals to imagine any world but the one received. Charles Scott writes that "our values and their evaluation have generated blindly some of our worst pain," not because of our ignorance but "because of the desperation by which we have sought to see in the dark."[39] We are often most attached to, and thus most unreflectively violent about, those imaginative visions that give us the most stability and confidence in the face of the darkness Elizabeth Cady Stanton imagined all those years ago.[40]

The effects of such violence can be as visceral as they are systemic. As Jonathan M. Metzl argues, for example, many Americans can hardly "imagine alternate realities or empathize with groups other than their own," not because they are apathetic but because thinking about the world from a nonwhite perspective amounts to "treason" against their ideological entrenchment in the increasingly overt discourses of white nationalism. The result: a country "dying of whiteness."[41] Metzel wrote those lines over a year before white Americans turned out to protest public health measures designed to protect them from COVID-19. If there is a point at which white nationalists will realize their ideology amounts to suicide, we have yet to find it. This is not merely a case where many citizens fail to imagine the humanity of their fellows, but a case where their own self-imaginations are too effective—where we could stand to see imagination failing more often.

US American politics in 2020 presents a litany of similar cases of self-destructive intransigence. Most Americans, for example, treat the abolishment of prisons and police as a radical proposal even as they support systems of incarceration and policing that empirically multiply, not mitigate, social harms, and do so in inescapably racist ways.[42] What would it mean to instead treat the "radical" positions like pragmatic, even necessary, possibilities? To truly ask the question we must loosen our grip on how we imagine society to function—on what we think police do, why we think prisons are necessary, and so on. The same goes, with equally dreadful exigency, for climate change, gun violence, and so many other societal problems that today seem unanswerable. Questions that have no answers may just be bad questions; if our body politic is stuck on systemic issues, it probably has something to do with our consistent inability to imagine ways of living and relating outside the (racist, cis-hetero-patriarchal, capitalist) status quo.

Such examples point up the usefulness of a term like *aphantasia* that can name not the failure to imagine, but imagination's inverse, the inability to envision a definite, fixed vision of something, a term that can call attention to the range of what goes unimagined at any point in time. In moments of aphantasic vertigo there exist opportunities to question what we previously presumed in norms of propriety. And this, in the end, strikes me as a way aphantasia allows rhetoric to play one of its most important roles: making way for reinvention. Amitav Ghosh writes that "to think about the world only as it is amounts to a formula for collective suicide." *Aphantasia* can work against this by, borrowing another phrase from Ghosh, "making possible the imagining of possibilities."[43] In so doing, it can be a force for inventing futures undreamed and solving problems heretofore unfixable.

In sum: we should speak less of imagination's failures and more of its inversions, and we can learn how to do so by theorizing *aphantasia* as the twisting of expectations and not the failure of normalcy. To grant this point is to move toward the adoption of some much-needed epistemic humility when it comes to how we think about mind, thought, and imagination. Such humility might involve awareness of how human knowledge amounts to Stanton's spark otherwise "shut in by a tremendous darkness,"[44] the figurative darkness of what we cannot understand and the literal darkness of what we cannot perceive. If "all epistemology begins in fear," as Lorraine Daston and Peter Galison argue,[45] then the root of that fear must be something like the fear of this dark, and our attempts to imagine the worlds around us amount to the record of our tries to look beyond the lit horizon and into the abyss of what we have not yet seen. To peer into this abyss, I hope, is to find ways "the unimagined" names neither danger nor void, but an inventive resource for thought, action, and change.

NOTES

1. Elizabeth Cady Stanton, "'The Solitude of Self': Speech by ECS to the House Judiciary Committee Speech Text," Voices of Democracy (blog), accessed April 15, 2019, http://voicesofdemocracy.umd.edu/the-solitude-of-self-speech-by-ecs-to-the-house-judiciary-committee-speech-text.

2. Ibid.

3. Ibid. For some justification behind the idea that finitude defines the human condition, see the following representatives of a few philosophical and mystic traditions that argue much the same: Arne Næss, *Scepticism* (New York: Routledge, 2015); Paul Tillich, *The Courage to Be* (New Haven: Yale University Press, 2014); Jalāl al-Dīn Rūmī, *Signs of the Unseen: The Discourses of Jalaluddin Rumi*, trans. W. M. Thackston (Boston: Shambhala, 1999); Dōgen, *Treasury of the True Dharma Eye: Zen Master Dogen's Shobo Genzo*, trans. Kazuaki Tanahashi (Boston: Shambhala, 2012); Charles E. Scott, *The Lives of Things* (Bloomington: Indiana University Press, 2002).

4. For a range of ancient and modern authorities on imagination in philosophy and rhetoric, see Plato, *Theaetetus and Sophist*, trans. C. J. Rowe, Cambridge Texts in the History of Philosophy (New York: Cambridge University Press, 2015); Ruth Webb, *Ekphrasis, Imagination and Persuasion in Ancient Rhetorical Theory and Practice* (New York: Routledge, 2016); Edward S. Casey, *Imagining: A Phenomenological Study*, 2nd ed. (Bloomington: Indiana University Press, 2000).

5. Michele Kennerly, "Getting Carried Away: How Rhetorical Transport Gets Judgment Going," *Rhetoric Society Quarterly* 40, no. 3 (2010): 269–91; Debra Hawhee, "Looking into Aristotle's Eyes: Toward a Theory of Rhetorical Vision," *Advances in the History of Rhetoric* 14, no. 2 (2011): 139–65; Jordan Loveridge, "Praise Bee!: Allegory and Interpretation in the Aberdeen Bestiary," *Rhetoric Society Quarterly* 49, no. 4 (2019): 409–27.

6. Darrel Enck-Wanzer, "Decolonizing Imaginaries: Rethinking 'the People' in the Young Lords' Church Offensive," *Quarterly Journal of Speech* 98, no. 1 (February 2012): 1–23; Armond R. Towns, "'What Do We Wanna Be?' Black Radical Imagination and the Ends of the World," *Communication and Critical/Cultural Studies* 17, no. 1 (March 2020): 75–80; Jacqueline Jones Royster and Gesa Kirsch, *Feminist Rhetorical Practices: New Horizons for Rhetoric, Composition, and Literacy Studies* (Carbondale: Southern Illinois University Press, 2012).

7. Dorthea Frede, "The Cognitive Role of *Phantasia* in Aristotle," in *Essays on Aristotle's* De Anima, ed. Martha C. Nussbaum and Amelie Oksenberg Rorty (Oxford: Clarendon Press, 1992), 279, 294.

8. Webb, *Ekphrasis*, 110–15.

9. Ibid., 38, 122, 127.

10. Henry George Liddell, Robert Scott, and Henry Stuart Jones, *A Greek-English Lexicon*, 9th ed. (Oxford: Clarendon Press, 1996), s.v. *aphantasiōtos*.

11. Plutarch, "De sollertia animalium" 960D, in *Moralia*, vol. 12, trans. W. C. Helmbold (Cambridge: Harvard University Press, 1957).

12. Plato, *Sophist* 234b5–10 (in Plato, *Theaetetus and Sophist*, trans. C. J. Rowe [New York: Cambridge University Press, 2015]).

13. Aristotle, *De Anima* 429a1, trans. C. D. C. Reeve (Cambridge, MA: Hackett, 2017).

14. For example, see Quintilian, *The Orator's Education* [*Institutio Oratoria*] 6.2.29–25, vol. 3, trans. Donald A. Russell (Cambridge: Harvard University Press, 2001); and Longinus, *On the Sublime* [*Peri hupsous*] 15.1–5, trans. W. H. Fyfe (Cambridge: Harvard University Press, 1995).

15. Demetrius, *On Style*, trans. Doreen C. Innes (Cambridge: Harvard University Press, 1995), 209.

16. Webb, *Ekphrasis*, 122.

17. Kennerly observes there is common contrast drawn between narcissistic fantasies—the stuff of daydreaming—and genuinely "civic *phantasia*"—that which prompts audiences to think and deliberate about useful topics. I take this distinction as one useful example for the more general habit of reading ethical and communal import into differing modes of imaginative practice. See Kennerly, "Getting Carried Away," 270.

18. Material metaphors used to describe sensation, memory, and *phantasia* reinforce

this point: the famous metaphor of imprints in a wax tablet, as Paul Ricoeur observed, made reckoning with the possibility of error necessary to any discussion of memory and imagination, since the idea of "marks" or "traces" can be interpreted in any number of ways and in any case leaves room for distortions, misrepresentations, and other general misprints between traces and what does the tracing. See Paul Ricoeur, *Memory, History, Forgetting*, trans. Kathleen Blamey and David Pellauer (Chicago: University of Chicago Press, 2010), 13–15.

19. Hawhee, on this note, writes that there is a "fuzziness" to *phantasia*, since it occurs "at some remove" from moments of direct perception. See Hawhee, "Looking into Aristotle's Eyes," 143.

20. Frede, "Cognitive Role of *Phantasia*," 287.

21. Rebecca Keogh and Joel Pearson, "The Blind Mind: No Sensory Visual Imagery in Aphantasia," *Cortex* 105 (August 1, 2018): 53–60, at 54.

22. For a summary of these debates, and an attempt to connect them to ancient ideas of *phantasia*, see Matthew MacKisack, "Painter and Scribe: From Model of Mind to Cognitive Strategy," *Cortex* 105 (August 1, 2018): 118–24.

23. Adam Zeman, Michaela Dewar, and Sergio Della Sala, "Lives Without Imagery—Congenital Aphantasia," *Cortex* 73 (December 1, 2015): 378–80.

24. Ibid., 378.

25. Christianne Jacobs, Dietrich S. Schwarzkopf, and Juha Silvanto, "Visual Working Memory Performance in Aphantasia," *Cortex* 105 (August 1, 2018): 61.

26. Keogh and Pearson, "Blind Mind," 53.

27. Jacobs, Schwarzkopf, and Silvanto, "Visual Working Memory Performance in Aphantasia," 72.

28. Keogh and Pearson, "Blind Mind," 59.

29. Ibid., 58.

30. Casey, *Imagining*, 40–46.

31. M. Remi Yergeau, *Authoring Autism: On Rhetoric and Neurological Queerness* (Durham: Duke University Press, 2018), 51.

32. Keogh and Pearson, "Blind Mind," 59.

33. MacKisack, "Painter and Scribe," 123.

34. Charles Taylor, *Modern Social Imaginaries* (Durham: Duke University Press, 2004), 23–25.

35. Keogh and Pearson, "Blind Mind."

36. MacKisack, "Painter and Scribe."

37. For a few touchstone examples, see: B. K. Axel, "The Diasporic Imaginary," *Public Culture* 14, no. 2 (April 1, 2002): 411–28; Benedict Anderson, *Imagined Communities: Reflections on the Origin and Spread of Nationalism*, rev. ed. (New York: Verso, 2016); Claudia Strauss, "The Imaginary," *Anthropological Theory* 6, no. 3 (September 1, 2006): 322–44.

38. Bradford Vivian, *Public Forgetting: The Rhetoric and Politics of Beginning Again* (University Park: Penn State University Press, 2010).

39. Charles E. Scott, *The Question of Ethics: Nietzsche, Foucault, Heidegger* (Bloomington: Indiana University Press, 1990), 212.

40. For a more psychological account of how violence is so often justified by virtues, see Alan Page Fiske and Tage Shakti Rai, *Virtuous Violence: Hurting and Killing to Create, Sustain, End, and Honor Social Relationships* (Cambridge: Cambridge University Press, 2015).

41. Jonathan Metzl, *Dying of Whiteness: How the Politics of Racial Resentment Is Killing America's Heartland* (New York: Basic Books, 2019), 11.

42. Mariame Kaba, "Yes, We Mean Literally Abolish the Police," *New York Times*, June 12, 2020, https://www.nytimes.com/2020/06/12/opinion/sunday/floyd-abolish-defund-police.html.

43. Amitav Ghosh, *The Great Derangement: Climate Change and the Unthinkable* (Chicago: University of Chicago Press, 2017), 172.

44. Stanton, "'Solitude of Self,'" 32.

45. Lorraine Daston and Peter Galison, *Objectivity* (New York: Zone, 2010), 371.

APPENDIX

(No) Uncertain Terms

Cory Geraths, Michele Kennerly, Mari Lee Mifsud, Bess R. H. Myers, Damien Smith Pfister, and Alessandra Von Burg

The preceding chapters of this volume demonstrate the promise of alpha privation for rhetorical theory, and there are many more alpha-privative concepts in want of development. Here, in the spirit of an unending asyndeton but in the form of a finite list, we present a few more.

amnēsia (noun; the state of being without memory, forgetfulness); _amnēmōn_ (adjective; without memory, unmindful, forgetful, forgotten, not mentioned)

The concepts of public memory and public forgetting organize work in Rhetorical Studies on cultural preservation and amplification, on the one hand, and cultural diminution and loss, on the other.[1] Two ancient Greek alpha privatives occasionally appear, the first linked to memory, the second to forgetting: *alētheia* and *amnēsia*.[2] The common translations of *alētheia* as "truth" and *amnēsia* as "forgetfulness," respectively, obscure their alpha-privative construction. Since alpha privation lays bare some of the privileges of the concept upon which it exercises its effect, offering a cumbersome literal translation can change our attention to a word. All alpha privatives hold a reminder of what they are without, but *amnēsia* boasts a peculiar poignancy because memory (*mnēmē*) remains, inactive but present.

Rhetoric's mnemonic systems and devices are well known.[3] What have these systems habituated generations of rhetoric students to forget about their own lives or cultures or to keep out of their speeches or writings for fear of the power of new or resurgent public memory? What might it mean to conceive of amnemonic systems of rhetorical training? And how, throughout the history of rhetoric, have processes of exclusion challenged memory-making practices? Canonization, to name one system, is a practice of inclusion (memory) through exclusion (forgetting), and it will always favor what is at hand.[4]

Mnemocide is an act that kills memory, such as book burning. For all the spectacular acts of violence meted out on repositories of cultural memory, however, there are many mundane acts that perform far more damage over time. For instance, plenty of ancient material does not survive simply because it was not copied in sufficient numbers. Sappho, herself a casualty of acts that withheld memory, was acutely aware of the importance of recollection: "I say someone in another time will remember [*mnasesthai*] us."[5] Hilary Ilkay estimates that "[the] poetic corpus of Sappho . . . is but a fractured shard of what once existed."[6] The ellipses of editors are haunting reminders of pasts for which we lack centuries of commemoration. Still, Ilkay maintains, "Even in the stark silences of bracketed text, Sappho speaks to her characters and to us with a clear, resonant voice."[7]

Amnēsia, then, corresponds to ongoing conversations about marginalized rhetors and their forgotten, overlooked, or recovered texts.[8] Similarly, the consequences of homophobia, transphobia, patriarchy, racism, and their intersections are abundant "archival absences," which conspire with other lacks to keep too much of the past in a state without memory.[9]

—CORY GERATHS

apistos (adjective; untrustworthy, unbelievable); *apistia* (noun; distrust, unbelief, the state of being without belief)

As established in the introduction, *pistis* is usually associated with the *Rhetoric* of Aristotle (though it appears in the *Rhetoric to Alexander*, too), since that is the word he uses to describe what *ēthos*, *pathos*, and *logos* create: trust, faith, or belief.[10] *Peri Apistōn* (literally, On the Unbelievable), a work attributed to Palaephatus, likely a contemporary of Aristotle, demystifies a whole procession of seemingly improbable stories, but the demystification is of a particular kind. As translator Jacob Stern puts it, Palaephatus's mode of "historical rationalization" has as its "fundamental purpose not the creating of disbelief, but rather the creating of belief" by getting at the likely and thus believable cause behind a story driven to bogus extremes.[11] Palaephatus takes on the stories of the Trojan horse, the walking statues of Daedalus, the fashioning of Pandora, and the three-headed hellhound Cerberus, to name but a few.[12] For each, he substitutes a believable explanation for the unbelievable tale while continuing to hold a cultural place for the objects and people in question.

Though *apistos* (untrustworthy, unbelievable) and *apistia* (distrust, unbelief) are nowhere to be seen in rhetorical theory and criticism today, that is not to say the disposition to which they refer is entirely absent. For instance, in their article "The Unnaturalistic Enthymeme: Figuration, Interpretation, and Critique After Digital Mediation," Damien Smith Pfister and Carly Woods focus on viewers of digital images who display a savvy distrust of the veracity of any digital image.[13] Pfister and Woods compare the method used by distrusting viewers to recognize and categorize the unrealism of a given digital image to the ancient *quadripartita ratio* of addition, subtraction, transposition, and substitution.[14] In a way, these viewers resemble Palaephatus: they see an image that ought to be considered unbelievable and they try to work back to its starting conditions. Though Pfister and Woods reflect on the public dangers of "skepticism in the visual realm," they also underscore the importance of disbelief within what they call a "hypersophistic visual culture" marked by speed, novelty, and a huge expansion in the number of image creators and viewers.[15]

Consider, too, the prospects of an "apistemic rhetoric"—though "apistemic" will admittedly make Greek readers cringe—that would pull from debates about epistemic rhetoric, which centered on what kind of knowledge rhetoric makes and how.[16] If we read apistemic rhetoric as a set of communicative attitudes and actions based in a state of being "without trust," then it could be parsed any number of ways.[17] The essential point is that *apistos* (untrustworthy, unbelievable) and *apistia* (distrust, unbelief) urge not the disavowal of trust and belief but rather the discovery of the conditions under which trust and belief are bestowed or withheld.

—MICHELE KENNERLY

***asylum* (noun; 2. a place of retreat and security; 3. (a) the protection or security afforded by an asylum. (b) a protection from arrest and extradition given especially to political refugees by a nation or by an embassy or other agency enjoying freedom from what is required by law for most people)**[18]

Right now, in the summer of 2020, the right to seek asylum is in peril around the world.[19] A global pandemic and the movement-forcing results of racism, colonialism, and capitalism have prompted governments to use nationalism and purported security concerns to all but close their borders. As stipulated by Article 14 of the United Nations Declaration of Human Rights, the right to seek asylum is a human right.[20] Generally, the condition of asylum requires two elements: a threat of persecution based on race, gender, religion, or political affiliation from the home nation, and the hospitality of a host nation to grant refuge from those threats.[21] Though anyone has the right to seek asylum, a host nation is not obliged to grant the petition. What is withheld when asylum is not granted? While alpha privatives often withhold something desirable, in the case of the word *asylum*, privation works differently.

Asylum originates from the alpha-privative ancient Greek adjective ἄσῦλος, meaning to be protected from seizure (from ἀ [without] and σύλη [seizure, plunder]).[22] The related ancient Greek word *asulon* denotes a place of refuge, usually an inviolate sacred area. The privative "a" stresses the right *not* to be removed, leading to the right to seek refuge and ask for protection from violence. In its very constitution, asylum suggests that seizure—disrespect, violence, capture—is the prevailing approach to something or someone unprotected and vulnerable.[23]

Today, arguments originating from the ancient sacred duty of protection have been replaced by arguments that employ the language of "deterrence, prevention, control."[24] Elena Isayev asks: Why and how did nations come to value immobility and hostility over mobility and hospitality?[25] She ends with a powerful call: "Being inhospitable is what needs to be explained."[26] Given the makings of the word *asylum* itself, this call seems counterintuitive, and that gives it vitality and truth.[27] Crucial, too, to understand are the varied mechanisms driving the holding and interning of would-be im/migrants, refugees, and asylees. Such violent forms of seizure pervert the notion of asylum, etymologically, legally, and morally.[28] Through what rhetorical acts are they sustained? How can they be challenged and changed?[29]

—ALESSANDRA VON BURG

asynchronous **(adjective; not simultaneous or concurrent in time: not synchronous; of, used in, or being digital communication [as between computers] in which there is no timing requirement for transmission and**

in which the start of each character is individually signaled by the transmitting device)[30]

To be synchronous is to be simultaneous, to co-occur, to coincide. Colloquially, people draw on the phrases "in sync" or "out of sync" to register their felt sense of how their own rhythms match up with others and their broader ecologies. Syncing a phone with a computer brings the devices into a relationship of simultaneity, so that the files on one match the files on the other. Synchronous communication is often thought of as a precondition for community, especially in antiquity, when public speech forged common senses of the world and ancient peoples' place in it. As Keith Lloyd observes, Aristotle's enthymeme is reliant on a "relatively synchronous pattern" of reasoning—a simultaneous gathering together of cultural assumptions and argument—that differs from more diachronic, archetypal patterns developed in ancient India and elsewhere.[31] What the enthymeme does on the local level, logistical media like clocks and calendars do on more macro scales.[32] Nicole Allen's study of national calendars demonstrates how they function as political myths to "synchronize social rhythms" through the designation of official holidays.[33] Synchronization is closely tied to digitalization, with "digital rhetorical performance . . . increasingly synchronous" on, for example, social networking platforms like Twitter.[34] It is also tied to capitalism, which requires different business units to synchronize their activities in order to maximize profits. The convergence of digitality and capitalism leads Bernard Stiegler to warn of the dangers of "hypersynchronization" with inhuman(e) values of efficiency, standardization, and presentism.[35]

To be *asynchronous*, then, implies nonsimultaneity, a divergence from co-incidence. The alpha privative opens up numerous possibilities for alternatives to synchronization, as many different temporal relations are possible under the not-synchronous. Consider John Hartley's frequencies of public writing as a catalog of *asynchronicity*: while high frequency communication (exemplified by Twitter) approaches the maximally synchronic, medium and low frequency communication model *asynchronic* temporalities.[36] The gap between production and reception increases from mid-frequency writing, like monthly magazines or academic journals, through low-frequency writing, like monuments and ruins. Archaeological remnants of ancient civilizations are the most *asynchronous* human communication we have access to, introducing radical problems of interpretation and radical opportunities for invention. While Hartley's frequencies offer different registers of *asynchronous* communication tied to *chronos*, there is also a kairotic dimension to the *asynchronous*. Amid the worldwide COVID-19 pandemic of spring 2020, when stay-at-home orders and social-distancing norms made synchronous contact with others more difficult, "asynchronous" suddenly adjectivalized a range of activities: work, instruction, telehealth, and more. The capacity to be asynchronous opened up a new dimension of privilege, as white-collar workers were able to shift to a new temporal arrangement with more flexibility than workers in warehouses, factories, and on the front line of pandemic response. Pandemic asynchrony (temporarily) interrupted the hypersynchronization of digital capitalism, forcing a larger cultural conversation about the perceived benefits of synchrony. Some advocates note that asynchronous learning is posited as better for students with different learning styles, while others observe that the differential spread of COVID-19 produced "asynchronous grief" that made developing a coherent global strategy for responding to the pandemic more difficult.[37] Cultural crises often disrupt synchronous ways of doing things, inverting our normative relationship to temporality and each other in ways that offer new possibilities. Thus, the asynchronous, following the logic of the alpha privative, suggests not just a denial of the synchronous, but an opening up of temporal potential beyond the synchronic.

—DAMIEN SMITH PFISTER

atelēs (adjective; without end, unending, not brought to an end or issue, as in a task unaccomplished); *atelos* (adjective; free from tax being taken, net; uninitiated)

Atelēs/atelos can be traced in both classical and critical cultural usage, starting with its root *telos*, "accomplishment of an aim," being most commonly used in English. Classical rhetorical theory positions *telos* in terms of rhetoric's genre and purpose. Deliberative rhetoric's *telos* is the good; forensic rhetoric's is justice; and epideictic rhetoric's is virtue or its opposite. The purpose of rhetoric is sometimes getting termed persuasion but more appropriately termed practical judgment, *phronēsis*. Whether in genre or purpose, the *telos* is to be accomplished. In classical rhetorical theory, to be *atelos* is to be a failure.

Negative associations of *atelēs* in the classical rhetorical tradition change as critical, post-humanisms and new feminist materialism mingle with Rhetorical Studies. The appearance of the term is rare, but the concept of being free from a *telos,* or figuring *telos* otherwise as an unending process rather than a fixed end to achieve, is prominent across this theorizing. Raymie McKerrow's critical rhetoric is a praxis that must remain nomadic, an act without end. The critic must remain committed to going wherever necessary to critique structures of power.[38] While affirming critical rhetoric, pushback comes in defense of *telos.* Maurice Charland argues that if engaged in endless critique of power, the critic "has no place to take a stand."[39] Kent Ono and John Sloop call in response to critical rhetoric for a commitment to *telos* so that the critic can move from offering critique of power to effecting change in present conditions.[40]

On the second and third definitions of *atlēs/atelos,* I have given an account of *atelos* as a rhetorical energy offering freedom from being taken.[41] To be free from deductions can refer to concepts of personhood and not just money. For example, what is taken, who is taxed, when whiteness is the rhetorical ecology of civic and professional life, of personhood? Starting with those particular terms, Bryan J. McCann, Ashley Noel Mack, and Rico Self expose what is taken, Black personhood, and what is taxed, Blackness. Being *atelic* supports being anti-racist, whether in the case of being free from being taken or from being initiated into white supremacy.[42]

As "being human" has been articulated historically as a *telos* of a liberal arts education, posthumanist and new materialist theories take issue, questioning that *telos,* or at least complicating "the human" by way of entanglements with machines, animals, matter, and meaning.[43] Their *atelic* turns do not yet go far enough. Black feminism and border materialism intervene to rupture the *telos* of "being human" exposing it as a trope in a psychically and physically violent ecology of antiblackness, misogynoir, and *feminicidio.*[44] Rupturing this *telos* of "being human" shows the contradictions of "the human" *telos* as a construct of patriarchy, capitalism, colonialism, and neoliberalism. Being *atelic* in action and imagination serves as a corrective in the "order of being" and offers what Saidiya Hartman attributes to Zakiyyah Iman Jackson's work, "a generative disordering of being, inhabiting other senses of the world, imagining the field of relation in ceaseless flux and directionless becoming."[45]

—MARI LEE MIFSUD

atropos (adjective; unchangeable, eternal, inflexible); *atropia* (noun; inflexibility)

While the essays in this collection press familiar rhetorical terms into new and uncertain realms, *atropia* (formed from *a* + *tropos*, from the verb *trepō*, "turn") and its adjectival form, *atropos*, fundamentally resist change. Hesiod names Atropos among the three Moirai ("Fates"), along with her sisters Clotho and Lachesis.[46] According to Plato, Clotho spun the thread of life, Lachesis measured out the thread to the appropriate length, and Atropos, the inflexible one, made the final fateful cut.[47] He also mapped each of the Fates onto a different period of time: Lachesis he associated with the past, Clotho the present, and Atropos the future.[48] Atropos, then, is determinism personified.[49]

On a universal scale, Jane Sutton speaks to the relationship between *atropia* and rhetoric itself. Sutton notes that, in his *Rhetoric*, Aristotle navigated between two competing philosophical worldviews of the time, namely, Heraclitus's aphoristic *panta rhei* ("everything flows") and Parmenides' belief in the unchanging *to eon* ("what is").[50] Aristotle employed a "model of rest," the effect of which was "a geocentric consciousness that animated change in terms of *telos*."[51] He characterized change as a movement that arrives at an appropriate end (*telos*) and, therefore, a state of rest. This compromise between movement and stillness, she contends, can be observed in the *Rhetoric*, in which Aristotle connected rhetoric, "long associated, in part through the sophists, with flow, relative change, and uncertainty—to an earth at rest so as to rouse the art to its systematization."[52]

Thus, we should question the inflexibility of *atropia*. While *atropia* is an uncommon word in ancient Greek texts, *tropos* and the modern "trope" are ubiquitous, in Rhetorical Studies and otherwise. For example, regarding the four ostensibly atropic "master tropes"—metaphor, metonymy, synecdoche, and irony—Randy Allen Harris proposes that *irony* should be replaced by *antithesis*.[53] Demonstrating the seemingly unyielding dominance of "master tropes" within theory even more poignantly, Henry Louis Gates Jr. called *signifyin(g)* "the slave's trope," which "subsumes other rhetorical tropes, including metaphor, metonymy, synecdoche, and irony (the "master" tropes), and also hyperbole, litotes and metalepsis. . . . To this list, we could easily add aporia, chiasmus, and catachresis, all of which are used in the ritual of signifying."[54] In this way, we see that the primary turns (*tropoi*) of phrase are at once recalcitrant and changeable, even when they are used to hint at unwavering truths.[55]

—BESS R. H. MYERS

NOTES

1. The literature is vast. Some of it is cited in the notes.

2. For example, Bradford Vivian draws upon *lēthē* and *alētheia* in reviewing Western conceptions of forgetting in *Public Forgetting: The Rhetoric and Politics of Beginning Again* (University Park: Penn State University Press, 2010), 19–38; Nathan Stormer titularly references amnesia, though he focuses on *anamnēsis* (remembering) in "In Living Memory: Abortion as Cultural Amnesia," *Quarterly Journal of Speech* 88, no. 3 (2002): 265–383. *Amnēsia* appears rarely in ancient Greek texts, and amnesia comes to have a medical meaning in the nineteenth century, per the OED.

3. *Imagines* and memory palaces, for example, appear first in the *Rhetorica ad Herennium*, which refers to memory as "the guardian of all the parts of rhetoric" (3.28). Wordplay, too, is important to memory; note the text's reference to "a ram's testicles" (*testiculos arietinos*) as a ballsy mnemonic device for recalling witnesses (*testium*) (3.33). [Cicero,] *Rhetorica ad Herennium*, trans. by Harry Caplan (Cambridge: Harvard University Press, 1954).

4. Classicist Verena Schulz is working on a project called "Forms of Forgetting in Antiquity" that asks such questions of ancient Greece and Rome. See, too, Bradford Vivian, "Deletion and Damnatio: Theses on the Eventfulness of Forgetting," *Currents in Electronic Literacy* (2012), https://currents.dwrl.utexas.edu/2012/deletion-and-damnatio-memoriae-theses-on-the-eventfulness-of-forgetting.html; Dave Tell, *Remembering Emmett Till* (Chicago: University of Chicago Press, 2019), on the politics, economics, and geographies of remembering and forgetting.

5. Sappho, fragment 147, in *Sappho: A New Translation of the Complete Works*, ed. and trans. Diane J. Rayor (New York: Cambridge University Press, 2014), 81; The Digital Sappho: Text and Commentary, https://digitalsappho.org/fragments/fr118–68/.

6. Hilary Ilkay, "Mixing Memory and Desire: Helen's Eidolon in Sappho 16," EIDOLON, April 26, 2016, https://eidolon.pub/mixing-memory-and-desire-helens-eidolon-in-sappho-16-bbe2243b0113.

7. Ibid. See also Susan C. Jarratt, "Sappho's Memory," *Rhetoric Society Quarterly* 32, no. 1 (2002): 11–43; as well as Melissa Broder, *The Pisces: A Novel* (New York: Hogarth, 2018).

8. See, among many examples, the recovery of queer and transgender rhetorics, e.g., Thomas R. Dunn, *Queerly Remembered: Rhetorics for Representing the GLBTQ Past* (Columbia: University of South Carolina Press, 2016); K. J. Rawson, "The Rhetorical Power of Archival Description: Classifying Images of Gender Transgression," *Rhetoric Society Quarterly* 48, no. 4 (2018): 327–51.

9. Pamela VanHaitsma, "Between Archival Absence and Information Abundance: Reconstructing Sallie Holley's Abolitionist Rhetoric Through Digital Surrogates and Metadata," *Quarterly Journal of Speech* 106, no. 1 (2020): 25–47.

10. For *pistis* in Aristotle and the *Rhetoric to Alexander*, see Manfred Kraus, "How to Classify Means of Persuasion: The *Rhetoric to Alexander* and Aristotle on *Pisteis*," *Rhetorica* 29, no. 3 (Summer 2011): 263–79.

11. Jacob Stern, introduction to Palaephatus, *On Unbelievable Tales*, ed. and trans. Jacob Stern (Wauconda, IL: Bolchazy-Carducci, 1996), 8–9.

12. Palaephatus, *On Unbelievable Tales*, 47–48; 52; 66; 71–72.

13. Damien Smith Pfister and Carly S. Woods, "The Unnaturalistic Enthymeme: Figuration, Interpretation, and Critique After

Digital Mediation," *Argumentation and Advocacy* 52 (Spring 2016): 236–53.

14. Ibid., 242.

15. Ibid., 245 and 251.

16. It starts with Robert L. Scott, "On Viewing Rhetoric as Epistemic," *Communication Studies* 18.1 (1967): 9–17. (Well, it starts well before Scott, if you want to get technical about it.)

17. Other crucial interlocutors would be: Debra Hawhee, *Rhetoric in Tooth and Claw: Animals, Language, Sensation* (Chicago, University of Chicago Press, 2016), chapter 4; Dana Cloud, *Reality Bites: Rhetoric and the Circulation of Truth Claims in U.S. Political Culture* (Columbus: Ohio State University Press, 2018); Jenny Rice, *Awful Archives: Conspiracy Theory, Rhetoric, and Acts of Evidence* (Columbus: Ohio State University Press, 2020); and, of course, Caddie Alford's chapter on *adoxa* in this volume.

18. Merriam-Webster Dictionary, s.v. *asylum*, https://www.merriam-webster.com/dictionary/asylum.

19. E.g., Nicole Narea, "Trump Is Quietly Gutting the Asylum System Amid the Pandemic," *Vox*, June 12, 2020, https://www.vox.com/2020/6/12/21288063/trump-immigration-asylum-border-regulation.

20. See the full text of the United Nations Universal Declaration of Human Rights at http://www.un.org/en/universal-declaration-human-rights. Work on asylum, refugees, and im/migrants is growing in Rhetorical Studies. See, e.g., Alessandra Von Burg, "Citizenship Islands: The Ongoing Emergency in the Mediterranean Sea," *Media and Communication* 7, no. 2 (2019): 218–29; Noor Ghazal Aswad, "Biased Neutrality: The Symbolic Construction of the Syrian Refugee in the *New York Times*," *Critical Studies in Media Communication* 36, no. 4 (2019): 357–75; Sara L. McKinnon, *Gendered Asylum: Race and Violence in U.S. Law and Politics* (Champaign: University of Illinois Press, 2016); Johanna Hartelius, ed., *The Rhetoric of U.S. Immigration: Identity, Community, Otherness* (University Park: Penn State University Press, 2015); Anne Teresa Demo, "Sovereignty Discourse and Contemporary Immigration Politics," *Quarterly Journal of Speech* 91, no. 3 (2005): 291–311.

21. *Asylum*, therefore, relates to *atopos* ("without a place") and *anostos* ("without a homecoming), but it differs importantly, since *asylum* relies on a notion of a place that is not (yet) home and that is set apart via law or custom from other places.

22. OED, s.v. *asylum*. In the fourteenth century, asylum entered English from Latin, and it entered Latin from ancient Greek. See Robert Garland, *Wandering Greeks: The Ancient Greek Diaspora from the Age of Homer to the Death of Alexander the Great* (Princeton: Princeton University Press, 2014), 115; Paula Perlman, *Ancient Greek Law in the 21st Century* (Austin: University of Texas Press, 2018), 94. For connections between exile and asylum practices in ancient Greece and in twenty-first-century nation-states, see Benjamin Gray, "From Exile of Citizens to Deportation of Non-Citizens: Ancient Greece as a Mirror to Illuminate a Modern Transition," *Citizenship Studies* 15, no. 5 (2011): 565–82.

23. Saskia Sassen, *Expulsions: Brutality and Complexity in the Global Economy* (Cambridge: Harvard University Press), 2014.

24. Heather Johnson, *Borders, Asylum, and Global Non-Citizenship: The Other Side of the Fence* (Cambridge: Cambridge University Press, 2014), 88.

25. Elena Isayev, "Hospitality: A Timeless Measure of Who We Are?" *Migration and Society: Advances in Research* 1 (2018): 7–21; see also Etienne Balibar, "Toward a Diasporic Citizen? From Internationalism to Cosmopolitics," in *The Creolization of Theory*, ed. Françoise Lionnet and Shu-mei Shih (Durham: Duke University Press, 2011), 207–25.

26. Isayev, "Hospitality," 18.

27. Arjun Appadurai argues that one challenge is that the stories of refugees "do not fit the narrative requirements of modern nation-states" (561), in Arjun Appadurai, "Traumatic Exit, Identity Narratives, and the Ethics of Hospitality," *Television and New Media* 20, no. 6 (2019): 558–65, at 558.

28. See, e.g., Andrew Jefferson, Simon Turner, Steffen Jensen, "Introduction: On Stuckness and Sites of Confinement," *Ethnos* 84, no. 1 (2019): 1–13; John Washington, *The Dispossessed: A Story of Asylum at the US-Mexican Border and Beyond* (New York:

Verso, 2020); Lisa A. Flores, "Stoppage and the Racialized Rhetorics of Mobility," *Western Journal of Communication* 84, no. 3 (2020): 247–63.

29. Betsy Hartmann, "Rethinking Climate Refugees and Climate Conflict: Rhetoric, Reality and the Politics of Policy Discourse," *Journal of International Development* 22, no. 2 (2010): 233–46; Anne Teresa Demo, *Moving Subjects: Migration and Moral Suasion in Immersive Documentary* (Columbia: Ohio University Press, 2021).

30. See https://www.merriam-webster.com/dictionary/asynchronous.

31. Keith Lloyd, "Culture and Rhetorical Patterns: Mining the Rich Relations Between Aristotle's Enthymeme and Example and India's Nyāya Method," *Rhetorica* 24, no. 1 (2011): 76–105, 77.

32. John Durham Peters, *The Marvelous Clouds: Toward a Philosophy of Elemental Media* (Chicago: University of Chicago Press, 2015): 37, 175–7.

33. Nicole Allen, "A Reconsidering Chronos: Chronistic Criticism and the first 'Iraqi National Calendar," *Quarterly Journal of Speech* 104, no. 4 (2018): 361–83, 362.

34. J. E. Porter, "Recovering Delivery for Digital Rhetoric," *Computers and Composition* 26 (2009): 207–24, at 213.

35. Bernard Stiegler, *Symbolic Misery*, vol. 1, *The Hyperindustrial Epoch*, trans. Barnaby Norman (Cambridge: Polity, 2014).

36. John Hartley, "The Frequencies of Public Writing," in *Democracy and New Media*, ed. Henry Jenkins and David Thorburn (Cambridge: MIT Press, 2003): 247–69.

37. S. A. Applin, "The Chaos of Asynchronous Grief," *Allegra Lab*, May 15, 2020, https://allegralaboratory.net/the-chaos-of-asynchronous-grief.

38. Raymie E. McKerrow, "Critical Rhetoric: Theory and Praxis," *Communication Monographs* 56, no. 2 (1989): 91–111.

39. Maurice Charland, "Finding a Horizon and Telos: The Challenge to Critical Rhetoric," *Quarterly Journal of Speech* 77 (1991): 71–74, at 71.

40. Kent A. Ono and John M. Sloop, "Commitment to Telos—a Sustained Critical Rhetoric," *Communication Monographs* 59, no. 1 (1992): 54.

41. Mari Lee Mifsud, "On Network," in *Ancient Rhetorics and Digital Networks*, ed. Michele Kennerly and Damien Smith Pfister (Tuscaloosa: University of Alabama Press, 2018), 28–47.

42. Bryan J. McCann, Ashley Noel Mack, and Rico Self, "Communication's Quest for Whiteness: the Racial Politics of Disciplinary Legitimacy," *Communication and Critical/Cultural Studies* 17, no. 2 (June 2020): 243–52.

43. Rosie Bradiotti, *The Posthuman* (Cambridge: Polity, 2013); Donna Haraway, "A Cyborg Manifesto: Science, Technology, and Socialist Feminism in the Late Twentieth Century," in *Simians, Cyborgs, and Women: The Reinvention of Nature* (New York: Routledge, 1991), 149–81.

44. Zakiyyah Iman Jackson, *becoming human* (New York: New York University Press, 2020); Nina Maria Lozano, *Not One More! Feminicidio on the Border* (Columbus: Ohio State University Press, 2019).

45. Saidiya Hartman, as quoted in blurb of Jackson, *becoming human*.

46. Hesiod, *Theogony; Works and Days; Testimonia*, trans. Glenn W. Most (Cambridge: Harvard University Press, 2018), lines 217–18 and 905.

47. Plato, *Laws*, vol. 1, trans. R. G. Bury (Cambridge: Harvard University Press, 1926), 12.960c. The division of labor among Moirai seems to be a philosophical distinction invented perhaps around the time of Plato rather than an archaic convention.

48. Plato, *Republic*, vol. 2, trans. Chris Emlyn-Jones and William Preddy (Cambridge: Harvard University Press, 2013), 10.617c.

49. On climatic determinism, see Liu Ye, "Between the Tropics: The Genealogies of the Empires and the Revolutions," trans. Orion Martin, *Times Museum Journal*, no. 1, https://timesmuseum.org/en/journal/south-of-the-south/between-the-tropics-the-genealogies-of-the-empires-and-the-revolutions. Ye notes how the invention of the "tropics" as a climatic zone was essential to the colonial project.

50. Jane S. Sutton, "The Earth Is Not at Rest and Neither Should Be Rhetoric," in Jane S. Sutton and Mari Lee Mifsud, *A Revolution in Tropes: Alloiostrophic Rhetoric* (Lanham: Lexington Books, 2015): 19–46.

51. Ibid., 28.

52. Ibid.

53. Randy Allen Harris, "The Fourth Master Trope, Antithesis," *Advances in the History of Rhetoric* 22, no. 1 (2019): 1–26. I cannot help noting the standing-in-place-of-ness of "antithesis" (*anti*, "in opposition to" or "in the place of" + *thesis*, "setting").

54. Henry Louis Gates Jr., "The 'Blackness of Blackness': A Critique of the Sign and the Signifying Monkey," *Critical Inquiry* 9, no. 4 (June 1983): 685–723, at 686–87.

55. On the changing opinions of individuals, see David Lévystone, "Socrates' Versatile Rhetoric and the Soul of the Crowd," *Rhetorica* 38, no. 2 (2020): 135–55.

BIBLIOGRAPHY

Aelian. *Historical Miscellany*. Translated by N. G. Wilson. Cambridge: Harvard University Press, 1997.

Aeschylus. *Oresteia: Agamemnon. Libation-Bearers. Eumenides.* Translated by Alan H. Sommerstein. Loeb Classical Library 146. Cambridge: Harvard University Press, 2009.

Ahmed, Sara. *Living a Feminist Life*. Durham: Duke University Press, 2018.

Alexander, Jonathan, and Jacqueline Rhodes. *Sexual Rhetorics: Methods, Identities, Publics.* New York: Routledge, 2015.

Algra, Keimpe. *Concepts of Space in Greek Thought.* New York: Brill, 1995.

Allen, Danielle. *Talking to Strangers: Anxieties of Citizenship Since Brown v. Board of Education.* Chicago: University of Chicago Press, 2004.

Allen, Ira J. *The Ethical Fantasy of Rhetorical Theory.* Pittsburgh: University of Pittsburgh Press, 2018.

Allen, Nicole. "A Reconsidering Chronos: Chronistic Criticism and the First 'Iraqi National Calendar.'" *Quarterly Journal of Speech* 104, no. 4 (2018): 361–83.

Anderson, Benedict. *Imagined Communities: Reflections on the Origin and Spread of Nationalism.* Rev. ed. New York: Verso, 2016.

Anderson, Dana. *Identity's Strategy: Rhetorical Selves in Conversion.* Columbia: University of South Carolina Press, 2007.

Anderson, Elijah. "The White Space." *Sociology of Race and Ethnicity* 1, no. 1 (2015): 10–21.

Andrejevic, Mark. "Surveillance in the Digital Enclosure." *Communication Review* 10, no. 4 (2007): 295–317.

"Apathy Disappearing." *The North American Review*, 154. New York: North America Review, 1918.

Appadurai, Arjun. "Traumatic Exit, Identity Narratives, and the Ethics of Hospitality." *Television and New Media* 20, no. 6 (2019): 558–65.

Applin, S. A. "The Chaos of Asynchronous Grief." *Allegra Lab*, May 15, 2020. https://allegralaboratory.net/the-chaos-of-asynchronous-grief.

Arendt, Hannah. *Eichmann in Jerusalem: A Report on the Banality of Evil.* New York: Viking Press, 1963.

———. *The Human Condition.* Chicago: University of Chicago Press, 1998.

———. "Philosophy and Politics." *Social Research* 57, no. 1 (1990): 73–103.

Aristotelis. *Ars rhetorica*. Edited by W. D. Ross. Oxford: Oxford University Press, 1959.

———. *De Arte Poetica Liber*. Edited by Rudolphus Kassel. Oxford: Oxford University Press, 1965.

Aristotle. *De Anima*. Translated by C. D. C. Reeve. Cambridge, MA: Hackett, 2017.

———. *Nicomachean Ethics*. Translated by H. Rackham. Cambridge: Harvard University Press, 1975.

———. *On Rhetoric: A Theory of Civic Discourse*. Translated by George A. Kennedy. New York: Oxford University Press, 1991.

———. *Politics*. Translated by H. Rackham. Cambridge: Harvard University Press, 1994.

———. *Topics*. Translated by Hugh Tredennick. Cambridge: Harvard University Press, 1960.

Arnhart, Larry. *Aristotle on Political Reasoning: A Commentary on the Rhetoric.* DeKalb: Northern Illinois University Press, 1981.

Arnold, Carroll. "Johnstone's 'Wedge' and Theory of Rhetoric." *Philosophy and Rhetoric* 20, no. 2 (1987): 118–28.

Aswad, Noor Ghazal. "Biased Neutrality: The Symbolic Construction of the Syrian Refugee in the *New York Times*." *Critical Studies in Media Communication* 36, no. 4 (2019): 357–75.

Atwill, Janet M. *Rhetoric Reclaimed: Aristotle and the Liberal Arts Tradition.* Ithaca: Cornell University Press, 1998.

Austin, J. L. *How to Do Things with Words.* Cambridge: Harvard University Press, 1962.

Avilez, Gershun. "Staging Social Death: Alienation and Embodiment in Aishah Rahman's *Unfinished Women.*" In *The Psychic Hold of Slavery: Legacies in American Expressive Culture,* edited by Soyica Diggs Colbert, Robert J. Patterson, and Aida Levy-Hussen, 107–24. New Brunswick: Rutgers University Press, 2016.

Axel, B. K. "The Diasporic Imaginary." *Public Culture* 14, no. 2 (April 1, 2002): 411–28.

Badham, John, dir. *WarGames.* Beverly Hills, CA: MGM, 1983.

Bailey, Moya. "They Aren't Talking About Me . . ." *Crunk Feminist Collective,* March 14, 2010. http://www.crunkfeminist collective.com/2010/03/14/they-arent -talking-about-me.

Balibar, Etienne. "Toward a Diasporic Citizen? From Internationalism to Cosmopolitics." In *The Creolization of Theory,* edited by Françoise Lionnet and Shu-mei Shih, 207–25. Durham: Duke University Press, 2011.

Ballif, Michelle. "Introduction: Keywords; A Prelude and an Appendix." *Rhetoric Society Quarterly* 48, no. 3 (2018): 232–33.

———, ed. *Theorizing Histories of Rhetoric.* Carbondale: Southern Illinois University Press, 2013.

Barad, Karen. "Posthumanist Performativity: How Matter Comes to Matter." *Signs: Journal of Women in Culture and Society* 28, no. 3 (2003): 801–31.

Barrett, A. Igona. *Black Ass: A Novel.* Minneapolis: Graywolf Press, 2015.

Barthes, Roland. *A Lover's Discourse: Fragments.* Translated by Richard Howard. New York: Hill and Wang, 2010 [1977].

———. *The Semiotic Challenge.* Translated by Richard Howard. New York: Hill and Wang, 1988.

Beard, Mary. *Women in Power: A Manifesto.* New York: Liveright, 2017.

Beecher, Catharine. "Essay on Slavery and Abolitionism with Reference to the Duty of American Females." 1837. http://utc .iath.virginia.edu/abolitn/grimkehp .html.

Beekes, Robert. *Etymological Dictionary of Greek.* Vol. 1. Leiden: Brill, 2010.

Bensimon, Estela Mara, and Lindsey Malcom. *Confronting Equity Issues on Campus: Implementing the Equity Scorecard in Theory and Practice.* Sterling, VA: Stylus, 2012.

Bessette, Jean. "Making Space." *Journal for the History of Rhetoric* 23, no. 3 (2020): 366–69.

Bhabha, Homi K. *The Location of Culture.* New York: Routledge, 1994.

Black Pride RVA. "Black and Prideful LGBTQ+ March." Twitter, June 11, 2020, 9:15 PM. https://twitter.com/Black PrideRVA/status/1271249646845931523 /photo/1.

Bond, Sarah E. "The Origins of White Supremacists' Fear of Replacement." *Hyperallergic,* August 22, 2019. https:// hyperallergic.com/514034/the-origins-of -white-supremacists-fear-of-replacement.

———. "Why We Need to Start Seeing the Classical World in Color." *Hyperallergic,* June 7, 2017. https://hyperallergic.com /383776/why-we-need-to-start-seeing -the-classical-world-in-color.

Bonifazi, Anna. "Inquiring into *Nostos* and Its Cognates." *American Journal of Philology* 130 (2009): 481–510.

Bourdieu, Pierre. Preface to *The Suffering of the Immigrant,* by Abdelmalek Sayad, translated by David Macey, xi–xiv. Malden, MA: Polity, 2004.

Bouteldja, Houria. *Whites, Jews, and Us: Toward a Politics of Revolutionary Love.* Translated by Rachel Valinsky. South Pasadena, CA: Semiotext(e), 2016.

Boyle, Casey Andrew. *Rhetoric as a Posthuman Practice.* Columbia: Ohio State University Press, 2018.

Bradiotti, Rosie. *The Posthuman.* Cambridge: Polity, 2013.

Bradshaw, Jonathan L. "Rhetorical Exhaustion and the Ethics of Amplification." *Computers and Composition* 56 (June 2020).

Brauw, Michael de. "The Parts of Speech." In *A Companion to Greek Rhetoric,* edited by Ian Worthington, 187–202. Malden: Blackwell, 2007.

Broder, Melissa. *The Pisces: A Novel.* New York: Hogarth, 2018.

Brookey, Robert Alan, and Kristopher L. Cannon. "Sex Lives in Second Life." *Critical Studies in Media Communication* 26, no. 2 (2009): 145–64.
Brown, James J., Jr. "Epicrisis for An Epic Crisis." *Amodern 9: Techniques and Technologies*, April 9, 2020. https://amodern.net/article/epicrisis.
Burke, Kenneth. *Attitudes Toward History*. Los Altos, CA: Hermes 1959.
———. *A Grammar of Motives*. Berkeley: University of California Press, 1945.
———. *Language as Symbolic Action*. Berkeley: University of California Press, 1966.
———. *Rhetoric of Motives*. Berkeley: University of California Press, 1969.
Burke, Kenneth, with Bernard Brock and Parke G. Burgess. "Dramatism as Ontology or Epistemology: A Symposium." *Communication Quarterly* 33, no. 1 (Winter 1985): 17–33.
Butler, Judith. *Gender Trouble*. 10th anniversary ed. New York: Routledge, 1999.
Butler, Samuel. "Hudibras." In *The Logic and Rhetoric of Hudibras*, lines 25–26. https://www.bartleby.com/380/poem/361.html.
Cacho, Lisa Marie. *Social Death: Racialized Rightlessness and the Criminalization of the Unprotected*. New York: New York University Press, 2012.
Cameron, James, dir. *Avatar*. Los Angeles: 20th Century Fox, 2009.
Campbell, Timothy C. *The Techne of Giving: Cinema and the Generous Form of Life*. New York: Fordham University Press, 2017.
Camper, Martin. "The Future of the History of Rhetoric is Religious." *Journal for the History of Rhetoric* 23, no. 1 (2020): 104–5.
Carey, Christopher. "'Artless' Proofs in Aristotle and the Orators." In *Oxford Readings in the Attic Orators*, edited by Edwin Carawan, 229–46. Oxford: Oxford University Press, 2007.
Carson, Anne. *Eros the Bittersweet: An Essay*. Washington, DC: Center for Hellenic Studies, 1986.
Casey, Edward S. *Getting Back into Place: Toward a Renewed Understanding of the Place-World*. Bloomington: Indiana University Press, 1993.
———. *Imagining: A Phenomenological Study*. 2nd ed. Bloomington: Indiana University Press, 2000.
———. "Public Memory in Place and Time." In *Framing Public Memory*, edited by Kendall R. Phillips, 17–44. Tuscaloosa: University of Alabama Press, 2004.
———. *The World at a Glance*. Bloomington: Indiana University Press, 2007.
Cervenak, Sarah Jane. *Wandering: Philosophical Performances of Racial and Sexual Freedom*. Durham: Duke University Press, 2014.
Charland, Maurice. "Finding a Horizon and Telos: The Challenge to Critical Rhetoric." *Quarterly Journal of Speech* 77 (1991): 71–74.
Chávez, Karma R. "Beyond Inclusion: Rethinking Rhetoric's Historical Narrative." *Quarterly Journal of Speech* 101, no. 1 (2015): 162–72.
———. *Queer Migration Politics: Activist Rhetoric and Coalitional Possibilities*. Urbana: University of Illinois Press, 2013.
Chirindo, Kundai. "Rhetorical Places: From Classical Topologies to Prospects for Post-Westphalian Spatialities." *Women's Studies in Communication* 39, no. 2 (April 2016): 127–31.
Church, Scott Haden. "Remix, *Śunyatā*, and *Prosopopoeia*: Projecting Voice in the Digital Age." In *Ancient Rhetorics and Digital Networks*, edited by Michele Kennerly and Damien Smith Pfister, 229–51. Tuscaloosa: University of Alabama Press, 2018.
Cicero. *On Ends* [*De finibus*]. Translated by H. Rackham. Cambridge: Harvard University Press, 1914.
[Cicero.] *Rhetorica ad Herennium*. Translated by Harry Caplan. Cambridge: Harvard University Press, 1954.
Cirucci, Angela, and Barry Vacker. *Black Mirror and Critical Media Theory*. Lanham, MD: Lexington, 2018.
Cixous, Hélène. "Sorties: Out and Out: Attacks / Ways Out / Forays." In *The Newly Born Woman*, edited by Hélène Cixous and Catherine Clément, translated by Betsy Wing, 63–131. Minneapolis: University of Minnesota Press, 1986.

Cline, Ernest. *Ready Player One*. New York: Broadway, 2012.

Cloud, Dana L. *Reality Bites: Rhetoric and the Circulation of Truth Claims in U.S. Political Culture*. Columbus: Ohio State University Press, 2018.

Cohen, Herman. *The History of Speech Communication: The Emergence of a Discipline, 1914–1945*. Annandale, VA: Speech Communication Association, 1994.

Collins, Patricia Hill. "Learning from the Outsider Within: The Sociological Significance of Black Feminist Thought." *Social Problems* 33, no. 6 (October–December 1986): s14–s32.

Conley, Donovan, and William O. Saas. "*Occultatio*: The Bush Administration's Rhetorical War." *Western Journal of Communication* 74, no. 4 (July–Sept. 2010): 329–50.

Connors, Robert J., Lisa S. Ede, and Andrea A. Lunsford. "The Revival of Rhetoric in America." In *Essays on Classical Rhetoric and Modern Discourse*, edited by Robert J. Connors, Lisa S. Ede, and Andrea A. Lunsford, 1–15. Carbondale: Southern Illinois University Press, 1984.

Consigny, Scott. "Rhetoric and Its Situations." *Philosophy and Rhetoric* 7, no. 3 (Summer 1974): 175–86.

Corbett, Edward P. J. "Rhetoric in Search of a Past, Present, and Future." In *The Prospect of Rhetoric*, edited by Lloyd F. Bitzer and Edwin Black, 166–78. Englewood Cliffs, NJ: Prentice-Hall, 1971.

———. "The Usefulness of Classical Rhetoric." *College Composition and Communication* 14, no. 3 (October 1963): 162–64.

Corrigan, Lisa M. *Black Feelings: Race and Affect in the Long Sixties*. Jackson: University of Mississippi Press, 2020.

Cortez, José M. "Atopic Peripheries: Rhetoric, Hybridity, and the Latin American Resistance." Unpublished dissertation, University of Arizona, 2017.

———. "Of Exterior and Exception: Latin American Rhetoric, Subalterity, and the Politics of Cultural Difference." *Philosophy and Rhetoric* 51, no. 2 (2018): 124–50.

Crenshaw, Kimberlé. "Demarginalizing the Intersection of Race and Sex: A Black Feminist Critique of Antidiscrimination Doctrine, Feminist Theory and Antiracist Politics." *University of Chicago Legal Forum* 8 (1989): 139–67.

Cresswell, Tim. *In Place / Out of Place: Geography, Ideology, and Transgression*. Minneapolis: University of Minnesota Press, 1996.

Crosby, Richard Benjamin. "Kairos as God's Time in Martin Luther King Jr.'s Last Sunday Sermon." *Rhetoric Society Quarterly* 39, no. 3 (2009): 260–80.

Crowley, Sharon. *Toward a Civil Discourse: Rhetoric and Fundamentalism*. Pittsburgh: University of Pittsburgh Press, 2006.

Crowley, Sharon, and Debra Hawhee. *Ancient Rhetorics for Contemporary Students*. 3rd ed. New York: Pearson, 2004.

Curland, Martin, dir. *Zerophilia*. N.p.: TLA Releasing, 2005.

Daston, Lorraine, and Peter Galison. *Objectivity*. New York: Zone, 2010.

Davis, Zachary. "A Phenomenology of Political Apathy; Scheler and the Origins of Mass Violence." *Continental Philosophy Review* 42 (2009): 149–69.

Deighton, Katie. "Hims Is Bolstering Its Internal Marketing Team as Media Plan of 'Experimentation' Pays Off." *Drum*, June 11, 2019.

Deleuze, Gilles, and Felix Guattari. *A Thousand Plateaus: Capitalism and Schizophrenia*. Translated by Brian Massumi. Minneapolis: University of Minnesota Press, 1987.

DeLuca, Kevin. "The Speed of Immanent Images: The Dangers of Reading Photographs." In *Visual Communication: Perception, Rhetoric, and Technology*, edited by Diane S. Hope, 76–90. New York: Hampton, 2006.

Demetrius. *On Style*. Translated by Doreen C. Innes. Cambridge: Harvard University Press, 1995.

Demo, Anne Teresa. "Sovereignty Discourse and Contemporary Immigration Politics." *Quarterly Journal of Speech* 91, no. 3 (2005): 291–311.

Demosthenes. "On the Accession of Alexander." In *Orations*, Vol. 1. Translated by J. H. Vince and C. A. Vince. Cambridge: Harvard University Press, 1926.

———. *On the Crown*. Edited by Harvey Yunis. New York: Cambridge University Press, 2001.

Dennie, Nneka D. "Black Male Feminism and the Evolution of Du Boisian Thought, 1903–1920." *Palimpsest* 9, no. 1 (2020): 1–27.

Derrida, Jacques. *Aporias*. Translated by Thomas Dutoit. Palo Alto: Stanford University Press, 1993.

———. "Signature Event Context." In *Limited INC*, edited by Gerald Graff, translated by Samuel Weber, 1–24. Evanston: Northwestern University Press, 1988.

———. *Writing and Difference*. Translated by Alan Bass. Chicago: Chicago University Press, 1978.

Di Cesare, Donatella. "Atopos: Die Hermeneutik und der Ausser-Ort des Verstehens." In *Das Erbe Gadamers*, edited by Andrzej Przylebski, 85–94. Frankfurt: Peter Lang, 2006.

Dickinson, Greg. *Suburban Dreams: Imagining and Building the Good Life*. Tuscaloosa: University of Alabama Press, 2015.

Dōgen. *Treasury of the True Dharma Eye: Zen Master Dogen's Shobo Genzo*. Translated by Kazuaki Tanahashi. Boston: Shambhala, 2012.

Doss, Erika. *Memorial Mania: Public Feeling in America*. Chicago: University of Chicago Press, 2010.

Dream Channel VR. "Dream Channel Trailer." YouTube, December 9, 2019. https://www.youtube.com/watch?v=OKtcyjk2sZA&feature=youtu.be.

duBois, Page. "A Passion for the Dead: Ancient Objects and Everyday Life." In *Representing the Passions: Histories, Bodies, Visions*, edited by Richard Evan Meyer, 270–88. Los Angeles: Getty, 1999.

Du Bois, W. E. B. "The Colored World Within." In *Dusk of Dawn*, in *W. E. B. Du Bois Writings*, edited by Nathan Huggins, 681–715. New York: Library of America, 1986.

———. "The Talented Tenth." In "Essays and Articles," in *W. E. B. Du Bois Writings*, edited by Nathan Huggins, 842–61. New York: Library of America, 1986.

———. "The White World." In *Dusk of Dawn*, in *W. E. B. Du Bois Writings*, edited by Nathan Huggins, 652–80. New York: Library of America, 1986.

Dunbar, G. S. "Some Early Occurrences of the Term 'Social Geography.'" *Scottish Geographical Magazine* 93, no. 1 (1977): 15–20.

Dunn, Thomas R. *Queerly Remembered: Rhetorics for Representing the GLBTQ Past*. Columbia: University of South Carolina Press, 2016.

Dutta, Mohan Jyoti, and Raka Shome. "Mobilities, Communication, and Asia: Introduction." *International Journal of Communication* 12 (2018): 3960–78.

Easterling, Keller. "Disposition." In *Cognitive Architecture: from Biopolitics to Noopolitics*, edited by Deborah Hauptmann and Warren Neidich, 251–65. Rotterdam: 010 Publishers, 2010.

———. *Extrastatecraft: The Power of Infrastructure Space*. New York: Verso, 2016.

———. *Medium Design*. Moscow: Strelka Press, 2018.

———. "No You're Not." *e-flux*, September 26, 2016. https://www.e-flux.com/architecture/superhumanity/66720/no-you-re-not.

Eatman, Megan. *Ecologies of Harm: Rhetorics of Violence in the United States*. Columbus: Ohio University Press, 2020.

Eberly, Rosa A., and Jeremy David Johnson. "Isocratean *Tropos* and Mediated Multiplicities." In *Ancient Rhetorics and Digital Networks*, edited by Michele Kennerly and Damien Smith Pfister, 132–53. Tuscaloosa: University of Alabama Press, 2018.

Eide, Tormond. "Aristotelian *Topos* and Greek Geometry." *Symbolae Osloenses* 70, no. 1 (1995): 5–21.

Eliasoph, Nina. *Avoiding Politics: How Americans Produce Apathy in Everyday Life*. London: Cambridge University Press, 1998.

Ellwanger, Adam. *Metanoia: Rhetoric, Authenticity, and the Transformation of the Self*. University Park: Penn State University Press, 2020.

Emmerich, Karen. *Literary Translation and the Making of Originals*. New York: Bloomsbury, 2017.

Enck-Wanzer, Darrel. "Decolonizing Imaginaries: Rethinking 'the People' in the Young Lords' Church Offensive." *Quarterly*

Journal of Speech 98, no. 1 (February 2012): 1–23.

Enoch, Jessica. "A Woman's Place Is in the School: Rhetorics of Gendered Space in Nineteenth-Century America." *College English* 70, no. 3 (2008): 275–95.

Eveleth, Rose. "The Biggest Lie Tech People Tell Themselves—and the Rest of Us." *Vox*, October 8, 2019. https://www.vox.com/platform/amp/the-highlight/2019/10/1/20887003/tech-technology-evolution-natural-inevitable-ethics?__twitter_impression=true.

Fantasy Coin Whitepaper. October 2018. https://www.fxxx.io/static/FXXX_White_Paper_300919B.pdf.

Farah, Martha J. *Visual Agnosia*. Cambridge: MIT Press, 2004.

Fink, Bruce. "Love and/in Psychoanalysis: A Commentary on Lacan's Reading of Plato's *Symposium* in Seminar VIII: Transference." *Psychoanalytic Review* 102, no. 1 (February 2015): 59–91.

Finkelstein, Naomi. "Unmentionables: The Erinyes as the Culmination of Alpha Privative and Negated Language in Aeschylus's *Oresteia*." Unpublished dissertation, Columbia University, 2010.

Fish, Stanley. *Doing What Comes Naturally*. Durham: Duke University Press, 1989.

Fisher, Roger. "Preventing Nuclear War." *Bulletin of the Atomic Scientists* 37, no. 3 (1981): 11–17.

Fiske, Alan Page, and Tage Shakti Rai. *Virtuous Violence: Hurting and Killing to Create, Sustain, End, and Honor Social Relationships*. New York: Cambridge University Press, 2015.

Flakne, April. "'No Longer and Not Yet': From Doxa to Judgment." *Graduate Faculty Philosophy Journal* 21, no. 2 (1999): 153–75.

Flores, Lisa A. "Creating Discursive Space Through a Rhetoric of Difference: Chicana Feminists Craft a Homeland." *Quarterly Journal of Speech* 82 (1996): 142–56.

———. "Stoppage and the Racialized Rhetorics of Mobility." *Western Journal of Communication* 84, no. 3 (2020): 247–63.

Flores, Nancy. "Area Nonprofit Fearful After 'Sanctuary Cities' Law's Passage." *Austin American-Statesman*, May 12, 2017. https://www.mystatesman.com/news/local/area-nonprofits-fearful-after-sanctuary-cities-law-passage/u3dwbKfiX6VDKYqMdNg5MK.

Foley, Megan. "Time for Epideictic." *Quarterly Journal of Speech* 101, no. 1 (2015): 209–12.

Foss, Sonja K., and Cindy L. Griffin. "Beyond Persuasion: A Proposal for an Invitational Rhetoric." *Communication Monographs* 62 (March 1995): 2–18.

Foucault, Michel. *The Birth of the Clinic*. Translated by A. Sheridan. New York: Random House, 1975.

———. *Fearless Speech*. Cambridge: MIT Press, 2001.

Frede, Dorthea. "The Cognitive Role of *Phantasia* in Aristotle." In *Essays on Aristotle's* De anima, edited by Martha C. Nussbaum and Amelie Oksenberg Rorty, 279–95. Oxford: Clarendon Press, 1992.

Gadamer, Hans-Georg. "Language and Understanding (1970)." Translated by Richard E. Palmer. *Theory, Culture and Society* 23, no. 1 (2006): 13–27.

———. "Rhetoric, Hermeneutics, and Ideology-Critique." In *Rhetoric and Hermeneutics in Our Time: A Reader*, edited by Walter Jost and Michael J. Hyde, translated by G. B. Hess and R. E. Palmer, 313–34. New Haven: Yale University Press, 1997.

Garcia, Sen. Sylvia R. "Reason for Vote." *Senate Journal: Eighty-Fifth Legislature—Regular Session* (Austin, Texas), May 3, 2017, 1617.

Garland, Robert. *Wandering Greeks: The Ancient Greek Diaspora from the Age of Homer to the Death of Alexander the Great*. Princeton: Princeton University Press, 2014.

Gates, Henry Louis, Jr. "The 'Blackness of Blackness': A Critique of the Sign and the Signifying Monkey." *Critical Inquiry* 9, no. 4 (June 1983): 685–723.

Gaze Coin Whitepaper, October 2017. https://media.gazecoin.io/whitepaper.

Gearhart, Sally Miller. "The Womanization of Rhetoric." *Women's Studies International Quarterly* 2 (1979): 195–201.

Gerdes, Kendall. "Trauma, Trigger Warnings, and the Rhetoric of Sensitivity." *Rhetoric Society Quarterly* 49 (2019): 3–24.

Gersh, Stephen. "Dialectical and Rhetorical Space: The Boethian Theory of Topics and Its Influence During the Middle Ages." In *Raum und Raumvorstellungen im Mittelalter*, edited by Jan A. Aersten and Andreas Speer, 391–401. New York: de Gruyter, 1998.

Ghosh, Amitav. *The Great Derangement: Climate Change and the Unthinkable*. Chicago: University of Chicago Press, 2017.

Giorgis, Hannah. "How Black Suffragettes Subverted the Domestic Sphere." *Atlantic*, August 18, 2019. https://www.theatlantic.com/entertainment/archive/2019/08/how-black-suffragettes-subverted-domestic-sphere/596284.

Goldsmith, Oliver. *She Stoops to Conquer; Or, the Mistakes of a Night: A Comedy*. Open access through Project Gutenberg: http://www.gutenberg.org/ebooks/383.

Graff, Richard, Arthur E. Walzer, and Janet M. Atwill, eds. *The Viability of the Rhetorical Tradition*. Albany: State University of New York Press, 2005.

Gray, Benjamin. "From Exile of Citizens to Deportation of Non-Citizens: Ancient Greece as a Mirror to Illuminate a Modern Transition." *Citizenship Studies* 15, no. 5 (2011): 565–82.

Grimké, Angelina. "Appeal to the Christian Women of the South." 1836. http://utc.iath.virginia.edu/abolitn/abesaegat.html.

Gross, Alan G., and William M. Keith, eds. *Rhetorical Hermeneutics: Invention and Interpretation in the Age of Science*. Albany: State University of New York Press, 1997.

Gross, Daniel. *The Secret History of Emotion: From Aristotle's Rhetoric to Modern Brain Science*. Chicago: University of Chicago Press, 2006.

Gunkel, David J. *Hacking Cyberspace*. New York: Westview Press, 2001.

Gutfeld, Greg. "Gutfeld on Elizabeth Warren's Apocalyptic Climate Change Rhetoric." Fox News, June 5, 2019. https://www.foxnews.com/opinion/gutfeld-on-elizabeth-warrens-apocalyptic-climate-change-rhetoric.

Halloran, S. Michael. "The Growth of the Rhetoric Society of America: An Anecdotal History." *Rhetoric Society Quarterly* 48, no. 3 (2018): 234–41.

Haraway, Donna. "A Cyborg Manifesto: Science, Technology, and Socialist Feminism in the Late Twentieth Century." In *Simians, Cyborgs, and Women: The Reinvention of Nature*, 149–81. New York: Routledge, 1991.

Hariman, Robert. "Status, Marginality, and Rhetorical Theory." *Quarterly Journal of Speech* 72 (1986): 38–54.

Harker, Michael. "The Ethics of Argument: Rereading Kairos and Making Sense in a Timely Fashion." *College Composition and Communication* 59, no. 1 (2007): 77–97.

Harris, Owen, dir. *Black Mirror*. Season 5, episode 1, "Striking Vipers." Aired June 5, 2019.

Harris, Randy Allen. "The Fourth Master Trope, Antithesis." *Advances in the History of Rhetoric* 22, no. 1 (2019): 1–26.

Hartelius, Johanna, ed. *The Rhetoric of U.S. Immigration: Identity, Community, Otherness*. University Park: Penn State University Press, 2015.

Hartley, John. "The Frequencies of Public Writing." In *Democracy and New Media*, edited by Henry Jenkins and David Thorburn, 247–69. Cambridge: MIT Press, 2003.

Hartman, Saidiya. *Wayward Lives, Beautiful Experiments: Intimate Histories of Social Upheaval*. New York: W. W. Norton, 2019.

Hartmann, Betsy. "Rethinking Climate Refugees and Climate Conflict: Rhetoric, Reality and the Politics of Policy Discourse." *Journal of International Development* 22, no. 2 (2010): 233–46.

Haskins, Ekaterina. "Choosing Between Isocrates and Aristotle: Disciplinary Assumptions and Pedagogical Implications." *Rhetoric Society Quarterly* 36, no. 2 (Spring 2006): 191–201.

———. *Logos and Power in Isocrates and Aristotle*. Columbia: University of South Carolina Press, 2004.

———. *Popular Memories: Commemoration, Participatory Culture, and Democratic Citizenship*. Columbia: University of South Carolina Press, 2015.

Hatfield, Joe Edward. "The Queer Kairotic: Digital Transgender Suicide Memories and Ecological Rhetorical Agency." *Rhetoric Society Quarterly* 49, no. 1 (2019): 25–48.

Hauser, Gerard A. "Aristotle on Epideictic: The Formation of Public Morality." *Rhetoric Society Quarterly* 29, no. 1 (1999): 5–23.

Havelock, Eric. *Preface to Plato*. Cambridge: Harvard University Press, 1963.

Hawhee, Debra. "Agonism and Aretē." *Philosophy and Rhetoric* 35, no. 3 (2002): 185–207.

———. "Looking into Aristotle's Eyes: Toward a Theory of Rhetorical Vision." *Advances in the History of Rhetoric* 14, no. 2 (July 2011): 139–65.

———. *Rhetoric in Tooth and Claw: Animals, Language, Sensation*. Chicago: University of Chicago Press, 2016.

Hawk, Byron. *A Counter-History of Composition: Toward Methodologies of Complexity*. Pittsburgh: University of Pittsburgh Press, 2007.

———. "Toward a Post-Techne—Or, Inventing Pedagogies for Professional Writing." *Technical Communication Quarterly* 13, no. 4 (2004): 371–92.

Hayles, N. Katherine. *How We Became Posthuman: Virtual Bodies in Cybernetics, Literature, and Informatics*. Chicago: University of Chicago Press, 1999.

Herrick, James A. *The History and Theory of Rhetoric*. 3rd ed. New York: Pearson, 2005.

Hesiod. *Theogony; Works and Days; Testimonia*. Translated by Glenn W. Most. Cambridge: Harvard University Press, 2018.

Hinds, Aimee. "Hercules in White: Classical Reception, Art and Myth." The Jugaad Project, June 23, 2020. https://www.thejugaadproject.pub/home/hercules-in-white-classical-reception-art-and-myth.

Hochschild, Arlie Russell. *Strangers in Their Own Land: Anger and Mourning on the American Right*. New York: The New Press, 2016.

Homer. *Iliad*. Translated by A. T. Murray. 2 vols. Cambridge: Harvard University Press, 1924.

———. *Odyssey*. Translated by A. T. Murray. 2 vols. Cambridge: Harvard University Press, 1984.

———. *Odyssey*. Translated by Emily Wilson. New York: W. W. Norton, 2018.

hooks, bell. *Black Looks: Race and Representation*. Cambridge, MA: South End Press, 1992.

Houdek, Matthew, ed. "Forum: Race and Rhetoric." *Communication and Critical/Cultural Studies* 15, no. 4 (2018): 292–357.

Houdek, Matthew, and Kendall Phillips, ed. "Rhetoric and the Temporal Turn: Race, Gender, Temporalities." *Women's Studies in Communication* (2021; Online First).

Hunt, Everett Lee. "Plato on Rhetoric and Rhetoricians." *Quarterly Journal of Speech Education* 6, no. 3 (1920): 33–53.

Hurri, Samuli. "Justice *Kata Nomos* and Justice as *Epieikeia* (Legality and Equity)." In *Aristotle and the Philosophy of Law: Theory, Practice and Justice*, edited by Liesbeth Huppes-Cluysenaer and Nuno M. M. S. Coelho, 149–61. New York: Springer, 2013.

Ilkay, Hilary. "Mixing Memory and Desire: Helen's Eidolon in Sappho 16." EIDOLON, April 26, 2016. https://eidolon.pub/mixing-memory-and-desire-helens-eidolon-in-sappho-16-bbe2243b0113.

Inabinet, Brandon, and Christina Moss. "Complicit in Victimage: Imagined Marginality in Southern Communication Criticism." *Rhetoric Review* 38, no. 2 (2019): 160–72.

Ingraham, Chris. "Serendipity as a Cultural Technique." *Culture, Theory, and Critique* 60, no. 2 (2018): 107–22.

Isayev, Elena. "Hospitality: A Timeless Measure of Who We Are?" *Migration and Society: Advances in Research* 1 (2018): 7–21.

Isocrates. *Against the Sophists*. In *Isocrates II*, edited by George Norlin. Cambridge: Harvard University Press, 1980.

Jackson, Ronald L., II. "White Space, White Privilege: Mapping Discursive Inquiry into the Self." *Quarterly Journal of Speech* 85, no. 1 (1999): 38–54.

Jackson, Zakiyyah Iman. *Becoming Human: Matter and Meaning in an Antiblack World*. New York: New York University Press, 2020.

Jacobs, Christianne, Dietrich S. Schwarzkopf, and Juha Silvanto. "Visual Working

Memory Performance in Aphantasia." *Cortex* 105 (August 1, 2018): 61.

Jarratt, Susan C. "Sappho's Memory." *Rhetoric Society Quarterly* 32, no. 1 (2002): 11–43.

Jasinski, James. "Epistemic, Rhetoric as." In *Sourcebook on Rhetoric: Key Concepts in Contemporary Rhetorical Studies*, 219–29. Thousand Oaks, CA: Sage, 2001.

Jefferson, Andrew, Simon Turner, and Steffen Jensen. "Introduction: On Stuckness and Sites of Confinement." *Ethnos* 84, no. 1 (2019): 1–13.

Jhally, Sut, dir. *Dreamworlds 3—Desire, Sex, and Power in Music Videos*. Northampton, MA: Media Education Foundation, 2007.

Johnson, David Kyle, ed. *Black Mirror and Philosophy: Dark Reflections*. Hoboken, NJ: Wiley Blackwell, 2019.

Johnson, David Kyle, Leander P. Marquez, and Sergio Urueña. "*Black Mirror*: What Science Fiction Does Best." In *Black Mirror and Philosophy: Dark Reflections*, edited by David Kyle Johnson, 3–6. Hoboken, NJ: Wiley Blackwell, 2019.

Johnson, Heather. *Borders, Asylum, and Global Non-Citizenship: The Other Side of the Fence*. Cambridge: Cambridge University Press, 2014.

Johnson, Nan. *Gender and Rhetorical Space in American Life, 1866–1910*. Carbondale: Southern Illinois University Press, 2002.

Johnson, Paul Elliott. "The Art of Masculine Victimhood: Donald Trump's Demagoguery." *Women's Studies in Communication* 40, no. 3 (2017): 229–50.

Johnstone, Henry W., Jr. "Bilaterality in Argument and Communication." In *Advances in Argumentation Theory and Research*, edited by Robert J. Cox and Charles Willard, 95–102. Carbondale: Southern Illinois University Press, 1983.

———. "Communication: Technology and Ethics." In *Communication, Philosophy, and the Technological Age*, edited by Michael J. Hyde, 38–53. Tuscaloosa: University of Alabama Press, 1982.

———. "On Schiappa Versus Poulakos." *Rhetoric Review* 14, no. 2 (Spring 1996): 438–40.

———. "Philosophical Argument and the Rhetorical Wedge." *Communication and Cognition* 24, no. 1 (1991): 77–91.

———. *The Problem of the Self*. University Park: Penn State University Press, 1970.

———. "Response to Carroll Arnold and George Yoos." *Philosophy and Rhetoric* 20, no. 2 (1987): 129–34.

———. "Rhetoric as a Wedge: A Reformulation." *Rhetoric Society Quarterly* 20, no. 4 (1990): 333–38.

———. *Validity and Rhetoric in Philosophical Argument: An Outlook in Transition*. University Park, PA: The Dialogue Press of *Man and World*, 1978.

Johnstone, Henry W., Jr., and Mari Lee Mifsud. "Wedge and Bridge: A Note on the Rhetoric of Distinction and Identification." *Rhetoric Society Quarterly* 29, no. 2 (1999): 75–78.

Kaba, Mariame. "Yes, We Mean Literally Abolish the Police." *New York Times*, June 12, 2020. https://www.nytimes.com/2020/06/12/opinion/sunday/floyd-abolish-defund-police.html.

Kalbfleish, Elizabeth. "Anxieties of Legitimacy: The Origins and Influence of the 'Classicist Stance' in American Rhetoric Studies." *Advances in the History of Rhetoric* 16, no. 1 (2013): 82–106.

Karenga, Maulana. "Nommo, Kawaida, and Communicative Practice: Bringing Good into the World." In *Understanding African American Rhetoric: Classical Origins to Contemporary Innovations*, edited by Ronald L. Jackson II and Elaine B. Richardson, 3–22. New York: Routledge, 2003.

Kastely, James. "In Defense of Plato's *Gorgias*." *PMLA* 106, no. 1 (1991): 96–109.

Katula, Richard A. "Quintilian on the Art of the Emotional Appeal." *Rhetoric Review* 22, no. 1 (2003): 5–15.

Keining, Alexandra-Therese, dir. *Girls Lost* [*Pojkarna* (The Boys)]. N.p.: Saffron Hill, 2015.

Kelley, Donald R. "Philodoxy: Mere Opinion and the Question of History." *Journal of the History of Philosophy* 34, no. 1 (1996): 117–32.

Kendi, Ibram X. *Stamped from the Beginning: The Definitive History of Racist Ideas in America*. New York: Nation Books, 2016.

Kennedy, George A. "A Hoot in the Dark: The Evolution of a General Rhetoric."

Philosophy and Rhetoric 25, no. 1 (1992): 1–21.

Kennedy, Rebecca Futo. "Why I Teach About Race and Ethnicity in the Classical World." EIDOLON, September 11, 2017. https://eidolon.pub/why-i-teach-about-race-and-ethnicity-in-the-classical-world-ade379722170.

Kennerly, Michele. "Getting Carried Away: How Rhetorical Transport Gets Judgment Going." *Rhetoric Society Quarterly* 40, no. 3 (June 1, 2010): 269–91.

———. "On Being and Seeming (Good)." EIDOLON, September 26, 2016. https://eidolon.pub/on-being-and-seeming-good-8f779ab34342.

———. "Socrates *Ex Situ*." *Advances in the History of Rhetoric* 20, no. 2 (2017): 196–208.

Kennerly, Michele, and Damien Smith Pfister. Introduction to *Ancient Rhetorics and Digital Networks*, edited by Michele Kennerly and Damien Smith Pfister, 1–27. Tuscaloosa: Alabama University Press, 2018.

Kennerly, Michele, and Carly S. Woods. "Moving Rhetorica." *Rhetoric Society Quarterly* 48, no. 1 (January 2018): 3–27.

Keogh, Rebecca, and Joel Pearson. "The Blind Mind: No Sensory Visual Imagery in Aphantasia." *Cortex* 105 (August 1, 2018): 53–60.

Kgrind Jonny. "Dream Channel POV." Vimeo, September 25, 2018. https://vimeo.com/292059222.

———. "Land Sale Walkthrough." Vimeo, September 27, 2018. https://vimeo.com/292059222.

King, Martin Luther, Jr. "Letter from Birmingham Jail." In *Why We Can't Wait*, 64–84. New York: Signet Classic, 2000 [1963].

Kinneavy, James L. *Greek Rhetorical Origins of Christian Faith: An Inquiry*. New York: Oxford University Press, 1987.

Kinneavy, James L., and Catherine R. Eskin. "*Kairos* in Aristotle's Rhetoric." *Written Communication* 17, no. 3 (July 2000): 432–44.

Kraus, Manfred. "How to Classify Means of Persuasion: The *Rhetoric to Alexander* and Aristotle on *Pisteis*." *Rhetorica* 29, no. 3 (Summer 2011): 263–79.

Kruse, Kevin M. "A Traffic Jam in Atlanta Would Seem to Have Nothing to Do with Slavery. But Look Closer . . ." The 1619 Project. *New York Times Magazine*, August 18, 2019, 48–49.

Kunkel, Adrianne Dennis, and Michael Robert Dennis. "Grief Consolation in Eulogy Rhetoric: An Integrative Framework." *Death Studies* 27, no. 1 (January 2003): 1–38.

Lacan, Jacques. *Le séminaire livre VIII: Le transfert*. Edited by Jacques-Alain Miller. Paris: Editions du Seuil, 1991.

Laclau, Ernesto. *The Rhetorical Foundations of Society*. London: Verso, 2014.

La Gorce, Tammy. "'Everybody Was Sick': Inside an ICE Detention Center." *New York Times*, May 15, 2020. https://www.nytimes.com/2020/05/15/nyregion/coronavirus-ice-detainees-immigrants.html.

Lanham, J. Drew. *The Home Place: Memoirs of a Colored Man's Love Affair with Nature*. Minneapolis: Milkweed Editions, 2016.

Larson, Stephanie R. "'Just Let This Sink In': Feminist *Megethos* and the Role of Lists in #MeToo." *Rhetoric Review* 38, no. 4 (2019): 432–44.

Law, Martin, and Lisa M. Corrigan. "On White-Speak and Gatekeeping: Or, What Good Are the Greeks?" *Communication and Critical/Cultural Studies* 15, no. 4 (2018): 326–30.

Lawlor, Andrea. *Paul Takes the Form of a Mortal Girl*. New York: Vintage, 2019.

Lefebvre, Henri. *The Production of Space*. Translated by Donald Nicholson-Smith. Oxford: Basil Blackwell, 1991 [1974].

Leff, Michael C. "The Topics of Argumentation in Latin Rhetorical Theory from Cicero to Boethius." *Rhetorica* 1, no. 1 (Spring 1983): 23–44.

Le Gaufey, Guy. "Le plus atopique des deux . . ." In *Lacan avec les Philosophes*, edited by Natalia S. Avtonomova, 166–70. Paris: Albin Michel, 1991.

Levenson, David B., and Thomas R. Martin. "Akairos or Eukairos? The Nickname of the Seleucid King Demetrius III in the Transmission of the Texts of Josephus' *War* and *Antiquities*." *Journal for the Study of Judaism* 40 (2009): 307–41.

Lévystone, David. "Socrates' Versatile Rhetoric and the Soul of the Crowd." *Rhetorica* 38, no. 2 (2020): 135–55.

Liddell, Henry George, Robert Scott, and Henry Stuart Jones. *A Greek-English Lexicon*. 9th ed. Oxford: Clarendon Press, 1996.

Lightman, Bernard. *The Origins of Agnosticism: Victorian Unbelief and the Limits of Knowledge*. Baltimore: Johns Hopkins University Press, 1987.

Lloyd, Keith. "Culture and Rhetorical Patterns: Mining the Rich Relations Between Aristotle's Enthymeme and Example and India's Nyāya Method." *Rhetorica* 24, no. 1 (2011): 76–105.

———, ed. *The Routledge Handbook of Comparative World Rhetorics: Studies in the History, Application, and Teaching of Rhetoric Beyond Traditional Greco-Roman Contexts*. New York: Routledge, 2020.

Longinus. *On the Sublime* [*Peri hupsous*]. Translated by W. Hamilton Fyfe. Cambridge: Harvard University Press, 1932.

Loraux, Nicole. *The Invention of Athens: The Funeral Oration in the Classical City*. Translated by Alan Sheridan. Cambridge: Harvard University Press, 1986.

Lorde, Audre. *Sister Outsider: Essays and Speeches by Audre Lorde*. Berkeley: Crossing Press, 2007 [1984].

Loveridge, Jordan. "Praise Bee!: Allegory and Interpretation in the Aberdeen Bestiary." *Rhetoric Society Quarterly* 49, no. 4 (August 8, 2019): 409–27.

Lozano, Nina Maria. *Not One More! Feminicidio on the Border*. Columbus: Ohio State University Press, 2019.

Lozano-Reich, Nina M., and Dana L. Cloud. "The Uncivil Tongue: Invitational Rhetoric and the Problem of Inequality." *Western Journal of Communication* 73, no. 2 (2009): 220–26.

Lu, Xing. "Chinese Rhetoric in Classical and Contemporary Times." ASHR.org. https://ashr.org/teaching-resources/diversifying-teaching/chinese-rhetoric-in-classical-and-contemporary-times.

———. *Rhetoric in Ancient China, Fifth to Third Century B.C.E.: A Comparison with Classical Greek Rhetoric*. Columbia: University of South Carolina Press, 1998.

Lyon, Arabella. "Imagining Confucian Audiences: Tactical Media and the Umbrella Movement." In *Ancient Rhetorics and Digital Networks*, edited by Michele Kennerly and Damien Smith Pfister, 48–66. Tuscaloosa: University of Alabama Press, 2018.

MacKisack, Matthew. "Painter and Scribe: From Model of Mind to Cognitive Strategy." *Cortex* 105 (August 1, 2018): 118–24.

Manderscheid, Katharina. "Social Space." In *Encyclopedia of Urban Studies*, edited by Ray Hutchison, 2:747–51. Thousand Oak, CA: SAGE Reference, 2010.

Manne, Kate. *Down Girl: The Logic of Misogyny*. New York: Oxford University Press, 2018.

Markovits, Elizabeth. *The Politics of Sincerity: Plato, Frank Speech, and Democratic Engagement*. University Park: Penn State University Press, 2008.

Maura, Andrew, and Byron Hawk. "Posthuman Rhetorics and Technical Communication." *Technical Communication Quarterly* 19, no. 1 (2019): 1–10.

McAllister, Joan Faber. "Space in Rhetorical Theory." *Oxford Research Encyclopedia of Communication* (2019). https://oxfordre.com/communication.

McCann, Bryan J., Ashley Noel Mack, and Rico Self, "Communication's Quest for Whiteness: The Racial Politics of Disciplinary Legitimacy." *Communication and Critical/Cultural Studies* 17, no. 2 (June 2020): 243–52.

McCoy, Marina Berzins. *Wounded Heroes: Vulnerability as a Virtue in Ancient Greek Literature and Philosophy*. Oxford: Oxford University Press, 2013.

McGeveran, Tom. "The New Media Religion: 'Platform Agnostic.'" *Observer*, August 4, 2008.

McKeon, Richard. "Creativity and the Commonplace." *Philosophy and Rhetoric* 6, no. 4 (Fall 1973): 199–210.

McKerrow, Raymie. "Critical Rhetoric: Theory and Praxis." *Communication Monographs* 56 (1989): 91–111.

McKinnon, Sara L. *Gendered Asylum: Race and Violence in U.S. Law and Politics*. Champaign: University of Illinois Press, 2016.

McPherson, Annika. "From Utopia to Atopia to Diaspora? Narratives of Social (Re-) Organization in a German Refugee Home." In *Transcultural Modernities: Narrating Africa in Europe*, edited by Elisabeth Bekers, Sissy Helff, and Daniela Merolla, 363–75. New York: Editions Rodopi, 2009.

"Meghan McCain Eulogy of John McCain: Celebrating Her Dad's Love and Influence While Criticizing Trump." *Arizona Republic*, September 1, 2018. https://www.azcentral.com/story/news/politics/arizona/2018/09/01/meghan-mccain-full-text-eulogy-john-mccain-trancript/1174328002.

Metzl, Jonathan. *Dying of Whiteness: How the Politics of Racial Resentment Is Killing America's Heartland*. New York: Basic Books, 2019.

Mifsud, Mari Lee. "Oh Popoi! Henry Johnstone, Homer, and the History of Rhetoric." *Communication Annual: Journal of the Pennsylvania Communication Association* 60 (2004): 73–90.

———. "On Being a Simple Judge: Exploring Rhetorical Citizenship in Aristotelian and Homeric Rhetorics." In *Contemporary Rhetorical Citizenship*, edited by Christian Kock and Lisa S. Villadsen, 223–38. Leiden: Leiden University Press, 2014.

———. "On Network." In *Ancient Rhetorics and Digital Networks*, edited by Michele Kennerly and Damien Smith Pfister, 28–47. Tuscaloosa: University of Alabama Press, 2018.

———. "On Rhetoric as Gift/Giving." *Philosophy and Rhetoric* 40 (2007): 89–107.

———. "On the Idea of Reflexive Rhetoric in Homer." *Philosophy and Rhetoric* 31, no. 1 (1998): 41–54.

———. "Revision and Immortality in Philosophical Argumentation: Reconsidering the Rhetorical Wedge." *Informal Logic* 21, no. 1 (2001): 51–60.

———. *Rhetoric and the Gift: Ancient Rhetorical Theory and Contemporary Communication*. Pittsburgh: Duquesne University Press, 2015.

Miles, Margaret R. *Carnal Knowing: Female Nakedness and Religious Meaning in the Christian West*. Boston: Beacon Press, 1989.

Miller, Bernard R. "Retrieving a Sophistic Sense of Doxa." In *Rhetoric in the Vortex of Cultural Studies: Proceedings of the Fifth Biennial Conference*, edited by Arthur Walzer, 32–41. Minneapolis: University of Minnesota Press, 1992.

Miller, Carolyn R. "Classical Rhetoric Without Nostalgia: A Response to Gaonkar." In *Rhetorical Hermeneutics: Invention and Interpretation in the Age of Science*, edited by Alan G. Gross and William Keith, 156–71. Albany: State University of New York Press, 1997.

———. "Genre in Ancient and Networked Media." In *Ancient Rhetorics and Digital Networks*, edited by Michele Kennerly and Damien Smith Pfister, 176–204. Tuscaloosa: University of Alabama Press, 2018.

———. "Should We Name the Tools? Concealing and Revealing the Art of Rhetoric." In *The Public Work of Rhetoric*, edited by David Coogan and John Ackerman, 19–38. Columbia: University of South Carolina Press, 2010.

Mirhady, David. "Non-Technical Pisteis in Aristotle and Anaximenes." *American Journal of Philology* 112, no. 1 (1991): 5–28.

Mitchell, Koritha. "Identifying White Mediocrity and Know-Your-Place Aggression: A Form of Self-Care." *African American Review* 51, no. 4 (Winter 2018): 253–62.

Montefusco, Lucia Calboli. "Die Topik in der Argumentation." In *Rhetorik zwischen den Wissenschaften*, edited by Gert Ueding, 21–34. Tübingen: Max Niemeyer Verlag, 1991.

Moore, Christopher. *Socrates and Self-Knowledge*. Cambridge: Cambridge University Press, 2015.

Morgan, Teresa. *Roman Faith and Christian Faith:* Pistis *and* Fides *in the Early Roman Empire and Early Churches*. New York: Oxford University Press, 2015.

Mortley, Raoul. "The Fundamentals of the Via Negativa." *American Journal of Philology* 103, no. 4 (Winter 1982): 429–39.

Mountford, Roxanne. "On Gender and Rhetorical Space." *Rhetoric Society Quarterly* 31, no. 1 (2001): 41–71.

Muckelbauer, John. *The Future of Invention: Rhetoric, Postmodernism, and the Problem of Change*. Albany: State University of New York Press, 2008.

Mulvey, Laura. "Visual Pleasure and Narrative Cinema." *Screen* 16, no. 3 (1975): 6–18.

Myers, Bess R. H. "Women Who Translate." *Eidolon*, August 5, 2019. https://eidolon.pub/women-who-translate-7966e56b3df2.

Myers, Kelly A. "*Metanoia* and the Transformation of Opportunity." *Rhetoric Society Quarterly* 41, no. 1 (2011): 1–18.

Næss, Arne. *Scepticism*. New York: Routledge, 2015.

Nakayama, Thomas K., ed. "Forum: Whiteness and Communication." *Communication and Critical/Cultural Studies* 17, no. 2 (2020): 199–266.

Nakayama, Thomas K., and Robert L. Krizek. "Whiteness: A Strategic Rhetoric." *Quarterly Journal of Speech* 81, no. 3 (1995): 291–319.

Narea, Nicole. "Trump Is Quietly Gutting the Asylum System Amid the Pandemic." *Vox*, June 12, 2020. https://www.vox.com/2020/6/12/21288063/trump-immigration-asylum-border-regulation.

Nelson, John S., and Allan Megill. "Rhetoric of Inquiry, Projects and Prospects." *Quarterly Journal of Speech* 72, no. 1 (1986): 20–37.

Nietzsche, Friedrich Wilhelm. "On the Uses and Disadvantages of History for Life." In *Untimely Meditations*, translated by R. J. Hollingdale, 57–123. Cambridge: Cambridge University Press, 1997.

Nussbaum, Martha C. *Monarchy of Fear: A Philosopher Looks at Our Political Crisis*. New York: Simon & Schuster, 2018.

Ochieng, Omedi. "African Philosophy and Rhetoric." ASHR.org. https://ashr.org/teaching-resources/diversifying-teaching/african-philosophy-rhetoric.

Odell, Jenny. *How to Do Nothing: Resisting the Attention Economy*. New York: Penguin Random House, 2019.

Olson, Christa J. "American Magnitude: Frederic Church, Hiram Bingham and Hemispheric Vision." *Quarterly Journal of Speech* 48, no. 4 (2018): 380–404.

———. "Performing Embodiable Topoi: Strategic Indigeneity and the Incorporation of Ecuadorian National Identity." *Quarterly Journal of Speech* 96, no. 3 (August 2010): 300–323.

———. "Places to Stand: The Practices and Politics of Writing Histories." *Advances in the History of Rhetoric* 15, no. 1 (2012): 77–100.

Ono, Kent A., and John M. Sloop. "Commitment to Telos—a Sustained Critical Rhetoric." *Communication Monographs* 59, no. 1 (1992).

Ore, Ersula J. *Lynching: Violence, Rhetoric, and American Identity*. Jackson: University of Mississippi Press, 2019.

Osborn, Michael. "Patterns of Metaphor Among Early Feminist Orators." In *Rhetoric and Community: Studies in Unity and Fragmentation*, edited by J. Michael Hogan, 3–26. Columbia: University of South Carolina Press, 1998.

Pagels, Elaine. *The Gnostic Gospels*. New York: Vintage, 1979.

Painter, Nell Irvin. *The History of White People*. New York: W. W. Norton, 2010.

Palaephatus. *On Unbelievable Tales*. Translated by Jacob Stern. Wauconda, IL: Bolchazy-Carducci, 1996.

Papamattheakis, George, and Keller Easterling. "Inside Keller Easterling's Personal *Medium Design*." *Strelka Mag*, September 18, 2019.

Peary, Alexandria. "The Role of Mindfulness in *Kairos*." *Rhetoric Review* 35, no. 1 (2016): 22–34.

Pease, Arthur Stanley. "Things Without Honor." *Classical Philology* 21 (1926): 27–42.

Pender, Kelly. *Techne, from Neoclassicism to Postmodernism: Understanding Writing as a Useful, Teachable Art*. Anderson, SC: Parlor Press, 2011.

Peralta, Dan-el Padilla. "Classics Beyond the Pale." *Eidolon*, February 20, 2017. https://eidolon.pub/classics-beyond-the-pale-534bdbb3601b.

Perl, Jeffrey M. *The Tradition of Return: The Implicit History of Modern Literature*. Princeton: Princeton University Press, 2014.

Perlman, Paula. *Ancient Greek Law in the 21st Century*. Austin: University of Texas Press, 2018.

Pernot, Laurent. "Thesaurus: The System of Ancient Rhetoric." In *Rhetoric in Antiquity*, 215–32. Translated by W. E. Higgins. Washington, DC: Catholic University of America Press, 2005.

Peters, Benjamin, ed. *Digital Keywords: A Vocabulary of Information Society and Culture*. Princeton: Princeton University Press, 2016.

Peters, John Durham. *The Marvelous Clouds: Toward a Philosophy of Elemental Media*. Chicago: University of Chicago Press, 2015.

Peterson, Anne Helen. "Jennifer Lawrence and the History of Cool Girls." *BuzzFeed*, February 28, 2014. https://www.buzzfeed.com/annehelenpetersen/jennifer-lawrence-and-the-history-of-cool-girls.

Pew Research Center. "Religious Landscape Study." https://www.pewforum.org/religious-landscape-study.

Pfister, Damien Smith, and Carly S. Woods. "The Unnaturalistic Enthymeme: Figuration, Interpretation, and Critique after Digital Mediation." *Argumentation and Advocacy* 52 (Spring 2016): 236–53.

Pierce, Lee M. "For the Time(d) Being: The Form Hate Takes in The Hate U Give." *Women's Studies in Communcation* (2021; Online First).

Plato. *Gorgias*. Translated by James H. Nichols. Ithaca: Cornell University Press, 1998.

———. *Laws*. Vol. 1. Translated by R. G. Bury. Cambridge: Harvard University Press, 1926.

———. *Meno*. Translated by W. R. M. Lamb. Cambridge: Harvard University Press, 1924.

———. *Platonis Opera*. Vol. 2. Edited by John Burnet. New York: Oxford University Press, 1995.

———. *Protagoras*. Translated by W. K. C. Guthrie. In *Plato: Collected Dialogues*, edited by Edith Hamilton and Huntington Cairns, 308–52. Princeton: Princeton University Press, 1989.

———. *Republic*. Vol. 2. Translated by Chris Emlyn-Jones and William Preddy. Cambridge: Harvard University Press, 2013.

———. *Theaetetus and Sophist*. Translated by C. J. Rowe. New York: Cambridge University Press, 2015.

Plutarch. "De sollertia animalium." In *Moralia*, vol. 12, translated by W. C. Helmbold. Cambridge: Harvard University Press, 1957.

Porter, J. E. "Recovering Delivery for Digital Rhetoric." *Computers and Composition* 26 (2009): 207–24.

Poulakos, Takis. "Isocrates' Use of 'Doxa.'" *Philosophy and Rhetoric* 34, no. 1 (2001): 61–78.

———, ed. *Rethinking the History of Rhetoric: Multidisciplinary Essays on the Rhetorical Tradition*. Boulder: Westview Press, 1993.

Price, Robert Grant. "Love in *Black Mirror*: Who Do We Really Love?" in *Black Mirror and Philosophy: Dark Reflections*, edited by David Kyle Johnson, 301–10. Hoboken, NJ: Wiley Blackwell, 2020.

Price-Mckell, Cheryl. "When Kairos Compels Composition: Women's Response to the 1924 Burpee Seed Company® Contest, 'What Burpee Seeds Have Done for Me.'" *Rhetoric Review* 38, no. 4 (2019): 463–81.

Pruchnic, Jeff. *Rhetoric and Ethics in the Cybernetic Age: The Transhuman Condition*. Abingdon: Routledge, 2013.

Puwar, Nirmal. *Space Invaders: Race, Gender, and Bodies Out of Place*. New York: Bloomsbury, 2004.

Quintilian. *The Orator's Education [Institutio oratoria]*. Vol. 3. Translated by Donald A. Russell. Cambridge: Harvard University Press, 2001.

Ralina, Joseph L. "What's the Difference with 'Difference'?: Equity, Communication, and the Politics of Difference." *International Journal of Communication* 11 (2017): 3306–26.

Ramírez, Cristina Devereaux. *Occupying Our Space: The Mestiza Rhetorics of Mexican Women Journalists and Activists, 1875–1942*. Tucson: University of Arizona Press, 2015.

Rand, Erin. *Reclaiming Queer: Activist and Academic Rhetorics of Resistance*. Tuscaloosa: University of Alabama Press, 2014.

Rawson, K. J. "The Rhetorical Power of Archival Description: Classifying Images of

Gender Transgression." *Rhetoric Society Quarterly* 48, no. 4 (2018): 327–51.
"Read the Full Text of Barack Obama's Speech at John McCain's Memorial Service." NBC News, September 1, 2018. https://www.nbcnews.com/politics/barack-obama/read-full-text-barack-obama-s-speech-john-mccain-s-n905721.
Reames, Robin. *Seeming and Being in Plato's Rhetorical Theory*. Chicago: University of Chicago Press, 2018.
Reeves, Joshua. "Suspended Identification: *Atopos* and the Work of Public Memory." *Philosophy and Rhetoric* 46, no. 3 (2013): 306–27.
Rice, Jenny. *Awful Archives: Conspiracy Theory, Rhetoric, and Acts of Evidence*. Columbus: Ohio State University Press, 2020.
———. *Distant Publics: Development Rhetoric and the Subject of Crisis*. Pittsburgh: University of Pittsburgh Press, 2012.
———. "The Rhetorical Aesthetics of More: On Archival Magnitude." *Philosophy and Rhetoric* 50, no. 1 (November 2017): 26–49.
Rickert, Thomas. *Ambient Rhetoric: The Attunements of Rhetorical Being*. Pittsburgh: University of Pittsburgh Press, 2013.
Ricoeur, Paul. *Memory, History, Forgetting*. Translated by Kathleen Blamey and David Pellauer. Chicago: University of Chicago Press, 2010.
Roberts-Miller, Patricia. *Demagoguery and Democracy*. New York: The Experiment, 2017.
Robertson, Benjamin J. *None of This Is Normal: The Fiction of Jeff VanderMeer*. Minneapolis: University of Minnesota Press, 2018.
Rollins, Brooke. "The Ethics of Epideictic Rhetoric: Addressing the Problem of Presence Through Derrida's Funeral Orations." *Rhetoric Society Quarterly* 35, no. 1 (2005): 5–23.
Roochnik, David. *Of Art and Wisdom: Plato's Understanding of Techne*. University Park: Penn State University Press, 1996.
Royster, Jacqueline Jones. "Disciplinary Landscaping, or Contemporary Challenges in the History of Rhetoric." *Philosophy and Rhetoric* 36, no. 2 (2003): 148–67.
Royster, Jacqueline Jones, and Gesa Kirsch. *Feminist Rhetorical Practices: New Horizons for Rhetoric, Composition, and Literacy Studies*. Carbondale: Southern Illinois University Press, 2012.
Rubin, Peter. *Future Presence: How Virtual Reality Is Changing Human Connection, Intimacy, and the Limits of Ordinary Life*. New York: Harper Collins, 2018.
Rubinelli, Sara. *Ars Topica: The Classical Technique of Constructing Arguments from Aristotle to Cicero*. New York: Springer, 2009.
Rumī, Jalāl al-Dīn. *Signs of the Unseen: The Discourses of Jalaluddin Rumi*. Translated by W. M. Thackston. Boston: Shambhala, 1999.
Said, Edward W. *Out of Place*. New York: Vintage, 2000.
Sappho. *Sappho: A New Translation of the Complete Works*. Edited and translated by Diane J. Rayor. New York: Cambridge University Press, 2014.
Sassen, Saskia. *Expulsions: Brutality and Complexity in the Global Economy*. Cambridge: Harvard University Press, 2014.
Scherlis, Lily. "Distantiated Communities: A Social History of Social Distancing." *Cabinet Magazine*, April 30, 2020. http://cabinetmagazine.org/kiosk/scherlis_lily_30_april_2020.php.
Schiappa, Edward. *The Beginnings of Rhetorical Theory in Classical Greece*. New Haven: Yale University Press, 1999.
Schiappa, Edward, and Omar Swartz. Introduction to *Landmark Essays on Classical Greek Rhetoric*, edited by Edward Schiappa, xi–xiv. Davis, CA: Hermagoras, 1994.
Scott, Charles E. *The Lives of Things*. Bloomington: Indiana University Press, 2002.
———. *The Question of Ethics: Nietzsche, Foucault, Heidegger*. Bloomington: Indiana University Press, 1990.
Scott, Robert L. "On Viewing Rhetoric as Epistemic." *Central States Speech Journal* 18 (1967): 9–17.
Sheard, Cynthia Miecznikowski. "Kairos and Kenneth Burke's Psychology of Political and Social Communication." *College English* 55, no. 3 (March 1993): 291–310.
———. "The Public Value of Epideictic Rhetoric." *College English* 58, no. 7 (1996): 765–94.

Shome, Raka. "Post-Colonial Interventions in the Rhetorical Canon: An 'Other' View." In *Contemporary Rhetorical Theory: A Reader*, edited by John Louis Lucaites, Celeste Michelle Condit, and Sally Caudhill, 591–608. New York: Guilford Press, 1999.

Simmel, Georg. "Der Fremde." In *Soziologie: Untersuchungen über die Formen der Vergesellschaftung*, 685–91. Leipzig: Duncker & Humbolt, 1908.

Sipiora, Phillip. Introduction to *Rhetoric and Kairos: Essays in History, Theory, and Praxis*, edited by Phillip Sipiora and James S. Baumlin, 1–22. Albany: State University of New York Press, 2002.

Slade, Darren M. "*Striking Vipers* and Closed Doors: How Meaningful Are Sexual Fantasies?" In *Black Mirror and Philosophy: Dark Reflections*, edited by David Kyle Johnson, 241–50. Hoboken, NJ: Wiley Blackwell, 2019.

Smith, Bromley. "Corax and Probability." *Quarterly Journal of Speech Education* 7, no. 1 (1921): 13–42.

———. "The Father of Debate: Protagoras of Abdera." *Quarterly Journal of Speech Education* 4, no. 2 (1918): 196–215.

———. "Gorgias: A Study in Oratorical Style." *Quarterly Journal of Speech Education* 7, no. 4 (1921): 335–59.

———. "Prodicus of Ceos: the Sire of Synonomy." *Quarterly Journal of Speech Education* 6, no. 2 (1920): 51–68.

Snorton, C. Riley. *Nobody Is Supposed to Know: Black Sexuality on the Down Low*. Minneapolis: University of Minnesota Press, 2014.

Spielberg, Steven, dir. *Minority Report*. Universal City, CA: DreamWorks, 2002.

———, dir. *Ready Player One*. Universal City, CA: DreamWorks, 2018.

Spivak Gayatri. *An Aesthetic Education in an Era of Globalization*. Cambridge: Harvard University Press, 2012.

Stafford, Andy. "*Classé, Surclasser, Déclassé*, or, Roland Barthes, Classification Without Class." *L'Esprit Créateur* 55, no. 4 (Winter 2015): 148–64.

Stanton, Elizabeth Cady. "'The Solitude of Self': Speech by ECS to the House Judiciary Committee Speech Text." Voices of Democracy (blog). Accessed April 15, 2019. http://voicesofdemocracy.umd.edu/the-solitude-of-self-speech-by-ecs-to-the-house-judiciary-committee-speech-text.

Staten, Henry. *Techne Theory: A New Language for Art*. New York: Bloomsbury, 2019.

Stern, Jacob. "Introduction." In Palaephatus, *On Unbelievable Tales*, edited and translated by Jacob Stern, 1–25. Wauconda, IL: Bolchazy-Carducci, 1996.

Sterne, Jonathan. "Communication as Techné." In *Communication as . . . : Perspectives on Theory*, edited by Gregory J. Shepherd, Jeffrey St. John, and Ted Striphas, 1–98. Thousand Oaks, CA: Sage, 2006.

Stiegler, Bernard. *The Age of Disruption: Technology and Madness in Computational Capitalism*. Translated by Daniel Ross. Cambridge: Polity, 2019.

———. *Symbolic Misery*. Vol. 1, *The Hyperindustrial Epoch*. Translated by Barnaby Norman. Cambridge: Polity, 2014.

Stillion Southard, Bjørn. *Peculiar Rhetoric: Slavery, Freedom, and the African Colonization Movement*. Jackson: University of Mississippi Press, 2019.

Stormer, Nathan. "In Living Memory: Abortion as Cultural Amnesia." *Quarterly Journal of Speech* 88, no. 3 (2002): 265–383.

Story, Louise. "A Media-Agnostic, Judging Campaigns of Others." *New York Times*, April 10, 2008.

Strauss, Claudia. "The Imaginary." *Anthropological Theory* 6, no. 3 (September 1, 2006): 322–44.

Sturken, Marita. *Tourists of History: Memory, Kitsch, and Consumerism from Oklahoma City to Ground Zero*. Durham: Duke University Press, 2007.

Summers, Brandi Thompson. *Black in Place: The Spatial Aesthetics of Race in a Post-Chocolate City*. Chapel Hill: University of North Carolina Press, 2019.

Sutton, Jane S. "The Earth Is Not at Rest and Neither Should Be Rhetoric." In *A Revolution in Tropes: Alloiostrophic Rhetoric*, by Jane S. Sutton and Mari Lee Mifsud, 19–46. Lanham, MD: Lexington Books, 2015.

Sutton, Jane S., and Mari Lee Mifsud. *A Revolution in Tropes: Alloiostrophic Rhetoric.* Lanham, MD: Lexington Books, 2015.

———. "Toward an Alloiostrophic Rhetoric." *Advances in the History of Rhetoric* 15, no. 2 (2012): 222–33.

Swearingen, C. Jan. "*Pistis*, Expression, and Belief: Prolegomenon for a Feminist Rhetoric of Motives." In *A Rhetoric of Doing: Essays on Written Discourse in Honor of James L. Kinneavy*, edited by Stephen P. Witte, Neil Nakadate, and Roger D. Cherry, 123–43. Carbondale: Southern Illinois University Press, 1992.

Taylor, Charles. *Modern Social Imaginaries.* Durham: Duke University Press, 2004.

Taylor, Diana. *The Archive and the Repertoire: Performing Cultural Memory in the Americas.* Durham: Duke University Press, 2003.

Tell, Dave. *Remembering Emmett Till.* Chicago: University of Chicago Press, 2019.

Theophrastus. *Characters.* Translated by James Diggle. Cambridge Classical Texts and Commentaries 43. Cambridge: Cambridge University Press, 2004.

Thompson, Roger. "Kairos Revisited: An Interview with James Kinneavy." *Rhetoric Review* 19, nos. 1–2 (2000): 73–88.

Thucydides. *The Peloponnesian War.* Translated by E. P. Dutton. London: J. M. Dent, 1910.

Tillich, Paul. *The Courage to Be.* New Haven: Yale University Press, 2014.

Timmerman, David M., and Edward Schiappa. *Classical Greek Rhetorical Theory and the Disciplining of Discourse.* New York: Cambridge University Press, 2010.

Tolentino, Jia. *Trick Mirror: Reflections on Self-Delusion.* New York: Random House, 2019.

Tosh, John. *A Man's Place: Masculinity and the Middle-Class Home in Victorian England.* New Haven: Yale University Press, 1999.

Towns, Armond R. "'What Do We Wanna Be?' Black Radical Imagination and the Ends of the World." *Communication and Critical/Cultural Studies* 17, no. 1 (March 2020): 75–80.

Trapani, William C., and Chandra A. Maldonado. "*Kairos*: On the Limits to Our (Rhetorical) Situation." *Rhetoric Society Quarterly* 48, no. 3 (2018): 278–86.

Tuitt, Frank, Chayla Haynes, and Saran Stewart, eds. *Race, Equity, and the Learning Environment: The Global Relevance of Critical and Inclusive Pedagogies in Higher Education.* Sterling, VA: Stylus, 2016.

United Nations Universal Declaration of Human Rights. http://www.un.org/en/universal-declaration-human-rights.

VanHaitsma, Pamela. "Between Archival Absence and Information Abundance: Reconstructing Sallie Holley's Abolitionist Rhetoric Through Digital Surrogates and Metadata." *Quarterly Journal of Speech* 106, no. 1 (2020): 25–47.

Villanueva, Victor. Afterword to *Rhetorics Elsewhere and Otherwise: Contested Modernities, Decolonial Visions*, edited by Romeo García and Damián Baca, 223–25. Conference on College Composition and Communication of the National Council of Teachers of English, Urbana, Illinois, 2019.

Vitanza, Victor J. "Big Rhetoric." Interviewed by Jimmy Butts. *Itineration*, 2013. https://vimeo.com/62108351.

———. *Negation, Subjectivity, and the History of Rhetoric.* Albany: State University of New York Press, 1997.

Vivian, Bradford. "Deletion and Damnatio: Theses on the Eventfulness of Forgetting." *Currents in Electronic Literacy* (2012). https://currents.dwrl.utexas.edu/2012/deletion-and-damnatio-memoriae-theses-on-the-eventfulness-of-forgetting.html.

———. *Public Forgetting: The Rhetoric and Politics of Beginning Again.* University Park: Penn State University Press, 2010.

Von Burg, Alessandra. "Citizenship Islands: The Ongoing Emergency in the Mediterranean Sea." *Media and Communication* 7, no. 2 (2019): 218–29.

Wagner, Russell H. "The Rhetorical Theory of Isocrates." *Quarterly Journal of Speech Education* 8, no. 4 (1922): 323–37.

Wanzer-Serrano, Darrel, ed. "#RhetoricSoWhite." Forum. *Quarterly Journal of Speech* 105, no. 4 (2019): 465–507.

Warner, Michael. *Publics and Counterpublics.* New York: Zone, 2002.

Washington, John. *The Dispossessed: A Story of Asylum at the US-Mexican Border and Beyond*. New York: Verso, 2020.

Webb, Ruth. *Ekphrasis, Imagination and Persuasion in Ancient Rhetorical Theory and Practice*. New York: Routledge, 2016.

Welch, Kathleen E. *The Contemporary Reception of Classical Rhetoric: Appropriations of Ancient Discourse*. New York: Routledge, 1990.

Wells, Susan. "Rogue Cops and Health Care: What Do We Want from Public Writing?" *College Composition and Communication* 47, no. 3 (1996): 325–41.

Westerman, Catherine Y. Kingsley. "How People Restore Equity at Work and Play: Forgiveness, Derogation and Communication." *Communication Studies* 6, no. 3 (July–August 2013): 296–314.

White, Eric Charles. *Kaironomia: On the Will-to-Invent*. Ithaca: Cornell University Press, 1987.

Williams, Raymond. Introduction to *Keywords: A Vocabulary of Culture and Society*. Rev. ed., 11–26. New York: Oxford University Press, 1985.

Wilson, Kirt H. *The Reconstruction Desegregation Debate: The Politics of Equality and the Rhetoric of Place, 1870–1875*. East Lansing: Michigan State University Press, 2002.

Wise, J. Macgregor. "Towards a Minor Assemblage: An Introduction to the Clickable World." In *Theorizing Digital Rhetoric*, edited by Aaron Hess and Amber Davisson, 68–82. New York: Routledge, 2017.

Witham, Keith, Lindsey E. Malcom-Piqueux, Alicia C. Dowd, and Estela Mara Bensimon. *America's Unmet Promise: The Imperative for Equity in Higher Education*. Washington, DC: Association of American Colleges and Universities, 2015.

Wohl, Victoria. *Law's Cosmos: Juridical Discourse in Athenian Forensic Oratory*. Cambridge: Cambridge University Press, 2010.

Woodruff, Paul. *First Democracy*. New York: Oxford University Press, 2005.

Woods, Carly S. *Debating Women: Gender, Education, and Spaces for Argument*. East Lansing: Michigan State University Press, 2018.

Wu, Ellen D. *The Color of Success: Asian Americans and the Origins of the Model Minority*. Princeton: Princeton University Press, 2013.

Wu, Tim. *The Attention Merchants: The Epic Scramble to Get Inside Our Heads*. New York: Random House, 2016.

Ye, Liu. "Between the Tropics: The Genealogies of the Empires and the Revolutions." Translated by Orion Martin. *Times Museum Journal*, no. 1. https://timesmuseum.org/en/journal/south-of-the-south/between-the-tropics-the-genealogies-of-the-empires-and-the-revolutions.

Yergeau, M. Remi. *Authoring Autism: On Rhetoric and Neurological Queerness*. Durham: Duke University Press, 2018.

Zeman, Adam, Michaela Dewar, and Sergio Della Sala. "Lives Without Imagery—Congenital Aphantasia." *Cortex* 73 (December 1, 2015): 378–80.

Zuboff, Shoshana. *The Age of Surveillance Capitalism: The Fight for a Human Future at the New Frontier of Power*. New York: Public Affairs, 2018.

Zuckerberg, Donna. "Make Comparisons Great Again." EIDOLON, June 6, 2016. https://eidolon.pub/make-comparisons-great-again-f778e953e691.

Zulick, Margaret D. "The Active Force of Hearing: The Ancient Hebrew Language of Persuasion." *Rhetorica* 10, no. 4 (Autumn 1992): 367–80.

Zulli, Diana. "Capitalizing on the Look: Insights into the Glance, Attention Economy, and Instagram." *Critical Studies in Media Communication* 2, no. 35 (2018): 137–50.

CONTRIBUTORS

CADDIE ALFORD is Assistant Professor of Rhetoric and Writing at Virginia Commonwealth University. Her work has appeared in *enculturation*, *Rhetoric Review*, *Media Ethics Magazine*, and *Rhetoric Society Quarterly*. She serves as the book review editor at *enculturation*. Her current manuscript project both examines and builds upon the intersections between opinion and social media rhetorics through the ancient Greek concept of *doxa*.

BENJAMIN FIRGENS is a PhD candidate in Penn State's Department of Communication Arts and Sciences. His research on social imagination and rhetorics of technology has won multiple disciplinary awards. His dissertation examines how public memories of major innovations in twentieth-century aerospace technology shape what Americans imagine the future to be.

CORY GERATHS is Assistant Professor of Communication at Eureka College. His research explores the rhetorical intersections of religion, gender and sexuality, and popular media. Cory's scholarship has appeared in *Critical Studies in Media Communication*, *Advances in the History of Rhetoric*, *Rhetoric Review*, *Communication Teacher*, and EIDOLON. In addition to his research, Cory also teaches courses in ancient rhetorical theory; digital rhetoric and media; and rhetoric, gender, and sexuality.

ANTHONY J. IRIZARRY is a PhD student in the Department of Communication Arts and Sciences at Penn State University. His research focuses on public memory and border rhetorics, with a special interest in mnemonic and political constructions of the home within civic communities. His most recent work examined the rhetorical efficacy of nostalgic natality following moments of crisis.

MICHELE KENNERLY is Associate Professor of Communication Arts and Sciences and, by courtesy, Classics and Ancient Mediterranean Studies at Penn State. She is the author of *Editorial Bodies: Perfection and Rejection in Ancient Rhetoric and Poetics* and coeditor of *Ancient Rhetorics and Digital Networks* (with Damien Smith Pfister) and *Information: Keywords* (with

Samuel Frederick and Jonathan E. Abel). Her current work considers invocations of ancient Athens in discourse about automation and digitization. She serves as president of the American Society for the History of Rhetoric and on the council of the International Society for the History of Rhetoric.

MARI LEE MIFSUD is Professor of Rhetoric and Women, Gender, and Sexuality Studies at the University of Richmond. She is the author of *Rhetoric and the Gift: Ancient Rhetorical Theory and Contemporary Communication* and coauthor and coeditor with Jane Sutton of *A Revolution in Tropes: Alloiostrophic Rhetoric*. Her work has appeared in *Philosophy and Rhetoric, Advances in the History of Rhetoric, Journal of International Women's Studies, Informal Logic, Rhetoric Society Quarterly,* and *Review of Communication*.

JOHN MUCKELBAUER is Associate Professor of English at the University of South Carolina, where he teaches rhetorical theory, classical rhetoric, and science fiction. His first book, *The Future of Invention: Rhetoric, Postmodernism, and the Problem of Change*, attempts to articulate an "affirmative" approach to the practice of invention. His current book project, *Thinking Through Style*, follows the Nietzschean lineage in continental philosophy in order to rethink the function of style for pedagogy and for writing.

BESS R. H. MYERS is the Assistant Director of First-Year Writing at the University of Memphis. Her research focuses on classical rhetoric and its reception, and appears in *Arethusa, Voices of Democracy,* and EIDOLON. Her current book project pursues the rhetorical significance of Plato's *Timaeus*.

DAMIEN SMITH PFISTER is Associate Professor of Communication at the University of Maryland studying the dynamic confluence of technology, digitally networked media, rhetorical practice, public deliberation, and visual culture. He is the author of *Networked Rhetorics, Networked Media: Attention and Deliberation in the Early Blogosphere* and coeditor of *Ancient Rhetorics and Digital Networks*. His work appears in journals like *Philosophy and Rhetoric, Argumentation and Advocacy, Rhetoric Review, Environmental Communication,* and the *Quarterly Journal of Speech*. *Always On: Fashioning Ethos After Wearable Computing* is the tentative title of his next book project, on the rhetorical and cultural implications of devices like mobile phones, head-mounted displays, activity trackers, and smartwatches.

NATHANIEL A. RIVERS is Associate Professor of English at Saint Louis University. His current research addresses topics such as environmentalism, locative media, and accessibility. He coedited *Kenneth Burke + The Posthuman* and *Thinking with Bruno Latour in Rhetoric and Composition*. His recent work has appeared in such journals as *Rhetoric Society Quarterly*, *amodern*, *enculturation*, *Technical Communication Quarterly*, and *Quarterly Journal of Speech*.

ALESSANDRA VON BURG is Associate Professor of Communication at Wake Forest University. She is affiliated faculty for American Ethnic Studies and Jewish Studies. Her research focuses on rhetorical theory, citizenship, mobility, noncitizens, and nonplaces. She has published in *Philosophy and Rhetoric*, *Advances in the History of Rhetoric*, *Quarterly Journal of Speech*, and other national and international outlets. She is coprincipal investigator for the Benjamin Franklin Transatlantic Fellows (BFTF) Summer Institute, a Department of State–funded summer program for international and American students; and the director and executive producer of the Where Are You From? Project. She is the cofounder of the Every Campus a Refuge (ECAR) chapter at Wake Forest University and the Incubator@WFU, residential programs for refugees and asylees.

INDEX

N.B., The keywords in their familiar and alpha-privative forms are not included here, since they tend to bunch in their respective chapters.